Esoteric Theravada

The Story of the Forgotten Meditation Tradition of Southeast Asia

Kate Crosby

SHAMBHALA

Shambhala Publications, Inc.
4720 Walnut Street
Boulder, Colorado 80301
www.shambhala.com

Some material in this book has been previously published or adapted, including substantial parts of chapters 4 and 5, from *Traditional Theravada Meditation and Its Modern-Era Suppression* (Buddha-dharma Centre of Hong Kong, 2013).

Cover art: bpk Bildagentur / Museum für Asiatische Kunst, Staatliche Museen, Berlin, Germany / Art Resource, NY
Cover design: Claudine Mansour Design
Interior design: Gopa & Ted2, Inc.

9 8 7 6 5 4 3 2 1

First Edition
Printed in the United States of America

♾ This edition is printed on acid-free paper that meets the American National Standards Institute Z39.48 Standard.
♻ This book is printed on 30% postconsumer recycled paper.
For more information please visit www.shambhala.com.
Shambhala Publications is distributed worldwide by Penguin Random House, Inc., and its subsidiaries.

LIBRARY OF CONGRESS CATALOGING-IN-PUBLICATION DATA
Names: Crosby, Kate (Religion scholar), author.
Title: Esoteric Theravada: the story of the forgotten meditation tradition of Southeast Asia / Kate Crosby.
Description: First edition. | Boulder, Colorado: Shambhala Publications, Inc., [2020] | Includes bibliographical references and index.
Identifiers: LCCN 2020011074 | ISBN 9781611807943 (trade paperback)
Subjects: LCSH: Borān kammaṭṭhāna. | Theravāda Buddhism—Southeast Asia—History.
Classification: LCC BQ5630.B67 C76 2020 | DDC 294.3/910959—dc23
LC record available at https://lccn.loc.gov/2020011074

In grateful and affectionate memory of
John Crosby (1935–2016)
Lance Cousins (1942–2015)
Surana Neil Burns (1965–2017)
Steven Collins (1951–2018)
Yey Oun Sophy (c. 1934–2019)

Contents

Acknowledgments

I offer my sincere thanks to Richard Gombrich, who, back in the early 1990s, first drew my attention to the meditation text, the *Amatākaravaṇṇanā*; to the late Heinz Bechert, who wrote the brief entry that had caught Richard's attention and encouraged me to undertake this research; and to Andrew Skilton and the late Lance Cousins, who both alerted me to the work of François Bizot. I was fortunate that in Lance's final years he made time to discuss meditation with me, with a refreshing open-mindedness, a serious consideration of practice, and an inspiring facility for detailed engagement in Abhidhamma. It was only after his death that I came to understand the significance of the practice element in Lance's approach. This was thanks to Grevel Lindop, Keith Munnings, and others of the Samatha Trust.

I would like to thank practitioners of meditation in Thailand and Cambodia for their assistance and support. While I name specific sources in the body of the text, I would like to highlight here the personal contributions of Ven. Veera Virandharo, former Director of the Dhammakaya International Society of the United Kingdom, and Ven. Veera Thanaveero of Wat Ratchasittharam, Thonburi. Of the many who have helped me in Cambodia, I would like to highlight the help of the late Achar Te Tong Yi, my teacher Ven. Neang Sam Ol, the late Yey Oun Sophy, and Yey Srean. I thank Ven. Uch Yoeurn for the repeated loan of his former *kuṭi*, and Elizabeth Guthrie, John Marston, and the late Ian Harris for their kindness and expertise. I would also like to thank my long-time friends and occasional assistants, Long Sarou and Chea Bunnary.

Deserving of special mention are those who worked with me in Thailand and London on materials related to this tradition and shared my enthusiasm for putting together the puzzle: Phibul Choompolpaisal, Andrew Skilton, and Amal Gunasena. For encouragement on the subject over the years, I would like to thank Phyllis Granoff, Gregory Schopen, and Paul Dundas. For the past decade, I have benefited from membership of the Theravada Civilizations Project established by Juliane Schober and the late Steven Collins, and from Steve's galvanizing comments and breathtaking enthusiasm. For their important work on the subject, as well as their kindness in sending me their writings, I thank François Bizot, Olivier de Bernon, Phibul Choompolpaisal, Oskar von Hinüber, François Lagirarde, Mano (erstwhile) Mettanando Laohavanich, Andrew Skilton, Barend (Baas) Terwiel, and Kitchai Urkasame.

For help in access to resources and references, I thank Mike Charney, Romola Dane, Alastair Gornall, Jotika Khur-Yearn, Atsuko Naono, Liz Harris, and Pyi Phyo Kyaw, whom I also thank for her expertise in Abhidhamma and important help of various kinds. For their practical support, I thank Isara Treesahakiat, Kampol Treesahakiat, and Patcharin Yimpatna.

In helping me to develop the subject and my understanding over the past decade, I should additionally like thank the co-organizers, contributors, and audiences at conferences on variety in Theravada meditation and on Abhidhamma, at King's College London in October 2014 and June 2015, at the École française d'Extrême-Orient in Siem Reap in July 2016, and at Shan State Buddhist University near Taunggyi in November 2019. The first three of these conferences were generously funded by Dhammakaya International Society of the United Kingdom and the Ji Chanqun Buddhist Studies funding of King's College London. I am also grateful to David Germano, colleagues and students at the University of Virginia, Charlottesville, and Kurtis Schaeffer and Andrew Quintman, who organized the thought-provoking 2017 IABS panel on Literatures of Contemplation, as well as students at King's and elsewhere, who all pushed me to think in different ways.

For both the path and the fruit, I would like to thank Nikko Odiseos, Breanna Locke, Katherine Ulrich, Matt Zepelin, and their colleagues at Shambhala. I also thank the Hong Kong Centre for Buddhist Studies for allowing me to reuse material from my now out-of-print work, *Traditional Theravāda Meditation and Its Modern-Era Suppression,* that they published in 2013.

The most recent period of research leading to this book has also been a period of farewells: to my father, John Crosby; my senior colleagues and mentors Steven Collins and Lance Cousins; Achar Te Tong Yi, who after the Pol Pot period resuscitated the lineage in which I practice in Cambodia; my guide Yey Oun Sophy and my dearest friend, Surana Neil Burns; deep in history, profound in reflection, and inspiring in the telling, all kind and generous teachers. My final expression of thanks is to my partner, Andrew Nash.

—Kate Crosby
Hastings, a little adrift off the coast of France
January 2020

Transliteration

For Pali and Sanskrit, I employ the standard international conventions stemming from *International Congress of Orientalists* at Geneva in 1894. Anglicized Indic terms are given in their anglicized form, unless being used in a technical sense or in quotation. For Thai, I use the Royal Thai General System of Transcription, except again with words that have been anglicized, such as Wat "monastic complex/temple" (Pali *vatthu*), or accepted transliterations that circulate within the tradition under discussion. Where there are multiple transcriptions and names in circulation, as there are for a number of Thai monks, I have tried to provide them all at the first main point of discussion of the person in question. For Cambodian names and Thai and Cambodian temple names, I have either employed an established romanization or given my own or my informant's phonetic transcription. For Sinhala, unless a standard romanization for a given name exists, I have used the UN system adapted from D. N. Sharma, with the exception that I do not mark short vowels with a short marker, thus short and long *o* and *e* are undifferentiated here. For countries, I have mostly used their modern names, such as "Sri Lanka," or both the modern name and the name at the time of the event under discussion where appropriate, such as "Siam/Thailand," although I have mainly used "Burma," rather than "Myanmar," since the name continued to be used throughout the period under discussion.

Esoteric Theravada

Introduction

Today we are surrounded by a rich profusion of meditation teachings from the Theravada world as well as the array of secularized Mindfulness practices that they have inspired. The early Buddhist texts that teach meditation are also familiar to many, widely available in translation, and have been for over a century. This situation might lead us to assume that these present-day practices represent unbroken, uncontested lineages of meditation teaching going back to the Buddha himself. Those more familiar with the history of how Theravada Buddhists had to fight for the survival of their religion, against the devastation and upheaval of the European colonial period, know that many of these modern offerings were stirred into life by that fight. It has been said that there was little or no meditation at all (or perhaps only isolated and fragmentary forest traditions) in Theravada countries before its well-documented reconstruction as part of that revival. There did exist, however, an extensive, older tradition of meditation. It was represented across the Theravada world at court and among the Sangha (monastic) hierarchy as much as in rural contexts. Reflecting its anteriority to the meditations of the revival period, I shall here refer to that system of meditation as *borān kammaṭṭhāna*, "the old meditation." This book is about its history, its distinctive practices, the evidence we have for it, how it sat within its broader cultural context, and why it disappeared.

This older tradition was marginalized and suppressed in the course of the reforms and revivals of Buddhism from the nineteenth century onward because of characteristics no longer seen as fitting in the new world order: sequential, body-based practices that internalize meditative experiences to create an enlightened being within, which utilize potent language and are transmitted in an esoteric teacher-pupil relationship. As such they reminded some modern observers of tantra, others of magical lore, and were dismissed as corruptions or as influences from beyond Theravada.

Hidden beneath those characteristics, however, is a rigorous framework of Abhidhamma, the orthodox Theravada teaching of how causality and transformation happen. This framework is not immediately visible to the casual observer or even the beginner practitioner. Moreover, many of the somatic characteristics that at first seem strange in fact point to the participation of meditators in scientific techniques unrecognized and unappreciated by Western observers and Buddhist modernizers. This book attempts to present a holistic view of the nature of this meditation system. I am particularly interested in its understanding of how change happens and how it relates to other technologies of transformation.

The Challenges of This Book

My task is complicated by the intersection of several factors:

1. Although the beginner levels of some modernized versions are widely accessible, *borān kammaṭṭhāna* has for most of its history been an esoteric tradition, not disseminated publicly but through initiation into closed teacher-pupil lineages. In this respect, *borān kammaṭṭhāna* presents similar ethical, access, and disclosure issues as does the scholarly exposition of Vajrayana and other esoteric tantric traditions within Mahayana Buddhism.
2. It is a meditation system, and meditation by its nature is a somewhat intractable subject of academic discourse.
3. Once widespread, the practice of this meditation has collapsed to the point of extinction. This collapse has occurred under a diverse range of factors including the impact of colonialism, modernism, reform, technological innovation, and geo-politics.

4. The evidence for the existence and former importance of *borān kammaṭṭhāna* is scanty, sometimes hidden, sometimes misunderstood, and sometimes discarded.
5. The meditation system is complex, employing a range of methods to induce transformation in the individual. Some of these methods are usually associated with other fields, especially generative grammar, ayurvedic obstetrics, and alchemy. These features of the practice take me into the technicalities of areas no longer seen as related either to Buddhism or spiritual transformation.

These factors mean that I am attempting to introduce a method of meditation that does not fit our preconceptions of what Theravada meditation is, particularly in its inclusion of mechanisms aimed at somatic transformation. To explain these unfamiliar aspects, I must delve into the technicalities of the practice itself, of Abhidhamma, and of pre-modern sciences. I must also trace the sometimes complex history of modern Theravada to explain how these practices were lost. Specialists in some areas may feel that I ride roughshod over subjects that deserve fuller treatment. Meanwhile, non-specialist readers may, at times, feel trampled by technical details. I have attempted to alleviate this second issue by providing introductions and conclusions to each chapter. These summarize key points, highlight the place of the chapter within the flow of the book, its contribution to our understanding of the workings and history of *borān kammaṭṭhāna*, or how it related to the scientific and political landscapes within which it thrived and disappeared.

Despite these challenges, the evidence for *borān kammaṭṭhāna*, once we know what we are looking for, is far more widespread, accessible, and unproblematic to deal with than other esoteric forms of Theravada meditation, such as, for example, the *weikza* meditation in Burma (Myanmar). For although the core practices of *borān kammaṭṭhāna* were esoteric, its existence was visible, sponsored as it was at the highest levels of court society as well as practiced at key points in the Buddhist and harvest calendar among the rural population. Moreover, the more practical aspects of it, such as its use in protection, are still visible today in what in the modern period have come to be labeled as the magical or apotropaic practices of Theravada Buddhists.

Drawing on texts, earlier studies, and practitioners' explanations, I presume to discuss traditional esoteric Theravada meditation in such a public forum under the active encouragement of practitioners who are concerned for its preservation. However, the understanding I present of it is my own, as are the flaws in this presentation. While I have been taught by teachers in several branches of this tradition, my experience as a practitioner is very limited.

What's New in This Book?

Almost a decade ago, I wrote a book on the disappearance of this meditation practice, primarily by looking at global developments and the impact of European knowledge systems on Theravada Buddhism.[1] Since then, both the field and my knowledge have developed. My colleagues and I have held several conferences to explore in and around the subject. New authors, whose work I shall reference in the following pages, have made discoveries and published important contributions, in part responding to that book. This has allowed a broader as well as a more nuanced picture to emerge. Far more of the material that practitioners left behind, in manuscripts and art, or through publications of the early to mid-twentieth century, is now visible. The response to this form of meditation by observers of the colonial period has been further explored. My predictions about the picture that would emerge as Thailand documented and made its manuscript collections more accessible have been not only confirmed but superseded. I have now understood why Abhidhamma is such a strong feature of the practice, underlying the process of transformation enacted. This confirms the fundamental role of Abhidhamma in the development of this meditation system, a speculation I had only mooted then against the backdrop of alternative theories. I have been able to participate in practice lineages, which I had back then only just encountered, as well as meet many more practitioners. This book reflects those developments. Here the global and European history that formed the structure of the previous work has been left behind, as have other theories about its origins, only touched on where necessary. We follow instead the practice and its foundations in Abhidhamma, the varieties of its manifestations, its history, dating, and disappearance. We can provide a clearer and more detailed account of the practice and have established a timeline. There is overlap with my previous book, as I have expanded upon the evidence known then. This particularly applies in the explanation of the parallel technologies of transformation, namely generative grammar, the harnessing of potent language, obstetrics, and chemistry, updated in chapters 4 and 5. Some historical aspects have also been reused but filled out. Meanwhile, in a separate publication, several authors, including me, have written about the various branches and aspects of the practice and the evidence available for them in more detail than space here allows.[2]

The Structure of This Book

In chapter 1, I look at attitudes to Theravada Buddhism and its meditation during the colonial period, in order to understand why *borān kammaṭṭhāna* was so invisible, even though it was still widely practiced. I examine various dichotomies that arose in the colonial period, between religion and science, between Theravada as a philosophy and as practiced, between the spiritual and material. This background will help us understand the shape that the revival of Buddhist meditation took, and why *borān kammaṭṭhāna* was marginalized and dismissed as contrived or corrupt. The criticisms made against it beg the question of what it was that outsiders disliked or found difficult to understand about this meditation.

Chapter 2 will seek to address this question, discussing the key features seen as unorthodox and looking at how it is practiced. This will entail looking at its distinctive use of *nimitta*, the "signs" seen in meditation, and how these are used to incorporate meditative attainments into the body. We shall compare *borān kammaṭṭhāna* with two more familiar systems of Theravada meditation. The first is the *Path of Purification*, the *Visuddhimagga*, an important and highly influential treatise by the fifth-century scholar-monk Buddhaghosa. The second is Vipassanā, the form of meditation developed as part of the Burmese revival of Buddhism, which went on to influence the modern Mindfulness movement. Looking in more detail at *borān* meditation instructions, we shall see how all three systems relate to Abhidhamma, the Theravada project to unravel the steps and possibilities of causality and human transformation. The pervasiveness of Abhidhamma in *borān kammaṭṭhāna* presents a conundrum. Is it the superimposition of Theravada orthodoxy on a pre-existing, non-Theravada tradition? Alternatively, does it reflect a detailed working out of the Abhidhamma path to liberation?

Chapter 3 looks at the evidence we can draw on to understand *borān kammaṭṭhāna* and its dating. There we also learn how the visibility of the practice was variously helped or hindered by the technologies of manuscript production and printing. This chapter begins to provide some of the history of *borān kammaṭṭhāna*, revealing how politics, both at the global and local levels, shaped the availability and visibility of the tradition. While chapter 2 had sought to explain the Abhidhamma underpinnings of *borān kammaṭṭhāna*, this did not account for many of the features that seem unorthodox, or rather unorthoprax, making it vulnerable at times of challenge and reform.

In chapters 4 and 5 we seek to account for these features by looking at technologies of the material world that were important in the pre-modern Theravada context. These help explain ideas about how transformation is brought about, ideas found in the somatic aspects of *borān kammaṭṭhāna* practice. First, in chapter 4, we look at ideas of language and generative grammar, which inform the use of potent language in *borān kammaṭṭhāna*. Then, in chapter 5, we turn to the medicine, particularly ayurvedic obstetrics, as well as the chemistry of the purification of mercury, to see how these too relate to meditation practice. They indicate shared understandings of how transformation may be brought about. I suggest that it was the suppression and disappearance of these resonating technologies that left *borān kammaṭṭhāna* isolated and vulnerable to being misunderstood at times of Buddhist reform.

Chapter 6 turns to the subject of revivals and reforms of Buddhism in the eighteenth to early twentieth centuries, to discuss the rise and fall of *borān kammaṭṭhāna* under the influence of Siam/Thailand. *Borān kammaṭṭhāna* had been the form of meditation at the heart of Buddhist revival in Sri Lanka in the mid-eighteenth century, brought there by missions from Ayutthaya, the then-capital of Siam. However, political events and the modernization of Siam/Thailand led to reforms in Buddhism and education. These contributed to the marginalization of *borān* meditation both there and in countries under its influence.

Chapter 7 traces the patterns of revival in the late nineteenth and twentieth centuries outside of Thailand in order to understand why certain meditations were selected and others deselected. This includes the effect of the rise of Vipassanā and text-based meditation. We look at how Marxist revolutions devastated the remaining strongholds of practice and the abortive revival of *borān kammaṭṭhāna* in Cambodia after the end of the Pol Pot period. We return to Thailand to see how the Cold War and local politics influenced meditation there, culminating with a look at those *borān kammaṭṭhāna* traditions that have survived, in adapted form, including the popularity of the modernized lineages stemming from Candasaro Sot of Wat Paknam.

Finally, we conclude by bringing together these different strands to make sense of the esoteric meditation tradition of Southeast Asia and how it is that we have come so close to both losing and losing sight of such a major strand of Theravada practice, the oldest living lineage of Theravada meditation, which brought together the insights of Abhidhamma and the sciences that surrounded it, only to be misunderstood and suppressed in the politics and rivalries of the modern period.

1

The Colonial Gaze

The Invisibility of Pre-Modern Theravada Meditation

> There are, it is true, many passages, especially among those that deal with meditation or with supernatural attainments, which entirely leave behind all that is human, natural, probable, all that is genial or attractive, and sail away into a region of empty abstraction, which it would be flattery to call a cloudland.
>
> Reginald Copleston, Bishop of Colombo, 1892[1]

Nowadays Buddhism is inextricably linked with meditation in popular imagination, scholarship, and global practice. How was it then that—little more than a century ago—in his best-selling book on Theravada Buddhism, Bishop Copleston, a highly regarded scholar, should so roundly dismiss the subject? In fact, he writes positively of the gentleness, calm, earnestness, and purity of Buddhist ideals and morality, and liberalism of its practice, but he struggles with what he regarded as a negative end goal: "for the Buddhist solitude is a withdrawal from all things to nothing, the Christian's, from other things to God . . . It is impossible to imagine a greater interval between two ideals [of Buddhist and Christian salvation] . . . between that which contains only the negative, and that which adds to it the infinite positive."[2] He does attempt to present some canonical material on the subject of meditation, and acknowledges the miraculous powers thought to attend it, but expected the practice to be simple: "The elaborate systems of what may be called mechanical meditation or self-mesmerism by mechanical processes (kammaṭṭhānaṃ) belong to a later phase."[3] Copleston was writing in Sri Lanka (then Ceylon), at a point when it had already suffered three centuries of European colonial control over substantial parts of the island. This began with the Portuguese at the end of the sixteenth century, followed by the Dutch and then, from the early nineteenth century, the British. Copleston's position may well have been the same had he been writing in Burma, colonized by the British over the course of the nineteenth century. His information seems to come entirely from texts, with no mention of living practitioners. His dismissal, then, is at once an act of reporting, reflecting a religious landscape depleted by colonial oppression, and an act of suppression, ridiculing Buddhism's key technology of spiritual transformation. This trivialization, the colonial disinterest in the subject, would facilitate resurgent forces to gather around this very practice, with meditation at the heart of the impending Buddhist revival.

The widespread practices we see today are testament to the work of important activists who revived and popularized meditation, a process underway as Copleston wrote. Often these revivalists drew on texts that went back to the early centuries of Buddhism, to create reenvisaged forms of practice, accessible en masse and adapted to the modern period. These would spread throughout the Theravada region of mainland Southeast Asia and Sri Lanka and, after the retreat of European colonialism, across the world.

This text-based revival in Burma and Sri Lanka may have been necessitated by a lack of living meditation lineages.[4] However, an extensive, living tradition of meditation was widely available at that time, namely the family of practices that I shall here call *borān kammaṭṭhāna*, "the old meditation." This name was applied to it by early twentieth-century scholars in Thailand as it disappeared, replaced by revivalist forms. It had been found at court and among the hierarchy of the monastic community, the Sangha, as well as in rural contexts. While today this type of meditation in its more traditional forms is confined to a few small pockets, it had dominated the Buddhism of Sri Lanka at the height of an earlier revival in the preceding century.[5] While it had died out there by the end of the nineteenth century, it still thrived in the regions now covered by Cambodia, southern Vietnam, Laos, and Thailand.

Thailand (then Siam) was never colonized, and Copleston's contemporary there, the British vice-consul to Siam, Henry Alabaster (1836–1884), presents a more informed picture of meditation in his *The Wheel of the Law: Buddhism Illustrated from Siamese Sources.*[6] His work is based on a Thai book by Chao Phya Thipakon, the former foreign minister for Siam. Alabaster is aware that meditation, far from being "a region of empty abstraction," has content, and he mentions some of the Theravada practices familiar to us today, such as the meditation on the thirty-two constituents of the body and the "divine abidings," *brahmavihāra*, in which one develops positive emotional responses beginning with loving kindness, *mettā*. Unlike Copleston, he does not elevate Christianity and is against conversion to it—"It is a pity to see good Buddhists turned into bad Christians."[7] However, his view of meditation is still disparaging:

> We find monastic Buddhism sharing the fate which must attend all religions which encourage a professional class of monks, or men who lead unnatural lives, that is cumbered with dogmas and absurdities, the result of warped, fantastic and prurient minds. . . . we find that the professional religious class, in the absence of a useful occupation, has invented an intolerable terminology, has multiplied ridiculous distinctions, has twisted the elementary principles into all manner of shapes, and has invented a system of meditation which, in lieu of expanding the mind, tends to contract it almost to idiocy.[8]

Here the objection is not only to meditation, but also to "intolerable terminology" and "ridiculous distinctions." These comments are possibly a reference to Abhidhamma, Buddhism's highly evolved and detailed analysis of causality, which seeks to explain ethics, experience, and the path to liberation (nibbana) from the cycle of death and rebirth (samsara). Alabaster's criticisms may differ in the specifics but share Copleston's colonial attitudes: the dismissal of local expertise that they did not acknowledge, and the expectations of what Buddhism and religion should and should not be.

Buddhism in the Emerging Religion-Science Divide

These attitudes reflect the dramatic reconfiguration of religion and science that developed over the course of the nineteenth century. In the West, having previously been considered aspects of a single quest to understand and harness God's creation, they were redefined as separate enterprises in such a way as to require a discourse explaining the relationship between them. In 1874, the acclaimed Protestant Christian writer John William Draper (1811–1882) published a best-selling work entitled the *History of the Conflict between Religion and Science.* He reflected the educated, Protestant view of his day when summing up the history of the relationship as "a narrative of the conflict of two contending powers, the expansive force of the human intellect on the one side, and the compression arising from traditionary faith and human interests on the other."[9] Draper's work is in essence a history of science that seeks to remold the meaning of religion such that true religion is in line with "Progress." Indeed, the title he originally intended for the book was "The Intellectual Development of Europe."[10] Like modern histories of religion and science, he began his account with Galileo's conviction for heresy in 1633, a story that by Draper's time was taught to schoolchildren, and on that basis represented Catholicism as the "traditionary faith" that compresses intellect.[11] Alabaster's reference to "a professional class of monks, or men who lead unnatural lives, . . . cumbered with dogmas," is also clearly leveled at Catholicism, a criticism extended to forms of Buddhism that look like it.

It was also in the nineteenth century that Western observers labeled and defined Buddhism as a discrete religion. By the mid-nineteenth century the congeries of idolatrous religious expression across Asia that had been derided by European observers in the past centuries was coalescing in the European consciousness into an atheistic philosophy or religion, now termed "Buddhism," recognized as having a common history and a single, historical founder, Gautama Buddha. The Buddha was now regarded as a human being whereas it had previously been assumed that he was some kind of god.

European scholars and missionaries, having studied classical Asian languages, claimed ownership of Buddhist canons and contributed to the popular understanding of original Buddhism as rational and scientific.[12] Comparing the divergent texts and practices of Buddhism, Protestant observers assessed the Buddhism of Tibet unfavorably against the Buddhism of Sri Lanka and Southeast Asia. The Buddhism of the latter region was identified as a form of *hīnayāna*, or pre-Mahayana Buddhism, so an early form of the religion. This label was later replaced with "Theravada," "doctrine of the elders," picking up on the self-description of its teachings found in fifth-century commentarial texts.[13] Theravada was regarded as the only survivor of a number of branches of early Buddhism, and elements of its practice that were seen as later developments were therefore seen as corruptions. Parallels were drawn with Christianity: Tibetan Buddhism was the "corrupt popery" of Catholicism; Theravada—in its proper form—the more authentic Protestantism. The discovery and excavation of Buddhist remains in British India, where Buddhism was long extinct in most regions, enhanced the British claim to ownership of early Buddhism. It was admired for its philosophy, its antiquity, its tolerance, its androcentrism, as well as for the artworks brought back by colonial officers, particularly Gandharan sculptures, found to be so reminiscent of Western classical art. Even that most alien of Buddhist theological presuppositions, rebirth, conjured up for Victorians the newly popular Darwinian theory of evolution.[14]

Emerging knowledge about Buddhism, and the attendant difficulties of fitting it into existing understandings of the term "religion," informed the redefining of the religion-science relationship. This is reflected in Draper's work. His appreciation of Buddhism is clear when he uses it to authorize his theory of "a vast spiritual existence pervading the universe, even as there is a vast existence of matter pervading it . . . In one of its forms, as we have seen, this idea was developed by Chakia Monni [Śākyamuni, the Buddha], in India, in a most masterly manner, and embodied in the vast practical system of Buddhism."[15] Another point we should note here is that Draper contrasts the spiritual with the material, and indicates that Buddhism deals with the former. This divide between the spiritual and physical realms would undermine aspects of Buddhism that relate to the physical, both in its practices and the engagement of the Sangha in practical matters.

While Draper wrote appreciatively of Buddhism, the "Progress" of which he wrote was elsewhere offered as an apologetic justification of European colonialism and missionizing. The ruthless wars of expansion in Asia and Africa in search of economic advantage were defended as bringing both progress and the hope of Christian salvation to primitive peoples eager for the benefits that the supposedly superior European had to offer.[16] The rhetoric of European superiority that pervades Draper's book had been widely employed during the period to justify the contemporary exploitation of Asia to secure the continuation of those very economic gains that had supported Europe's scientific and social advances in the first place. While Draper acknowledges the reverse influence of Asia on Europe in the past, he is silent on Asia's scientific present and on the new advances stemming from contemporary interactions with her. This mirrors the ways in which Asia's contributions were downplayed and her institutions ignored by the instruments of colonial power of the day.

Since millions of those in the newly benefiting territories of Asia were Buddhists, this contributed to radically contrasting attitudes to Buddhism, on the one hand, and to Buddhists, on the other.

Europeans writers increasingly represented Buddhists themselves as incapable of understanding the true meaning of the texts they had been preserving for the previous two millennia and depicted them as following only a debased and corrupted form of the religion. "Buddhism, *as he taught it*, is not the religion of the five hundred millions who are said to reverence his shrines," wrote the Countess of Jersey, an admirer of the Buddha but not of Buddhists. "Much of which its founder never dreamed was introduced into the system, and which, had he heard it, he would have treated as foolishness or presumption. Simple as his teaching was, his disciples have spun it out into an affair so lengthened and prolix, that it requires the labour and patience of years to disentangle its intricacies," complained the challenged author of the entry on Buddhism in the *Journal of Sacred Literature* in 1865.[17] Complexities in Buddhism were not to be taken seriously, since they were mere corruptions of an originally simple message.

These dissonant attitudes to Buddhism and Buddhists, coupled with the disestablishment of Buddhist institutions in territories colonized by European powers, would in turn influence the ways in which the peoples of these colonies and emerging nations in Asia came to redefine and adapt their own traditional forms of Buddhism. This was particularly true of mainland Southeast Asia and Sri Lanka, which were dominated by French and British colonialists, and a rapidly modernizing Siam (Thailand), Siam in turn being reshaped by its efforts to retain its sovereignty. The new European desire to distinguish religion from science and to modify one's religion in response was assimilated in these countries too. The result was that Buddhism was reformed in the light of what was then considered rational and scientific.

Buddhism as Mind-Science

The colonialist idea that Buddhism had become corrupt and now fell short of the Buddha's original ideal resonated with indigenous Buddhist beliefs about the inevitable decline over the centuries of the Buddha's teachings and institutions. The collective term for these is *sāsana*, "teaching," in a broader sense than that conveyed by the term *dhamma*, "truth," "reality." The decline of the *sāsana* would be marked by devastating warfare, disease, and other hardships, exactly what people were witnessing with the arrival of European colonialism. Whereas previous reforms throughout the history of Buddhism had emphasized the continued preservation of the texts and a pure monastic lineage, and these concerns continued in reforms of the modern period, the modern approach to reform also discarded or marginalized "accretions" regarded as not conforming to "pure," "original" Buddhism.

Another taxonomic division being negotiated and explored during this period of Western discourse was the axiomatic separation of body and mind, or between *physis* and *psyche*, reflected in Draper's division between materiality and spirituality. For modernist Christians, religion concerned only the latter. This approach was reflected in the increasing acceptability among Christians of non-literal interpretations of biblical statements on the material world, such as the creation myth in the book of Genesis.

Early Buddhism also divided the world, particularly living beings and what they experienced, into a broad taxonomy of materiality or form, *rūpa*, and mentality or consciousness, literally "naming," *nāma*. Theravada Buddhism, however, teaches the interdependence of materiality and consciousness in a well-known analysis of the individual into a set of five aggregates that coexist interdependently in an ever-changing flux. These five aggregates (*khandha*) are (1) *rūpa*, materiality; (2) *vedanā*, sensation; (3) *saññā*, apperception; (4) *saṅkhārā*, volitional responses; and (5) *viññāṇa*, consciousness. This list can be further analyzed under three main headings. The first is still *rūpa*, materiality, the first of the five *khandha*, which consists of the material elements and matter derived from them. The other four *khandha* are divided into two: aspects of consciousness, *cetasika*, and states of consciousness, *citta*. An important function of Abhidhamma, which Alabaster and the challenged contributor to the *Journal of Sacred Literature* had found so objectionable, was to explain how these different categories combine and mutually cause one another. The result is a highly complex analysis of the human condition.

Abhidhamma underpins Buddhism's practical path of ethics and self-transformation, but was dismissed by external observers as a form of unnecessary scholasticism, secondary to Buddhism. Despite similarities in the overall recognition of materiality and consciousness, Buddhism does not, therefore, share the Cartesian mind-body distinction. Nevertheless, the dominance of the latter in European thinking meant that the resonances that can be found, particularly in Buddhist teachings on the primacy of the mind, would be influential in forming new emphases in Buddhism itself. It influenced meditation, which came to be seen more as a mind-science and less concerned with the physical realm. Those meditation practices that were associated with cognitive change from realizing Buddhist truths such as impermanence, suffering, and no-self were emphasized, while those more associated with physical transformation and material power were marginalized.

The resulting perception that meditation was primarily concerned with the mind and *psyche* to some extent protected it from colonial scrutiny, since scientific research of the period on the whole ignored the *psyche*, choosing the physical world as the focus of research.[18] Only in the second half of the twentieth century in the West did an explicit interest in Buddhist meditation become part of the continuing redefinition of religion and of the emerging study of consciousness and the brain.[19] This later interest in Buddhism's potential contribution to cognitive science built upon another, related shift in attitudes that saw its origins in the colonial period. Back then, in the face of European hegemony in the physical realm, evinced initially in military technology and later in medical procedures and medicines, Asians began to claim superiority in the realm of the mind. Buddhism's superiority, then, was to be found specifically in its mind-culture, particularly the technology of meditation and the analysis of mental processes. These were activities dismissed or ignored by colonial writers on Buddhism.

These approaches to Buddhism in the colonial period are neatly reflected in the early twentieth-century writings of the Burmese scholar Shwe Zan Aung (1871–1932), who both accepted and countered them, drawing on Abhidhamma. Whereas colonial-period external observers and modernist reformers in Thailand, such as those who had influenced Alabaster (above), regarded Abhidhamma as a form of dry scholasticism that developed after the Buddha, revivalists in Burma saw it as the fundamental teaching of the Buddha, representing the realization of his omniscience. Indeed, predictions of the decline of the *sāsana* identified the Abhidhamma section of the Buddhist scriptural canon as the most vulnerable, the first to disappear. In response, Burmese monks and laypeople dedicated themselves to the serious study and practice of Abhidhamma as a way of protecting Buddhism, leading to the expertise in Abhidhamma found throughout Myanmar to this day.[20]

As both a retired government servant for the British and a committed lay student of Burmese monks learned in Abhidhamma, Shwe Zan Aung was uniquely instrumental in conveying the knowledge of Abhidhamma to a global audience, providing the first translation of an Abhidhamma text in English.[21] In an article replete with Abhidhamma terminology, entitled "Buddhism and Science," he writes, "There is no essential difference between scientific and Buddhistic methods. . . . There is Buddhism in every science which accepts the theory of change, the theory of causation and the theory of evolution." Drawing parallels with Darwinism in terms of the content and its initial treatment by skeptics, he proceeds to point out Buddhism's strengths: "Psychology is the stronghold of Buddhism. Buddhist psychology is at once complete and comprehensive, providing a place for every possible form of thought known or unknown in Western psychology."[22] By way of example, he includes an astute analysis of the anteriority and superiority of Buddhism's practice of hypnotism, which had "only recently been recognized as a science in the West."[23] Shwe Zan Aung is, of course, referring on the Buddhist side to meditation, as can be seen from his observation, "The Western method begins with a subject, while the Buddhist method begins with the operator himself." As might be expected of an experienced administrator writing at a point when British-educated Burmese were challenging the colonial system from within, Shwe Zan Aung also reacts to the prevailing assumption of Buddhists' lack of expertise in materiality: "Buddhism has been held to be weakest in the physical sciences."[24] He does this in part by explaining Buddhist cosmology as an allegory, in part by pointing out the knowledge of the physical world displayed in Abhidhamma.

The Rise of Vipassanā

The conceptual divisions of the period between mind and body and religion and science, coupled with the emerging belief in the superiority of the Asian mind, influenced other aspects of the response of Buddhists to the fear that the long-prophesied demise of the Buddha's teaching was imminent. As colonial powers increasingly followed policies of non-involvement in religion, this meant that there was no royal authority to provide sponsorship to ensure the maintenance of the material fabric of Buddhism or deal with disputes within the Sangha. This policy of non-involvement therefore increased anxiety about the demise of the *sāsana*. At the same time, it made religion an arena within which to express dissent, leading to an association between Buddhism and emerging national identities.[25] In Burma, the increasing emphasis on personal salvation or liberation in this life, while the Buddha's teachings were still available, led to a revival of meditation as the most direct path to liberation. People turned to the teachings on meditation preserved in the sacred texts of the Pali canon and to the guidance provided in authoritative commentaries on those texts. While local attempts had been made to popularize meditation among monks in eighteenth-century Burma, it was in the second half of the nineteenth century that such endeavors proved effective. Without a king to protect the religion, it was now the responsibility of everyone, monk and non-monk alike, to do so.

One of the most influential figures in this project, popularizing meditation among both monastics and laypeople, was the Burmese monk Ledi Sayadaw (1846–1923). His mentor, who influenced both his clear writing style and his treatment of Buddhism as a scientific enterprise, was King Mindon's minister Hpo Hlaing (1830–1883). Hpo Hlaing had an avid interest in European scientific works and even wrote a meditation text that drew on Western anatomy.[26] The meditation techniques that first developed out of these influences—spreading first to the rest of the region, then worldwide during the twentieth century—were therefore informed by contemporary cosmopolitan learning as well as by the return to the earlier Pali texts.

As we will see when examining different systems of meditation, these techniques emphasized the transformative insight into reality as taught by the Buddha. The word for insight is *vipassanā*. As a result, the meditations that emerged at this time are themselves called Vipassanā, "Insight." They de-emphasized other outcomes of meditation, called *samatha*, "calming" techniques, that trained the mind, making it more receptive to insight. *Samatha* was sometimes associated with suprahuman powers and with gaining access to different realms of traditional Buddhist cosmology, two aspects of religious belief challenged by Western worldviews. Suprahuman powers included the ability to master the physical realm, for example by visiting different realms of the Buddhist cosmology, increasingly now seen as allegorical. The emphasis on insight was in part an attempt to speed up the transformative process of meditation, to create a fast track to the liberating insights into reality while the *dhamma* was still accessible. It was also a response to the *psyche-physis* divide, seen in the writings of Draper, and the colonial dominance of the material world.

In the revivals of the nineteenth and early twentieth centuries, Buddhist meditation focused on insight and the development of the mind, rather than on physical transformation. This selectiveness facilitated the later uptake and adaptation of these forms of meditation in the West, when Buddhist meditation practices were increasingly adopted by Westerners. This, in turn, informed scientific developments in the newly developing fields of cognitive science and psychology, including therapy. Buddhist meditation, and applications derived from it, have since the last decades of the twentieth century become of interest for the treatment of a range of psychological issues including depression, anxiety, pain management and, more recently, cognitive reserve in aging. Empirical testing has confirmed the value of meditation in these areas, and yet these applications have been developed from only a limited range of the technologies of transformation comprised within meditation practice, those that—through their emphasis on mental culture—successfully navigated the transition into the modern world. *Borān kammaṭṭhāna* is a major missing strand.

Dismissal of Pre-modern Theravada Meditation

This history begs two questions. (1) What happened to the forms of meditation that were still practiced in the nineteenth and early twentieth centuries, at least in those parts of the Theravada world not colonized by the British? (2) Given that meditation within Theravada Buddhism itself was not new—even if its teaching en masse in centers specially constructed for the purpose was a new departure—and given that science is in itself a culturally constructed approach to knowledge, what was the relationship between meditation and "science" (or its analogous cultural counterparts) before these new developments?

As we shall see, some of those pre-existing living traditions of meditation adapted to become more in line with the revisionist tendencies. Practices were checked against early authoritative texts on the subject and aligned with expectations of Buddhist meditation as mind-science. At the same time, those that were not adapted, including practices referred to here as "the old meditation" (*borān kammaṭṭhāna*), began to disappear. They began to disappear at exactly the time when Vipassanā and the other meditation practices based on normative Pali texts began to spread and increase in popularity. This family of older practices came to be referred to as the "traditional or old." This appears to have happened in the early twentieth century as new practices, especially modern Vipassanā and the practice of a newly established revisionist wing of the Thai forest tradition, were gaining currency. The phrase *boran kammatthan* (Thai) is found in texts about the tradition published by Jai Yasothararat in 1936.[27] The same distinction is used in Cambodia to contrast *borān* "traditional" with *samay* "modern" practice, a division that initially referred to divisions within the majority "Mahanikay" monastic lineages of Cambodia as Thai and then French colonial authorities sponsored modernizing approaches to Buddhism and the modern study of Pali. The Khmer and Thai term *boran* is the equivalent of Pali *purāṇa*, meaning "former," "ancient." In commentarial Pali texts from the fifth century, the Pali term *kammaṭṭhāna* meant meditation exercise or practice, but by the early modern period it had come to mean meditation in general or meditation path.[28] The phrase I am using is composite, Khmer/Thai (*borān*) "old/former" and Pali (*kammaṭṭhāna*) "meditation." The Pali *purāṇa*, although written the same way and having the same literal meaning as Khmer/Thai *borān*, is not used with the same connotation. The term *kammaṭṭhān(a)* is recognized in all three languages, as is its Sanskritized counterpart, *karmasthāna*, in Sinhala, to refer to both a specific meditation topic or exercise and meditation practice in general.

While in the early twentieth century these methods were labeled "old," there is no such mention of being "old," or consciousness of being a separate tradition, indicated in the texts belonging to these traditions themselves. The terms used in *borān kammaṭṭhāna* practice manuals are standard terms for meditation from within Theravada: *kammaṭṭhāna*, *samatha*, *vidarśanā*, and *vipassanā*. This indicates that the practitioners did not, before the modern period, see a need to differentiate their training as a distinctive form of meditation. This practice was just *kammaṭṭhāna*, "meditation," although—on the basis of both living and earlier documented practice—we can assume that people sought out different masters for different levels of initiation and for different perspectives. One surviving example of the tradition at Wat Ratchasittharam, Thonburi, Bangkok, describes this system as *majjhima-kammaṭṭhāna-baep-lamdap*, "the progressive development of meditation subjects on the middle path."[29]

Although it was an esoteric tradition, sufficient evidence of *borān kammaṭṭhāna* survives for us to gain some understanding of how it differed from the reform practices of the modern period, and how it related to the scientific world it inhabited. In fact, the first book on Theravada Buddhist meditation ever to be published in the West was a manual of *borān kammaṭṭhāna* from Sri Lanka. It was published in 1896, just a few years after Copleston's book. The manual, given the title *The Yogāvacara's Manual*, was edited by T. W. Rhys Davids, who had founded the Pali Text Society in 1881 to promote the publication and understanding of Pali literature. The basis of the edition was a copy of a manuscript composed in a mixture of Pali and Sinhala lent to Rhys Davids by the renowned Sri Lankan Buddhist revivalist Anagarika Dharmapala.

Anagarika Dharmapala was personally interested in the practice of meditation, so one might say meditation here was in safer hands.[30] However, for those with more positive interest in the subject, meditation was influenced by the same shifts in attitudes to religion that had informed Draper. Particularly influential was the Theosophical Society, set up in 1875. Theosophists assumed that meditation represented a universal mysticism underlying a number of religions, the variations between them being merely skin-deep. While drawing on Buddhism, they also incorporated other strands of thought influential at the time, such as the magnetic healing of Franz Anton Mesmer, particularly as reenvisaged in relation to trance states and clairvoyance by his student Armand Marie Jacques de Chastenet.[31] This influence is seen in Bishop Copleston's reference to mesmerism, which influenced the later development of hypnosis referenced by Shwe Zan Aung. The influence of Theosophy on attitudes to meditation at the time is reflected in remarks made by the colonial officer Hugh Nevill (1847–1897) in relation to the content of some texts related to *The Yogāvacara's Manual* found in manuscripts that he was collecting in Sri Lanka at around the same time:

> I myself regard the whole treatment as an attempt to pass a Buddhist paramattha gloss [using the Buddhist term for "ultimate truth," but possibly a reference to Abhidhamma] over an established system of bhāvānā [(*sic*) meditation], which amounted to what we should call a magnetic concentration of thought on any subject, not necessarily a Buddhist dhyāna [meditative state], and consequent clairvoyance.[32]

No attempt appears to have been made to study the method with a living practitioner and when, twenty years later, a translation was produced, the last known living practitioner in Sri Lanka had already died. The result was that the practice represented by the text was not understood. T. W. Rhys Davids's wife, Caroline, wrote a preface to the new translation, dismissing it as the product of seventeenth-century "decadence."[33]

Caroline Rhys Davids had little experience to go on in making her remarks, but significant textual knowledge by this time. To have learned more about meditation as a practice would have required her studying under a meditation master, controverting the hierarchy of the European-Asian relationship of the period. As it was, her own edition of Buddhaghosa's fifth-century treatise, the *Visuddhimagga*, was to be published in 1920,[34] and she may have been contrasting the content of the earlier publication—which she had typed out at her husband's dictation[35]—with her textual knowledge of the latter text. The *Visuddhimagga*, which we will explore later, was already influencing text-based revivals of Buddhism. In 1897 Dharmapala himself used it as the basis of teaching meditation at Greenacre in Maine, an important center for the dissemination of Asian spirituality to the United States.[36]

Over half a century later, the *borān* meditation system published in *The Yogāvacara's Manual* would again be the subject of a negative assessment. The Sri Lankan monk Mātara Ñāṇārāma, seeking textual sources as the basis for the revival of practice for a new forest meditation tradition, declared: "It is not a method of meditation." Michael Carrithers, reporting on Ñāṇārāma's work, expands on this: "I suspect that here we have an example of an imaginative but not very insightful attempt to revive meditation from the texts, for the texts seem to have been treated as repositories of magical lore."[37]

Interestingly Carrithers notes a Thai work by T. Magness on meditation, "which does much the same for the analytic categories so important to the *Visuddhimagga*. This is what happens when the sense of such categories is lost."[38]

Unwittingly Carrithers had recognized the family connection between two lineages of *borān kammaṭṭhāna*. In the 1950s–1970s, Terence Magness had been, as we shall explore later in chapter 7, a student in the lineage of Candasaro Sot (1884–1959), the abbot of the Wat Paknam, a royal temple in Bangkok. Sot's method forms the basis of the teachings of the Dhammakaya Foundation, a network of temples led by Wat Phra Dhammakaya, a temple established in the 1970s in Pathumthani. The meditation teachings of this latter temple, which now has thousands of adherents worldwide, have also been widely criticized as unorthodox, even in recent years, most notably by the highly regarded and influential Thai scholar-monk Payuth Payutto (b. 1938). Western scholars have also proposed that it developed under the influence of Tibetan tantra.[39] As we shall see, Candasaro Sot had studied in one of the lineages transmitted from the senior monks of eighteenth-century Ayutthaya, which was also the source of the lineage represented by *The Yogāvacara's Manual*.

While negative assessments of Buddhist meditation in general may be a thing of the past, negative estimations of the family of practices here termed *borān kammaṭṭhāna* have remained. Yet the evidence, which we shall discuss more fully in chapter 3, indicates that its practice and transmission was widespread before the modern period. Particularly compelling is the further material that began to be published in the 1970s–1990s, informed by the texts, oral traditions, and living practices of Cambodia and neighboring Laos by François Bizot and other colleagues of the École française d'Extrême-Orient, recorded just prior to the devastation of Buddhism by Marxist revolutions in those countries. Unhindered by the expectations of a classical training in Pali, the usual route to textual scholarship on Theravada Buddhism, Bizot's works indicate the extraordinary depth and richness of this tradition, as well as how it sits within the Theravada culture of the region.[40] In the past decade a substantial amount of new textual material has come to light, and works have been published examining the systems of practice that this material represents.

Why then, given the significant body of evidence and an increasing number of publications on this family of related traditions, has *borān kammaṭṭhāna* been so negatively assessed? Why has it remained relatively unknown, even among scholars of Buddhism? Its neglect in scholarship reflects two things: its esoteric nature and its marginalization as "unorthodox" within the reform-oriented Buddhism that dominated Sri Lanka and mainland Southeast Asia from the nineteenth century onward. As an esoteric practice it was closed to the uninitiated. Moreover, its connection with Buddhist understandings of causality, as explained in the Abhidhamma Piṭaka, is not obvious until one reaches high-level stages of the practice. This meant that its place in relation to Theravada Buddhist orthodoxy was not recognized by outsiders and unclear even to those who had practiced its lower stages. As an esoteric practice, it also could not be advertised or publicly defended. From the teachers' perspective, it was available only to those whose past *kamma* (actions) and inclinations drew them to it, and who were accepted as worthy disciples. A further development that has led to its dismissal is that in the modern period, expectations of what Theravada meditation should entail have been dominated by the understanding of meditation as mind-science. *Borān kammaṭṭhāna*, in contrast, also takes into account the somatic aspects of Buddhist transformation. As we have seen, this understanding of meditation as mind-science, which developed in response to colonialism in the revival of meditation, has continued to grow and develop further in the post-independence period. It has done so at the expense of the earlier somatic approach.

Conclusion

This chapter has examined expectations of what Buddhism and meditation are, and how these, coupled with other developments of the colonial and post-independence period, have taken their toll on the recognition of *borān kammaṭṭhāna*. In its more traditional forms, it has disappeared and is now on the verge of extinction. Meanwhile, some modernized forms from Sot's lineage thrive but are primarily associated with specific groups within Thai Buddhism and are subjected to the discourse that emerges from competition between rival allegiances. In the next chapter, we shall look at what it was about *borān kammaṭṭhāna* that went against expectations of what Theravada meditation should be. We shall discuss the main features of its practice, compare it with more familiar forms of Theravada meditation, and then examine how it was understood by its practitioners to work as a system of spiritual transformation. This requires a consideration of Abhidhamma, the Theravada system of thought that explains experience, ethics, and causality and offers a detailed map of the spiritual path. After considering the evidence for the tradition and the methods of transformation it seeks to harness in more detail in subsequent chapters, we shall return to the colonial context more fully equipped to understand how this affected the perceptions of this tradition and its fate in the modern period.

2

Abhidhamma and Practice

The Path in Theravada Meditation Systems

> Sit comfortably in a position which you can hold for hours if necessary. Then fold your hands in your lap. . . . Close the eyes and try to imagine that you are concentrating the mind in the opening of the right nostril. I want you then to repeat the words *samma arahan* three times. Next, concentrate the mind at the inside corner of the right eye and repeat the words as before. Next, try to concentrate your whole attention at the centre of the skull. Then to the back of the mouth just above the uvula. Then to the bottom of the throat. Then right down to the navel. And finally at a position two fingerbreadths from the navel. At each of these positions you are to repeat *samma arahan* three times, but when you come to the last position you should keep on repeating the words. If you find that the mind wanders come straight back to the final position: do not go through all positions again. From this you will learn much. If you have success you will be conscious of a pinpoint of light seen as if in the mind's eye.
>
> —Candasaro Sot[1]

These were the first instructions in meditation given to the British monk Kapilavaḍḍho in 1954 at the temple Wat Paknam in Bangkok by its abbot Candasaro Sot, who was instrumental in popularizing a modernized, more accessible form of *borān kammaṭṭhāna*. Even this simplified instruction begins to give us some idea of what is unusual or distinctive: the importance of pinpoints of light, sometimes referred to as crystal spheres or gems; the use of mantra, sacred phrases, called *parikamma*, "aids," in this tradition; the attention to a pathway of physical locations from the nostril to a place two fingers' breadth from the navel. This last location is referred to as the "womb," *gabbha*, regardless of the gender of the practitioner.

We shall look at different teaching lineages in the next chapter, where we will be able to locate Candasaro Sot's teachings within the broader family of *borān kammaṭṭhāna*. First, I want to examine here what it was that outside observers found strange or unorthodox about the practice. Then I shall consider how we might nonetheless understand much of *borān kammaṭṭhāna* in relation to Theravada Buddhist understandings of causality, and how to bring about change.

Distinctive Features of Esoteric Theravada Meditation

This section explores a few of the most striking features of *borān kammaṭṭhāna* that mark it out as distinctive from all other forms of Theravada meditation practice. As we shall see, some of these features go against expectations of Theravada as an early, simple form of Buddhism.

Five Pīti *as the Initial Practice*

A distinctive feature of *borān kammaṭṭhāna* is that the practices—at least in the non-modernized forms—invariably begin with the five *pīti*, or joys. These are a subdivision of the *pīti*, joy or thrill, experienced during the first *jhāna*. The *jhāna* are a sequence of successively more refined states of calm and concentration associated with the *samatha*, "calming," effects of meditation practice. The subdivision of *pīti* had been established by the time of the fifth-century commentaries on the Pali canon. Beginning with *pīti* breaks the path down into more manageable stages. Rather than try to attain the first *jhāna* in one go, progress is broken down into its components.[2] Possibly also relevant is the theory found in Buddhist texts that beings in the higher planes of Buddhist cosmology, above the realm of desire (*kāmadhātu*), are nourished by *pīti*, which functions as a form of subtle food. As noted previously, there is a correlation between Buddhist meditative attainments and cosmology, particularly in relation to *samatha* practice. Before the recognition of the umbilical cord, mentioned in one fifth-century Buddhist commentary, it was speculated that the developing embryo in the womb was also nourished on such subtle food.[3]

The Fetus as Model for Spiritual Transformation

The imagery of the womb as the locus of practice is not merely to provide a guide to the rough location of meditative focus. Fetal development and embryology are found everywhere in premodern *borān kammaṭṭhāna*, including in rebirthing rituals.[4] Of the thirty-three constituents of the human body, found in Theravada analysis, twelve are equated with qualities of the mother of the fetus and the remaining twenty-one with the qualities of the father. We also find a division between right hand as male and left hand as female, alongside other male-female divisions. A more striking feature of *borān kammaṭṭhāna*, found nowhere in the Pali canon or its commentaries, is the practice of bringing the meditative attainments beginning with the five *pīti* into the body. This is done by drawing the visual representation of each attainment along a pathway from the intranasal cavity inside the nostril down to the womb. The attainments are usually represented in the form of spheres of light or other *nimitta*, "signs," that emerge during meditation. Once brought to the womb, they are rearranged in various combinations and deposited there. We shall return to this process, and the relationship between these meditations and the traditional medical treatment of the developing embryo in ayurvedic obstetrics, in chapter 5.

The Potency of the Pali Language

The language of the Theravada scriptural canon, Pali, is treated as a sacred language at least as far back as the fifth century C.E. The implications of this sanctity are taken to greater lengths in *borān* culture, with the Pali alphabet understood as a creative and potent force, used in letter symbolism and letter alchemy. For example, the *Buddhanorakan*, a *borān kammaṭṭhāna* text from northeastern Thailand edited by Kitchai Urkasame, provides a cosmogonic myth in which nothing exists prior to the Pali phonemes *ma*, *a*, and *u*. These are then equated with different sets of three: illumination, light, and rays of six colors; the Buddhist virtues of good conduct, inner *dhamma*, and generosity; and life, breath, and mind. Indologists will immediately associate these three syllables with an inversion of the components of the Sanskrit syllable *oṃ*, to which similar cosmogonic potency is attributed in Hinduism. *Oṃ* breaks down into *a*, *u* and *m/ṃ*.[5] We shall explore another cosmogony based on the Pali alphabet in chapter 4. In terms of practice, this conception of Pali means that Pali syllables are treated as potent, able to represent components of the cosmos and the Buddha's teaching. They are used in symbolism and in the mechanism of transformation, by using syllables to impart the qualities that they represent, just like the *nimitta* mentioned above. This letter alchemy is found not only in meditation but in protective practice to create sacred diagrams, *yantra*, made up of Pali syllables, to protect from danger. This practice has now spread globally through the popularity of tattoos from Thailand and Cambodia, although its association with meditation and the potency of Pali is now largely forgotten. This approach to Pali corresponds with the treatment of Sanskrit in the Indic cultural sphere. Moreover, to outsiders it looks similar to tantra, or even—for secular and Protestant colonial observers—the *hocus pocus* of dismissed Catholic incantations, and thus appears alien to Theravada.

Numerology

Numerology or number symbolism is also important in *borān kammaṭṭhāna*, particularly in relation to the number five. Rather than the standard set of three gems or refuges, namely the Buddha, Dhamma, and Sangha, we find five with the addition of the meditation practice itself as the fourth gem and the meditation teacher as the fifth. The offerings made to the Buddha and to the teacher ahead of beginning each stage of the practice are made in fivefold sets of candles, incense, popped rice, water, et cetera. This numerology combines with the use of potent syllables. For example, the set of five syllables *na mo bu ddhā ya*, in exoteric Pali meaning "homage to the Buddha," are said to represent various sets of five, such as the five elements (earth, water, fire, wind, and space), or the five *khandha* (aggregates) that make up the individual, or the five *pīti*. In the last instance, this means that the syllables *na mo bu ddhā ya* may represent the five *pīti* when incorporating the meditative attainments into the body.

Similarities with Tantra

In addition to letter alchemy and numerology, a number of other features may have led to an association between these practices and tantra. These include the creation of a Buddha or enlightened being (arhat) within the body of the practitioner, the process that will be the focus of this chapter. As with tantra, we also see a differentiation between these different types of application, between the internal transformation of oneself, the practitioner, and external transformation of and for others. The latter include methods for healing, bestowing invincibility, or even harming others. The "internal" practice is referred to as the right-hand path and the "external" as the left-hand path. Right-hand/left-hand categorization is found elsewhere in traditional Theravada. It is found in physical symbolism such as the association of the right-hand side with male and the left-hand with female, already noted above, and also in the organization of the Sangha at the national and the monastery level. The right-hand division has priority over that of the left-hand. Although the right-hand/left-hand divide is also found in Śaiva Hindu and Vajrayana Buddhist tantra, the use of the phrase "left hand" in *borān kammaṭṭhāna* does not have the antinomian connotations that it can have there. In other words, we do not see it referring to the charnel ground practices, sexual intercourse and caste transgression, or the consumption of impure substances found in Indic tantra.

Another similarity with tantra is the need for initiation from a teacher in order to practice, though this is not found in the initial stages of the more modernized lineages. The litany used for initiation includes a formula for the teacher taking on any *pāpa* (evil or bad karma) accrued by the initiate and giving the initiate their *puṇya* (merit or good karma), as found in tantric initiation.

Abhidhamma and the Question of Orthodoxy

These and other features make *borān kammaṭṭhāna* look unorthodox in the light of both canonical scripture and contemporary understandings of what Theravada should be. However, alongside these features, we find others that seem entirely in accord with Theravada. The most significant of these is the pervasive presence of Abhidhamma terminology. We have already met with Abhidhamma, the Theravada analysis of the universe and causality, primarily from the perspective of our embodied experience. It provides a framework for understanding how transformation from an unenlightened individual to an arhat, or Buddha, can take place, including a detailed understanding of consciousness and ethics. Contained in the third section of the Pali canon, the Abhidhamma Piṭaka, it represents ultimate truth from the Theravada perspective. As such, it is the most authoritative expression of the Dhamma, the truth taught by the Buddha. Because it is more detailed and systematized than the teachings in the Sutta Piṭaka, it represents orthodoxy. The seventh book of the Abhidhamma Piṭaka, the *Paṭṭhāna* focuses on synthesis, explaining how all the components of reality, *dhammas* (as distinct from *dhamma* in the singular), interact. The *Paṭṭhāna* is believed to be an expression of the Buddha's omniscience.

Abhidhamma continued to develop and has remained a living tradition of exegesis, scholarship, and practice to this day. As we shall see, *borān kammaṭṭhāna* uses extensive Abhidhamma terminology, drawn not from the canon, but from the fifth-century commentarial literature. A useful comparator from that period is the influential treatise, the *Visuddhimagga*, *Path of Purification*, which provides a systematic account of the path to becoming an arhat through the practice of good conduct and meditation, culminating in those meditations leading to liberating wisdom (*paññā*) or insight, as we shall explore further below. The *Visuddhimagga* is a work of Abhidhamma, applied to the path of practice. Highly authoritative, it can also be taken to represent Theravada orthodoxy, making it a valuable reference point.

Since Theravada has existed alongside brahmanical Hinduism and various traditions of Hindu and Buddhist tantra in Southeast Asia and Sri Lanka, an obvious question is whether *borān kammaṭṭhāna* developed from the placing of a Theravada mantel over a body of practice that is essentially brahmanical or tantric. In other words, is the Abhidhamma terminology a superimposition, an attempt to make non-orthodox teachings appear orthodox? Such a process could have taken place at a time when court sponsorship in one of the regions that are Theravada today switched to Theravada from Śaivism or Vajrayana, for example. Alternatively, is *borān kammaṭṭhāna* a development within Abhidhamma-based Buddhism that formed organically within Theravada, perhaps under some of the same influences that shaped those other traditions too? This question is particularly intriguing in the absence of any direct indication of borrowing from tantra, such as a tantric pantheon, the sublimation of sexual union, or the specifics of any tantric rituals known from elsewhere. Kitchai Urkasame's extensive study of *borān kammaṭṭhāna* materials from Thailand provides a thorough and useful consideration of features associated with *borān kammaṭṭhāna* that might be considered tantric in nature. He compares them with examples from non-Theravada sources that are explicitly tantric, confirming the lack of direct borrowing. He also looks at the possibility of local developments to explain some of the distinctive features.[6]

Here, I shall examine *borān kammaṭṭhāna* within the context of Theravada meditation and doctrine. First I shall consider it as a path of practice alongside other Theravada systems of meditation that we more commonly associate with Theravada orthodoxy. I shall then look at instructions on how to perform *borān* meditation in the light of the Abhidhamma terminology it uses. At the end I shall return to this question of whether Abhidhamma is fundamental or superficial to *borān kammaṭṭhāna*. Not all features of the *borān kammaṭṭhāna* processes of transformation apparent in the meditation instructions can be understood with reference to Abhidhamma. I shall identify some of these, so that we can consider them in subsequent chapters.

Comparing Systems of Theravada Meditation

While there are many meditation traditions in Theravada, and they are often influenced by one another, I shall discuss *borān kammaṭṭhāna* as a meditation system in the context of two comparators:

1. The normative, highly influential account of meditation derived from and authorized by the fifth-century-C.E. commentator Buddhaghosa in his *Visuddhimagga*.
2. The modernized, also highly influential reform method of meditation usually referred to as Vipassanā, originating in late nineteenth-century Burma. Here I shall use *Vipassanā*

for this type of meditation in contrast to *vipassanā* to refer to "insight" as an outcome of meditation.

In order to help make sense of the discussion as it develops I shall include here a brief description of each meditation system, by which I mean the structure of the path rather than the individual practices, followed by an outline of *borān kammaṭṭhāna* to give an indication of what it shares with these systems, as well as how it differs. Parts of this description are fairly technical, because the systems of meditation all relate to the Abhidhamma accounts of the types of transformative purification that lead to Awakening.

Buddhaghosa

The name of Buddhaghosa's highly influential treatise, the *Visuddhimagga*, means *Path of Purification* and refers to the sequence of seven purifications, *visuddhi*, that it describes.[7] It does this in three sections, with meditation being described in the second and third of these. The *Visuddhimagga* differentiates two types or outcomes of meditation: calming *samatha* and insight *vipassanā*. Both are predicated on the primary "purification of good conduct," *sīla* (*visuddhi* 1). (I number these purifications in parentheses for the purpose of clarification.) *Sīla* is the subject of the first of the three sections.

The process of calming meditation is achievable in varying degrees through the forty *kammaṭṭhāna* or meditation methods described in the *Samādhi* or concentration section, the second of the three sections of the *Visuddhimagga*. It prepares the mind, making it focused, supple, positive, and receptive. This preparation is described in the *Visuddhimagga* as the "purification of mind" (*visuddhi* 2). Leaving aside the psychological and a range of secondary outcomes of specific *samatha* meditations, the primary desired outcome of *samatha* practice is entry into a sequence of successively more refined states of calmness and concentration, termed *jhāna*, in which the mind becomes completely focused, literally "one-pointed consciousness," *ekaggacitta*.

Samatha meditation is preparatory for reflective *vipassanā* meditation processes found in the final *Paññā*, "Wisdom," section of the *Visuddhimagga*. The *vipassanā* meditation processes are presented as methods that precipitate "insight," *vipassanā*, the transformative cognitive insight into "the way things are," which lies at the heart of Buddhism and which constitutes Awakening. *Vipassanā* techniques involve the observation of experience and the reductive analysis of that experience, following the analyses offered by Abhidhamma. This is achieved through a sequence of three further purifications (*visuddhi* 3, 4, and 5). "Purification of view" (*visuddhi* 3) is achieved by analytic review of the body and mind. This review of the body and mind is performed using one of a number of deconstructions into their interrelating components: the five aggregates, *khandha*, that constitute consciousness, aspects of consciousness, and physicality that make up the individual and their experience, as discussed in the previous chapter;[8] the twelve bases, *āyatana*, of experience, namely the six senses (the five physical senses and mind) and their objects (the five types of tangible object, and thoughts); or the eighteen "elements," *dhātu*, which consist of the twelve *āyatana* plus their corresponding consciousness. In the case of the eye, the *āyatana* are the parts of the eye that see and the visible object, whereas the *dhātu* add the corresponding consciousness, namely sight, to this pair. The next *vipassanā*-related *visuddhi*, "purification of doubt" (*visuddhi* 4), entails realizing the application of the twelve links of dependent origination, *paticcasamuppāda*, the early Buddhist explanation of the chain of causality that perpetuates samsara, the cycle of death and rebirth. The final *vipassanā* purification is "purification of knowledge and vision of the right and wrong path" (*visuddhi* 5), through understanding precisely how all phenomena, beginning with states that are familiar to the practitioner, embody the three characteristics (*lakkhaṇa*) of conditioned existence: impermanence (*anicca*), suffering (*dukkha*), and non-self (*anattā*).

Progress in this system has two aspects: on the one hand, there is progress in *samatha*, which is measured through the practitioner's attainment and control of *jhāna*; and on the other hand, the practitioner also needs to progress through this sequence of three *vipassanā* "purifications" described in the previous paragraph in order to access two further and final purifications. The first of the two final purifications consists of a series of nine sequential insights collectively known as the "purification by knowledge and vision of the Way" (*visuddhi* 6), *paṭipadā-ñāṇa-dassana-visuddhi* (Vism XXI 1–128). This culminates in the second of the two final purifications. This final stage is the acquisition of the four "paths and fruits" (*magga-phala*) of the supramundane states, in which the practitioner transcends the mundane existence of the ordinary person and enters the stages of personal transformation that lead out of samsara. The four stages are "stream enterer," "once-returner," "non-returner," and "worthy one" or "arhat," this last being the Pali term for one who has attained Awakening under the teaching of a Buddha. This supramundane stage is known as the "purification by knowledge and vision" (*visuddhi* 7), *ñāṇa-dassana-visuddhi* (Vism XXII 1–32). The entire series of insight knowledges can be summarized as involving a deepening insight into the three characteristics (*lakkhaṇa*).[9]

Buddhaghosa's approach therefore proposes a hierarchical relationship between *samatha* and *vipassanā* meditation, since it is *vipassanā* that delivers the decisive insights of Buddhist Awakening. At the same time, the two have a symbiosis in that the preparations of *samatha* are presented as a necessary foundation for successful *vipassanā*. Implicit in this system is that soteriological Buddhism requires the transformation of the individual. While the methods of meditation are described in detail, the mechanisms of the transformation that takes place are not discussed. It nevertheless requires the combination of *samatha* and *vipassanā* to achieve that transformation.

The terminology and techniques discussed by Buddhaghosa became the standard terms and techniques contended by all successive Theravada meditation traditions. Even though Buddhaghosa's account of meditation became authoritative for much of Theravada, it should be noted that his account is a selective synthesis of canonical materials that discarded some practices described in the Pali canon, the set of authoritative texts believed by Theravada Buddhists to record the teachings of the Buddha.

Vipassanā, or Insight Meditation

In discussing Vipassanā meditation in this book, I am primarily referring to traditions developed in Burma from the late nineteenth century onward. The most influential lineages emerged from teachings primarily associated with two Burmese monks of the late nineteenth–early twentieth centuries: U Nārada, the first Mingun Sayadaw (1868–1955), and U Ñāṇadhaja, the Ledi Sayadaw (1846–1923). Similar reforms were instigated by other Theravada masters in the same period. The lineage from the first Mingun Sayadaw via Mahasi Sayadaw is also known as the "New Burmese Method" or the "Mahasi Method," or sometimes as "rising and falling." Both lineages were concerned to revive the practice of meditation, in part by simplifying it and in part by making it accessible for practice by lay followers. For textual authority both look back to the two closely related canonical texts, the *Satipaṭṭhāna Sutta* and the more expansive *Mahāsatipaṭṭhāna Sutta*, as seen through the explanations of them in the fifth-century commentaries by Buddhaghosa.[10] Indeed, while the laicization of practice has been seen as a response to various aspects of colonialism and modernity, the direct inspiration may be Buddhaghosa's commentary to the *Mahāsatipaṭṭhāna Sutta*, which describes the ideal country as one where meditation is practiced by all, and the subject of lively conversation by ordinary people as they go about their business.

The overall thrust of Vipassanā as a system is to emphasize the direct practice and experience of *vipassanā* insight meditation. This is achieved in a large part by de-emphasizing *samatha* meditation. Some go so far as to suggest that Vipassanā maintains that *samatha* is completely unnecessary, but different traditions vary on this aspect. *Samatha* is used in a restricted fashion, for example, by the popular Goenka system of Vipassanā in the Ledi lineage through U Ba Khin, which employs mindfulness of breathing, *ānāpānasati*, a *samatha* technique, as a precursor to intensive review of bodily sensations section by section. The Mahasi technique has the practitioner observing the rising and falling of their abdomen as they sit and labeling these sensations, or any other observations on posture or action that arise, with single words—thus, "rising" or "falling," et cetera.

Progress in Vipassanā is measured primarily in relation to the practitioner's experience of insight knowledges, *vipassanā-ñāṇa*.[11] We came across these in the *Visuddhimagga* as the set of nine sequential insights collectively known as the "purification by knowledge and vision of the Way," which constitute the sixth purification (*visuddhi* 6). The Burmese Vipassanā tradition looks to a different formulation of these found in the highly influential twelfth-century *Comprehensive Manual of Abhidhamma,* the *Abhidhammatthasaṅgaha*. This text lists a set of ten *vipassanā-ñāṇa* by combining "purification of knowledge and vision of the right and wrong path" (*visuddhi* 5) in the *Visuddhimagga* with the nine sequential insights that constitute *visuddhi* 6 of the *Visuddhimagga* path.[12]

While the higher attainments are not strictly secret—after all, they are described explicitly in the *Visuddhimagga* and elsewhere—discussion of them in Vipassanā circles is a matter of one-to-one interaction between teacher and pupil, subject to expectations of privacy and decorum. In contrast, basic entry-level practices are widely and freely taught, often to large groups.[13]

As the above summary indicates, there emerged two uses of the term *vipassanā*, "insight." The first is as the desired outcome of meditation. For clarity, we are using *vipassanā* to represent this usage. The second is as the name given to a system of meditations that focuses on achieving this outcome, while downplaying the value of its partner outcome, *samatha*. For clarity, I shall use

"Vipassanā" to represent this usage, referring to the types of meditation that developed in nineteenth–twentieth century Burma and spread worldwide. It is primarily Vipassanā that has been adapted as "Mindfulness" in the Western therapeutic context, with input from other sources such as Zen.

Borān Kammaṭṭhāna

Here I provide an overview of *borān kammaṭṭhāna* in order to locate it within Theravada meditation and contrast it with more familiar systems. Despite its differences from them, *borān kammaṭṭhāna* describes itself as system of *samatha-vipassanā* meditation, in other words, a meditation system that achieves both the *samatha* and *vipassanā* outcomes, so the full Buddhist path, as found also in the *Visuddhimagga*. Like the *Visuddhimagga*, it presupposes the Abhidhamma worldview attested by the fifth century in a number of ways, playing close attention to its understanding of how causality works.

One aspect of this worldview is the concept of momentariness, which elaborated on the early Buddhist teaching of impermanence. All phenomena or aspects of reality, *dhammas* have only momentary existence and are then substituted by other *dhammas*. The constant termination and substitution of *dhammas* provide the appearance of continuity. *Dhamma* in the sense of phenomena or aspects of reality are divided into four kinds: *rūpa*, materiality; *citta*, states of consciousness; *cetasika*, aspects of consciousness; and nibbana, enlightenment. Momentariness and substitution apply to the first three. Progression on the path from ordinary person to arhat entails inculcating positive attributes or factors of consciousness (*cetasika*) in the development of the beautiful mental states (*sobhana citta*). The *sobhana citta* consist of the skillful, resultant, and functional states (*kusala*, *vipāka*, and *kiriya citta*). Functional states are those experienced by arhats, the equivalent of skillful and resultant states of consciousness of those lower on the path but without any attendant karmic consequences. All the *sobhana citta* feature in *borān* manuals as the practitioner, having discarded unskillful mental states, progresses very gradually from skillful to functional states.

In Abhidhamma, the process of substitution is carefully worked out. Only certain types of *citta* may be replaced by other type of *citta*, meaning that change follows certain sequences and is not random. *Borān kammaṭṭhāna* follows those rules of possible causality, the possible permutations that allow one to progress on the path. The most significant difference in practice between it and the *Visuddhimagga* and *Vipassanā* systems of meditation is that *borān* methods then explicitly use the *sobhana citta* and *cetasika dhamma* to create a new, enlightened body. This is achieved by the practitioner pervading their body, their physical form (*rūpa*), with the positive mental states (*citta*), and aspects of consciousness (*cetasika*) as they are developed in meditation. In other words, the practice is extended beyond altering the quality of consciousness and attainment of insight to altering the physicality of the practitioner. In some lineages this is clearly envisaged as building a Buddha within the practitioner's "womb," or core of their body.

These somatic aspects of the practice may seem alien to modern practitioners who think of meditation primarily in terms of mind-science, but they in fact reflect a detailed understanding of the relationship between mentality and physicality found in Abhidhamma. The process uses physical locations within the body, centering on the heart-base (*hadayavatthu* in Pali) and the navel (*nābhi*), important also in the *Visuddhimagga*. Whereas Abhidhamma canonical texts do not identify a specific physical basis or seat for consciousness, the commentaries identified the *hadayavatthu* as that basis, and it is to be found within the heart, the physical organ. The *Visuddhimagga* mentions it also as a "prenascence condition" for mind-consciousness. This means that the *hadayavatthu* is a precondition for the arising of mental consciousness, an internal physical basis for thought, parallel to the eye as the internal physical basis for seeing, et cetera. While the Abhidhamma commentaries identify it as being implicit but unexpressed in the canon, it seems likely that they identified it as implicit in response to new knowledge in Indic anatomical understanding that arose after the Buddhist canonical scripture began to be composed, in around the fifth century B.C.E, and before the commentaries on the canon were written, from around the fifth century C.E. onward. This new anatomical knowledge is found in ayurvedic medical treatises such as the *Suśruta Saṃhitā* and *Caraka Saṃhitā* that were composed during this intervening period.[14]

The somatic aspects of *borān* practice thus take seriously the Abhidhamma understanding of the complex interrelationship between consciousness, aspects of conscious, and materiality, and thus draw on developments in understanding of *rūpa*. The concept of *cittaja-rūpa*, materiality (*rūpa*) that arises (*ja*) from consciousness (*citta*), seems to be relevant here, even though not explicitly named, because the process seems to involve creating new form, a new body (*rūpa*), by bringing the *citta* and *cetasika* into these physical locations in the body. While we have seen that *borān kammaṭṭhāna* drew on the Abhidhamma material formulated between the closing of the canonical material and the fifth-century commentarial period, it does not explicitly include the more detailed analysis of materiality found in later Abhidhamma such as the influential twelfth-century compendium of Abhidhamma, the *Abhidhammatthasaṅgaha,* which further breaks down the form of materiality (for example, into particles, *kalāpa*). Nonetheless, the process of transformation described in the latter is helpful for understanding the model of change underlying *borān* meditation because the *Abhidhammatthasaṅgaha* explains how causality in relation to *rūpa*, *citta*, and *cetasika* works. Since the *Visuddhimagga* offers an explanation of progression in relation to meditation practice, both texts are useful for understanding how *borān kammaṭṭhāna* conceptualized progress toward arhatship in terms of the causality of *rūpa*, *citta*, and *cetasika*, and what this means in terms of meditation.

Comparing the *Amatākaravaṇṇanā* and the *Visuddhimagga*

For a more direct comparison with the *Visuddhimagga* in terms of meditation topics, let us examine the broad contents of a *borān kammaṭṭhāna* meditation manual from Sri Lanka called the *Amatākaravaṇṇanā*, "Account of the Mine of Immortality." The *Amatākaravaṇṇanā* is one of most the extensive of the extant *borān* manuals. It was recorded in Pali by disciples of the Siamese meditation masters who brought the method from Ayutthaya to Kandy in the middle of the eighteenth century.

The *Amatākaravaṇṇanā* employs all but one of the *kammaṭṭhāna* that are listed by Buddhaghosa under *samatha* meditation. It combines them with another six components so as to create a thirteen-stage path. This adds three additional stages at the start of the *kammaṭṭhāna,* which consists of different types of *cetasika* important in the development of *jhāna*. Then come seven types of practice classified as *samatha* in the *Visuddhimagga* but in a slightly different configuration. Then we move into the *vipassanā* stage, with the ten insight knowledges (*vipassanā-ñāṇa*) of Vipassanā, which combines *visuddhis* 5 and 6 of the *Visuddhimagga,* then the supramundane states (*magga-phala*), and finally nibbana. The *kammaṭṭhāna* on the physical elements, *dhātu,* is not given as a separate meditation subject in the *Amatākaravaṇṇanā*. There are five physical elements, namely earth, water, fire, wind, and space, and they make up all materiality, *rūpa*. The reason no *kammaṭṭhāna* dedicated to the elements is found here is because, rather than being a separate meditation, they are found throughout all the meditations. This is because of the method of incorporating the desired *citta* and *cetasika* into the body, through combination with the elements that make up the materiality, *rūpa*, of the body.

The aim of this path to Awakening is for the practitioner to embody the full constituents of Buddhahood. The process takes the practitioner through all the stages of mental and physical development via the step-by-step development of the appropriate

Figure 1
Comparison of the *Kammaṭṭhāna* Lists of the *Amatākaravaṇṇanā* and the *Visuddhimagga*

No.	Path of the *Amatākaravaṇṇanā*	Forty *Kammaṭṭhāna* of the *Visuddhimagga*
1	*pañca-pīti* – five joys (5)	
2	*cha-yugala* – six pairs (12)	
3	*kāyacittasukha* – ease of body and mind	
4	*ānāpānasati* – mindfulness of breathing (1)	*(one of the 10 anussati, below)*
5	*kasiṇa* (10)	10 *kasiṇa* – the ten visual devices
6	*asubha* (10)	10 *asubha* – the ten impurities
7	*kāyagatāsati* – mindfulness of the body (32)	10 *anussati* – the recollections
8	*buddhānussati*, etc. (10)	
9	*arūpāvacara* (4)	4 *arūpāvacara* – the formless realms
10	*brahmavihāra* (4)	4 *brahmavihāras* – the four "divine abidings"
11	*dasañāṇa* – the ten knowledges (10)	
12	*catummaggaphala* – the four "paths and results/fruits" (8)	
13	*amata-nibbana* – the deathless state of Awakening (1)	
		the repulsiveness of food
	No separate elements section, but elements employed "longitudinally" to assist the integration of all *nimitta*.	the elements (4)

cetasika, aspects of consciousness, and *citta*, states of consciousness. In this path, for each component, or each of its subsets, until the higher levels, the practitioner's concentration leads them to experience a *nimitta* or "sign," usually an intensely vivid, eidetic image. *Nimitta* are explained in detail in the *Visuddhimagga*, but they are not as pervasive there as they are in *borān* practice.[15] The *Amatākaravaṇṇanā* provides *nimitta* for almost all stages, although some of the advanced stages have no corresponding sign. Those stages are said to lack any equivalent sign, so are "without sign," *animitta*. The *Amatākaravaṇṇanā* then—and this is what makes *borān kammaṭṭhāna* distinctive—instructs the meditator to internalize the *nimitta* for each of the thirteen stages into the body, from the tip of the nostril to the practitioner's navel. What are variously described as meditation objects, processes, or states in the *Visuddhimagga* are here all treated as being akin to subtle objects that can be physically manipulated inside the body of the practitioner, in combination with different aspects of consciousness and physicality. The practice thereby combines the desirable states of consciousness (*citta*), aspects of consciousness (*cetasika*), and materiality (*rūpa*), the three types of phenomena or aspects of reality (*dhamma*) according to Abhidhamma.

As noted above, traditional *borān* practice begins with the five *pīti*, aspects of consciousness (*cetasika*) present in the first *jhāna*, itself a state of consciousness, *citta*. The subsequent two stages also bring in *cetasika* important in the early stages of meditation. Next we have the *yugala*, "pairs," six pairs of positive attributes of body and mind. These *cetasika* act as antidotes to the five hindrances that block progress in meditation: desire, ill will, sloth and torpor, restlessness and worry, and doubt. Once the hindrances have been removed it is possible to attain the next set, *kāyacittasukha*, "ease or happiness of body and of mind." These are in turn necessary for attaining three levels of focus or concentration, *samādhi*: momentary, access, and absorption concentration, important at successive levels of transformation. The third of these, absorption *samādhi*, allows full experience of *jhāna*. It also enables the consciousness to avoid falling back into its habitual resting state within samsara, so is crucial in the attainment of arhatship.[16]

While many of the stages of meditation in the *Amatākaravaṇṇanā* correlate with those found in the *Visuddhimagga*, the *Amatākaravaṇṇanā* uses a "delivery method" that is very distinctive to *borān kammaṭṭhāna* and is not found in the *Visuddhimagga* or in Vipassanā. My reason for using the phrase "delivery method" is that once an experience has been established, such as the experience of the first *pīti*, or joy, that comes with initial *jhāna* experience, it must be taken into the body just as a pharmaceutical substance might be delivered into the body in medicine. It is this taking in of the experiences into the body that constructs the Buddha within. The *nimitta* corresponding to the desired experiences are key to this delivery. The *Amatākaravaṇṇanā* gives instructions for how to incorporate the meditation stages into the practitioner's body using the *nimitta*. Before looking at that delivery method, let us first consider the place of *nimitta* in Theravada meditation.

Nimitta in Theravada Meditation

Both the *Visuddhimagga* and the *Amatākaravaṇṇanā* teach the *nimitta* as the primarily visual characteristic of experiencing the outcome of a meditation, but their use in *borān* texts is far more extensive. Early on in the manual, some attention is given to describing what they are like, so that the practitioner and teacher can both recognize that a stage has been successfully reached. Here is the first mention of the *nimitta* experience in the *Amatākaravaṇṇanā* in relation to the first *pīti*, or joy:

> With his eye consciousness focused on the tip of his nose, he should establish the consciousness of his mind on the supports [*ārammaṇa*, objects of cognition] that are the in and out breaths. While watching in this way drops of foam or rays of smoke-like lines appear. He should recognize this as the acquiring sign (*uggahanimitta*).[17]

Here alternative appearances for the *nimitta* are given because they may be seen differently by different people. In the higher stages of some of the Sri Lankan manuals the experience of *nimitta* is briefly said to correlate to the *nimitta* for earlier stages; in other words, the physical and visual experiences are reused to represent different meditation results at different stages in the practice.

In the *Visuddhimagga*, although *nimitta* are also noted as arising in a number of other practices, the most extensive explanation of them and their use comes in the section on the *kasiṇa* practices, the ten contemplations of colored disks and other visual objects.[18] In the *borān* traditions, the use of *nimitta* is found with most stages of the practice, where the visual experience of the *nimitta* often has no obvious correlation with the meditation from which they develop. While meditators of non-*borān* methods often report the experience of *nimitta* even with practices such as *mettā*, because of their correlation with *jhāna* experience, they may treat them as interesting but ultimately as side effects of meditation. In contrast, the *borān* tradition systematizes them. It treats them as both diagnostics of achievement and as the medium for transporting what they represent into the body.[19] Here is how the *Amatākaravaṇṇanā* chapter on the *brahmavihāra* practices begins its summary of the *nimitta* for *mettā* (loving kindness, the first *brahmavihāra*):

> The preliminary sign is like a firefly. The acquiring sign is like the feathers of a peacock's tail. The counterpart sign has the color of a *kālaguṇa* stone.[20] Such are the distinguishing marks of *mettā*.[21]

Three stages of *nimitta* are mentioned here. They are explained in the *Visuddhimagga* in terms of the stages of progress in using a *kasiṇa* as a basis for meditation. The first, the preliminary sign, *parikamma-nimitta*, is what the practitioner sees when relying on the external object. The second, the acquiring sign, *uggaha-nimitta*, is when the practitioner is able to see the object with their eyes shut as clearly as with them open. The third is the counterpart sign, *paṭibhāga-nimitta*, which is a mental image of the meditation object that the practitioner can manipulate independently of the initial object. The counterpart sign is the object of *jhāna citta*, the states of consciousness that constitute the experience of *jhāna*.[22] As Eric Greene points out, the final stage, the counterpart sign, *paṭibhāga-nimitta*, is of an altogether different quality from the other two. It is more pure than the original object and functions as a kind of essence of it.

> The counterpart sign is *not* the perfect, "eidetic" *visualization* . . . of the initial object of meditation, but rather something like the purified essence of the object. For the water *kasiṇa*, for example, both the original object and the "acquired sign" have bubbles, froth, and other such details, while the counterpart sign "appears inactive, like a crystal fan set in space" . . . (There is thus actually a *loss* of visual "resolution" relative to the original physical object, as one moves from the acquired sign to the counterpart sign.) Significantly, the counterpart sign is sometimes described in visual terms even when the initial meditation object itself is not in any sense a "visual" one. Thus in the case of meditation on the breath, . . . it is said that the counterpart sign appears "to some like star or a cluster of gems," and to others "like a stretched-out cobweb or a film or cloud or a lotus flower or a chariot wheel or the moon's disk or the sun's disk."[23]

It is this purified essence that the *Amatākaravaṇṇanā* draws down into the body.[24] The counterpart sign is particularly important in that it can lead to the absorption *samādhi*, crucial in *jhāna* attainment.

While the *Amatākaravaṇṇanā* appears to add additional stages to the meditation in comparison with the *Visuddhimagga*, for example by treating the *cetasika* of the early stages of *jhāna* and the attainment of the eight supramundane states as separate meditation exercises, it is clear that the more discursive explanation of the *Visuddhimagga* is often helpful in explaining the concepts the *Amatākaravaṇṇanā* mentions. In fact, while treated as separate *kammaṭṭhāna*, all these additional topics are found in the *Visuddhimagga*. Let us return to the comparison between the *Amatākaravaṇṇanā* and *Visuddhimagga* that we began above. There we provided a broad comparison of the meditation topics, the *kammaṭṭhāna*, found in each, which revealed the broad correlation between the two, but also revealed the additional stages found in the *Amatākaravaṇṇanā*. Here Figure 2 shows how each of the components within the thirteen meditation stages contained in the *Amatākaravaṇṇanā* are all in fact also found in the *Visuddhimagga*. The right-hand column provides the parallel occurrences in the *Visuddhimagga* for each of the topics found in the *Amatākaravaṇṇanā*.

Figure 2
Correspondence between Topics in the *Amatākaravaṇṇanā* and Subjects Discussed in the *Visuddhimagga*

No.	*Amatākaravaṇṇanā*	*Visuddhimagga*
1	*pañcapīti* – five joys, aspects of consciousness (*cetasika*) that arise in early stages of *jhāna*, the increasingly elevated, focused state of body and mind that results from successful meditation practice.	Vism IV 94–99; pp. 141–142
2	[*cha-*]*yugala* – six pairs – positive attributes of body and mind. Again *cetasika*, in this case the antidotes to the five hindrances.	Vism XIV 145–149; pp. 468–469

No.	*Amatākaravaṇṇanā*	*Visuddhimagga*
3	*kāyacittasukha* – ease/ happiness of body and of mind. The prelude to the three levels of concentration: momentary, access, and absorption concentration.	Vism IV 99–100; p. 142
4	*ānāpānasati* – mindfulness of breathing	Vism VIII 145–244; pp. 259–285
5	*kasiṇa* – the ten visual devices that can be employed as objects of concentration	Earth Kasiṇa: Vism IV 2–198; pp. 118–165 Remaining Kasiṇa: Vism V 1–42; pp. 166–172
6	*asubha* – the ten ugly sights of a corpse	Vism VI 1–94; pp. 173–190
7	*kāyagatāsati* – mindfulness of the body including awareness of its thirty-two constituent parts	Vism VIII 42–144; pp. 235–259
8	*buddhānussati* – the ten recollections or applications of mindfulness *sati*, beginning with the recollection of the Buddha	Recollection of the Buddha: Vism VII 2–67; pp. 192–209 Recollection of the Dhamma: Vism VII 68–88; pp. 209–215 Recollection of the Sangha: Vism VII 89–100; pp. 215–218 Recollection of virtue: Vism VII 101–106; pp. 218–219 Recollection of generosity: Vism VII 107–114; pp. 219– 221 Recollection of deities: Vism VII 115–118; pp. 221–222 Recollection of death: Vism VIII 1–41; pp. 225–235 Recollection of the body: Vism VIII 42–144; pp. 235–259 Recollection of breathing: Vism VIII 145–244; pp. 259–285 Recollection of peace: Vism VIII 245–251; pp. 285–287

No.	*Amatākaravaṇṇanā*	*Visuddhimagga*
9	*arūpāvacara* – the formless realms – i.e., non-material *jhāna*	Vism X 1–66; pp. 320–336
10	*brahmavihāra* – the four "divine abidings" meditations: *mettā*, loving-kindness; *karuṇā*, compassion; *muditā*, sympathetic joy; and *upekkhā*, equanimity	Vism IX 1–124; pp. 288–319
11	*dasañāṇa* – the ten knowledges or insights. These are Purifications (5) and (6) of the *Visuddhimagga*, and the *vipassanā-ñāṇā* of Vipassanā.	1. *sammasana-ñāṇa* knowledge of comprehension Vism XX passim 2. *udaya-vyaya-dassana-ñāṇa* knowledge of rise and fall Vism XX 93–104; pp. 652– 656 and Vism XXI 3–9; pp. 662–663 3. *bhaṅgānudassana-ñāṇa* knowledge of dissolution Vism XXI 10–28; pp. 663–668 4. *bhayatupaṭṭhāna-dassana-ñāṇa* knowledge of appearance as terror Vism XXI 29–34; pp. 668–669 5. *ādīnavānudassana-ñāṇa* knowledge of danger Vism XXI 35–42; pp. 670–673 6. *nibbidānudassana-ñāṇa* knowledge of dispassion Vism XXI 43–44; pp. 673–674 7. *muccitu-kamyatā-dassana-ñāṇa* knowledge of desire for deliverance Vism XXI 45–46; pp. 674 8. *paṭisaṅkhānupassanā-ñāṇa* knowledge of reflection Vism XXI 47–52; pp. 674–676 9. *saṅkhārupekkānupassanā-ñāṇa* knowledge of equanimity about formations Vism XXI 61–65; pp. 678–679 10. *anuloma-anupassanā-ñāṇa* conformity knowledge Vism XXI 128–136; pp. 692–695

No.	*Amatākaravaṇṇanā*	*Visuddhimagga*
12	*catummaggaphala* – the four "paths and results/fruits" – i.e., the four stages on the path to arhatship, beginning with stream entrance, divided into eight, the path and the result	Vism XXII 3–31; pp. 696–702 The first path – first noble person The first fruition – second noble person The second path – third noble person . . . The fourth fruition – eighth noble person
13	*amata-nibbana* – the deathless state of Enlightenment	The attainment of cessation: Vism XXIII 15–60; pp. 730–740

This means that there is resounding overlap in terms of technical language and the envisaged pathway of transformation between the *Amatākaravaṇṇanā* and the *Visuddhimagga*, even while the internalization of the meditation attainments into the body through the combining of the *citta* and *cetasika* with the *rūpa* of the body is absent from the latter.

Initial Generation of *Nimitta*

Different lineages of *borān* practice teach the initial steps leading to *nimitta* differently. In the more traditional versions of the practice at Wat Damrei Sar in Cambodia and at Wat Ratchasittharam in Thonburi, Thailand, the practitioner is specifically not told what to expect from their meditation. The *nimitta* must arise spontaneously. In the former, one is taught how to breathe while reciting *arahaṃ* and given a question to find the answer to, even though the meaning of the question is not obvious. At Wat Ratchasittharam, one again begins with a basic breathing practice, this time specifically focusing on the area two-fingers breadths below the navel, while repeating the phrase *bu-ddho*.[25] As the mind settles and gains focus, the *nimitta* arise and these are reported to the teacher. In other lineages, such as that used by the Dhammakaya network of temples, one actively visualizes the crystal gem or crystal-like Buddha image. This practice is therefore more akin to *kasiṇa* practice, but with different objects of meditation to start with. One might conjecture that providing the practitioner with a description of what to look for is a feature of the modernization of the practice to make it easier to teach in large groups, or at speed. However, Phibul Choompolpaisal has recently identified it as deriving from the practice associated with a group of fifty-six unnamed meditation teachers from Ayutthaya, so dating back to at least the eighteenth century.[26] Sot's instruction to Kapilavaḍḍho, quoted at the outset of this chapter, represents a midway point between these two ends of the spectrum. Sot told Kapilavaḍḍho what to expect, but not to actively visualize it.

More traditional lineages also include a preliminary stage prior to the actual meditation practice. At the preliminary stage, the practitioner invites the *dhamma*, the desired phenomenon that he wishes to experience, usually the appropriate *cetasika*, to arise. The Pali term for the invitation is *ārādhanā*, from the verb *ārādheti*, "to please, propitiate." The same term is used when inviting a god to attend a ceremony at a temple. In Wat Damrei Sar in Cambodia, although the *dhammas* are regarded as external realities, there is no detailed litany for this. Rather, the *nimitta* representing these *dhamma* arise spontaneously in the correct order in response to the practitioner seeking answers to the "question" the teacher has posed. However, Wat Ratchasittharam in Thonburi, Thailand, preserves a process of invitation that closely corresponds to the more elaborate invitations found in the Sri Lankan manuscripts of the eighteenth-century practitioners. One such text is a litany called the *Vākkapprakaraṇa* to be used in conjunction with the *Amatākaravaṇṇanā*. When the practitioner invites the *dhammas* in the Wat Ratchasittharam practice, he uses honorifics that reflect the treatment of them as high-status, independent entities. These honorifics are also applied to the *kammaṭṭhāna*, the meditation exercises themselves, which ties in with them being one of the five refuges. The Thai honorifics are *ong* and *phra* before the term, both used in Thai culture before the name or term for something sacred such as a Buddha image and a Buddhist monk, and *chao* used after. Thus the *cetasika* desired in the first stage of meditation practice, the *pīti* or delights, is addressed as *ong-phra-pitithamma-chao*.[27] The use of an invitation to the desired *dhamma* reflects the understanding that they have a certain amount of autonomy, even though they are conditioned. This may correspond with the Abhidhamma analysis of *citta* as internal, *ajjhattika*, and *cetasika* as external, *bāhira*, like visitors, despite the fact that *citta* cannot arise without a minimum of seven concomitant *cetasika*.

We know from current practice, from the diagrams in the Sri Lankan and Lao manuals, and from other *borān kammaṭṭhāna* evidence that the *nimitta* may be experienced as spheres of light. These may be marked by individual Pali syllables, such as *a*, *ra*, or *haṃ* if it is a set of three, or *na mo bu ddhā ya* if it is a set of five. This relates to the *borān* conceptualization and use of sacred language. The expectation is that these are in Khom script, the Cambodian script used for the Pali language across the Khmer-Tai cultural region until the modern period. Simple *nimitta*, then, appear as colored lights or spheres, on their own or with Buddha images or sacred syllables, and may be attended by physical symptoms such as coolness, tingling, or horripilation. Phibul Choompolpaisal has recently provided a detailed survey of the varied types of *nimitta* found in manuals from Thailand and Laos from the seventeenth century onward, which were published in the 1930s.[28]

In some lineages, *nimitta* may become more complex and even narrative. This is a feature characteristic of the Cambodian tradition, where the *nimitta* may become didactic or give access to living beings in other realms. Thus the *nimitta* of the lower stages of the path at Wat Damrei Sar in Cambodia not only indicate attainment of the five *pīti*, but also such important cultural values as the qualities of parents, family, and teachers, as well as important Buddhist teachings such as rebirth and *asubha*, the impurity and impermanence of the body. It is also believed that through the practice people may also meet with the dying, deceased, and inhabitants of other realms, either deliberately or spontaneously. This last aspect explains the role of meditation practitioners in Cambodian funerals, a role that continues in name even as the availability of actual meditation practitioners has become more scarce. With these more complex *nimitta*, we find an interesting parallel between *borān kammaṭṭhāna* and Tibetan dream yoga. In the latter, the illusory nature of the external world may be harnessed to move between dream, life, and interlife states. In Theravada, by contrast, the external world really exists, creating the reverse relationship: the *nimitta* experienced by the practitioner are indicative of external realities. Both worldviews allow the harnessing of meditation experience to navigate this life and the next.

Incorporation of the *Nimitta*

Keeping for now with the simple *nimitta* in the forms of spheres of light, the practitioner, after developing the *nimitta*, grasps or catches (Pali *gaṇheti*) each sphere of light at the tip of the nose, one by one, and repeatedly moves them inside through the nostril. Male practitioners bring the visual image through the right nostril, female practitioners through the left nostril. This right-hand/left-hand division is parallel to the treatment of male and female embryos in Ayurveda, a point to which we shall return later, but we shall see from this point on correspondences between the treatment of the baby-to-be in traditional South Asian medicine and the treatment of the Buddha-to-be in *borān kammaṭṭhāna*.[29] From the nostril the practitioner moves the visual images down to place them (*ṭhapeti*) in the energy bases in the body. The list varies, but always starts with the tip of the nose and ends up in the "womb," two fingers' width from the navel, as seen in the instruction to Kapilavaḍḍho at the start of this chapter. In fuller lists, the *nimitta* is moved from the tip of the nose, to the back of the nose between the eyes, between the eyebrows, to the top of the head, at the back of the head, the epiglottis, the heart, the navel, and finally the place situated at a distance two fingers' width from the navel. Some manuals, including the *Amatākaravaṇṇanā*, do not mention the bases between the nostril and the epiglottis. Other Sri Lankan manuals include locations around the mouth and further down in the body, including the groin.[30] Again, this use of energy channels from the right or left nasal cavity down to the womb parallels the use of delivery pathways to deliver medicine to treat a male and female embryo respectively in traditional obstetrics. While the locations may be reminiscent of the *cakra* centers used in yoga and tantra, or the *marma* of traditional Indian medicine, I have found no use of these terms in the manuals I have examined to date. I have, however, found the term *nāḍī*, "energy channel."

After placing these visual representations of the meditative experiences in or near the navel, the practitioner combines them at that point, in different arrangements within the body, both vertically, especially between the heart and navel, and horizontally, on the plane at the level of the navel. In other words, the navel functions as the central location of a horizontal plane across the body, around which these *nimitta* can be moved. It seems that this is the way for them to enter the "interior of the womb" (*antogabbhasmiṃ*) two fingers' width from the navel. Although the womb imagery might suggest that the practitioner, whether male or female, is identified as female, at least symbolically, this issue is nowhere raised in the existing teachings. The practitioner repeatedly draws down along this channel from the nostril to the womb the successive *jhāna* and *dhammasaññā*, "realization of the quality" sought in relation to each of the *kammaṭṭhāna* to build the enlightened being within. They draw the qualities in, first in order, *anuloma*, and then in reverse order, *paṭiloma*, terms also used in Abhidhamma in relation to the positive and negative ordering of permutations to represent all the possible combinations of causality.[31]

The practitioner continues the process of internalization by invoking the five elements (earth, water, fire, wind, and space) that make up all physicality, including the human body, and plants them also at the place on which the meditation is focused, the navel, again in different arrangements. The practitioner brings further aspects of the meditation such as the skillful, resultant, and functional (*kusala, vipāka, kiriya*) states of consciousness and aspects of consciousness (*citta* and *cetasika*) into this physical location, again bringing the *jhāna* and placing them on the points they had been previously. Increasing combinations are brought into the body in relation to each *kammaṭṭhāna* including a grammatical element, the "six sounds." These are the six places of articulation that allow different phonemes to be produced in the mouth.[32] After completing the various cycles of combination, the practitioner now "ties" (Pali *bandhati*) each element of this new Buddha body into the fabric of their own physical being and, in so doing, recreates themselves as an arhat or a Buddha.

The various manuals from Sri Lanka all teach the same process but vary in what information they provide and how fully they represent the techniques. This indicates that they were composed as a record of the practice by individual practitioners. Sometimes these give us additional details. For example, one manual mentions an inspiring sermon as an occasion that might lead to the experience of *pīti*. Small snippets like this in manuals that are otherwise dry and technical remind us that even where the early stages of the process are not described, the ritualistic aspects of this practice harness actual experiences. They do not appear to be purely formulaic, yet for the most part they leave the process for inculcating the experience unspoken.

This movement of desirable aspects and states of consciousness between and at specific places throughout the body reflects premodern South Asian understandings of consciousness as mobile, while the reconstructing of these aspects in different combinations relates to the Abhidhamma understanding of consciousness as composite and ever-changing. The rapid iteration of the process, as well as reflecting the Abhidhamma understanding of momentariness, may reflect the process of transformation found in the purification of mercury and gold, as we shall discuss later, when looking at parallels with traditional chemistry. Here, embryology is again relevant, since traditional mercury purification was also thought of in terms of the creation of a new being through the union of male and female elements.

Progression in *borān kammaṭṭhāna* is obviously aimed at reaching the supramundane states from stream entrant to arhat. In practical terms it is measured by the practitioner's experience of the *nimitta* and other signs—experiences that are recognized and interpreted by their teacher—as well as by their ability to control the process of internalization of *nimitta* and the construction of the internal Buddha. How the progressive incorporation of the qualities of consciousness into the body relates to nibbana is not completely explained in any of the manuals. Some accounts of this path refer to the discarding of the transient, physical body on death, at which point the successful practitioner enters full nibbana.

Orthodoxy, Orthopraxy, and Abhidhamma

The extensive use of Abhidhamma concepts, path, and terminology in *borān kammaṭṭhāna* locates it within Theravada "orthodoxy." The earliest high-profile criticism of *borān kammaṭṭhāna* as unorthodox came from the monk Vajirañāṇa, Prince Mongkut, later King Rāma IV (1804–1868). When he was still a monk and was trained in these practices, Mongkut dismissed them as unorthodox because they were not visible in canonical and commentarial texts. As Mongkut became more powerful, meditation practitioners responded to this critique by aligning their practices with normative textual sources. We shall return to the reforms of Buddhism in the modernization of Thailand later, but here I want to consider the possibility that such criticism altered how *borān* texts were presented, to make them look more orthodox. In other words, is the Abhidhamma of *borān* material the result of what is referred to in textual studies as "contamination," the changing of one recension of texts under the influence of a different lineage?

This process of making the manuals look more orthodox could certainly apply from the time of Mongkut onward. According to

Olivier de Bernon, we can see the normalization of texts within the tradition by comparing two printed texts of the *borān kammaṭṭhāna* manual entitled the *Mūlakammaṭṭhāna* published in 1931 and 1934, both based on the same now-lost eighteenth-century manuscript from Wat Ratchathiwat (Wat Samoray) in Bangkok, which contained a manual belonging to the late eighteenth-century abbot of that temple. The second version of this text was published by Phrayakosakonvijan (also known as Boonsri Praphasiri, 1882–1963), a senior officer in the Thai Government.[33] According to Bernon, Phrayakosakonvijan altered the text, trying to make sense of it by adding passages from the normative *Visuddhimagga* and *Abhidhammatthasaṅgaha*, both mentioned above, into the texts.[34] In this same period, in 1936, Yasothararat produced an edition of multiple *borān kammaṭṭhāna* texts, whose range in geography and time, from regions now covered by Laos and Thailand between the sixteenth to early twentieth centuries, makes it one of the most important sources of evidence for the chronology and range of *borān kammaṭṭhāna* in Southeast Asia. In his introduction, he mentions comparing the texts with the *Abhidhammatthasaṅgaha* and *Visuddhimagga*, which, as Phibul Choompolpaisal points out, begs the question of contamination in his edition.[35]

However, the *Amatākaravaṇṇanā* manual explored above stems from the eighteenth century. If we turn to *borān kammaṭṭhāna* evidence that predates Mongkut or falls outside of his sphere of influence, we find that the concordance with Abhidhamma and the categories and worldview of the *Visuddhimagga* is ubiquitous. The related Phitsanulok *dhammakāya* inscription of 1549, and the longer versions of the *dhammakāya* text that circulate, use Abhidhamma terminology.[36] A particularly striking piece of evidence for the compatibility of normative Pali texts and *borān kammaṭṭhāna* is the Cambodian royal decree of 1920. This decree sought to suppress traditional Cambodian Buddhism of which *borān* meditation is just one aspect. It names attainments of which practitioners should not boast, yet these attainments are instantly recognizable from the "orthodox" account of progress in Abhidhamma, and they are found listed in the *Visuddhimagga*. These include the following results of successfully following the path of Theravada meditation, terms all found in our discussion above, in both *borān* texts and the *Visuddhimagga*: *jhāna*, *vimokkha*, *samādhi*, *sampat*, *magga*, and *phala*. However, for me it is the very detail of the path to nibbana laid out in texts such as the *Amatākaravaṇṇanā* and other manuals compiled in Sri Lanka following the meditation mission from Ayutthaya in the mid-eighteenth century that confirms the extensive correspondence between *borān kammaṭṭhāna* and Abhidhamma. It is too fundamental to the structure and the practice to be the result of superimposition.

The *Amatākaravaṇṇanā* and its accompanying litany, the *Vākkapprakaraṇa*, break down the entire path toward the practitioner's goal of achieving nibbana into progressive stages, through a process of discarding unskillful mental factors (*akusala cetasika*), and developing skillful mental states (*kusala citta*) and their attendant mental factors (*kusala cetasika*) and the higher beautiful mental states in ways that demonstrate a detailed understanding of the Abhidhamma analysis of causality. Phibul Choompolpaisal has pointed out that some of the modernization of *borān* methods entailed a simplification of the practice by focusing on individual sections, rather than following the entire sequence of practices.[37] As we have seen, it is the sequence that clarifies the relationship with the Abhidhamma analysis of the path. The modernization methods seem to obscure rather than clarify or enhance the relationship with Abhidhamma. This may explain why the extent to which the few surviving lineages of *borān kammaṭṭhāna* recognize the extent of the relationship with Abhidhamma varies. Indeed, in Thailand reform Buddhists emphasized the first two of the three sections of the Pali canon, the Vinaya Piṭaka on Monastic Discipline and the Sutta Piṭaka, to the detriment of expertise in the Abhidhamma Piṭaka, facilitating a rift between meditation and Abhidhamma. The loss of expertise in Abhidhamma may have contributed to the lack of recognition of the processes envisaged in *borān* practice.

It is possible, then, that the additions of sections of the *Visuddhimagga* and *Abhidhammatthasaṅgaha* and their consultation in publications of the 1930s were an attempt to provide clarity, prompted by the recognizable Abhidhamma character of the material before the redactor, just as we have drawn on these same texts above. For if this "orthodoxy" is a superimposition onto an unorthodox underlay or framework, it must have been imposed prior to any of our existing evidence for the tradition, prior to the different branches of *borān kammaṭṭhāna* spreading throughout the Theravada world, and long prior to any of the accusations of unorthodoxy made in the modern period. There is no evidence of an unorthodox "framework."

Rather than speculating about alternative sources for which there is no evidence, we can have better success in construing the issue not as a question of orthodoxy, correct doctrine, but as one of orthopraxy, correct practice. The ways in which the realization and embodiment of those orthodox doctrines are *delivered* to the practitioner, through a process of internalization into the body, are not described in the Pali canon or the *Visuddhimagga*. The delivery methods of *borān kammaṭṭhāna* are what make it distinctive and at first sight hard to understand. While not mentioned in such texts as the *Visuddhimagga*, these too appear to be a working out of causality and how change is brought about, based on Abhidhamma conceptions of momentariness and an Indic model of consciousness. The Abhidhamma substructure to the practice does not explain all aspects of it. Why the mechanism employed took the exact form that it did will be examined in subsequent chapters. For now, let us consider the issue of physical change as an aspect of spiritual transformation in Theravada Buddhism. *Borān kammaṭṭhāna* goes beyond the meditation systems with which we have compared it by providing a process of ensuring that the changes in consciousness (*citta* and *cetasika*) bring about a change in materiality (*rūpa*). In other words, the practitioner's body is changed, not just their mentality: meditation is not just a mind-science. How does this compare with Abhidhamma expectations of enlightenment? Was it envisaged purely as a matter of consciousness, or also somatic transformation?

Abhidhamma makes a direct link between our consciousness and resulting physical manifestations. This applies not only to ordinary humans but to enlightened beings. When, in Theravada, the concept of the Buddha was subjected to analysis, a more detailed conception emerged of both the "wisdom" and "physical" attributes or strengths of the Buddha (*ñāṇabala* and *kāyabala*).[38] Enlightenment transforms the Buddha psychosomatically, in a way that precludes the dichotomy that isolates body from mind.

The following account is taken from the commentary on the *Paṭṭhāna*, the seventh book of the Abhidhamma. The *Paṭṭhāna* encapsulates the Buddha's omniscience in relation to the doctrine of causality that underpins Theravada understanding of samsara and the path to nibbana. The physical transformation described here takes place after the Buddha's enlightenment when he is contemplating the Abhidhamma, but it only takes place once he contemplates the *Paṭṭhāna* in particular, which, as noted above, explains how all the components of reality, *dhammas*, interact. The six rays that emanate from the Buddha, described below, are first mentioned in the canonical *Paṭisambhidāmagga* (III 1.2). They recur throughout *borān kammaṭṭhāna* materials, with some variation in the colors ascribed to them, where various functions are attributed to them.[39]

> But when coming to the Great Book [*Paṭṭhāna*], he [the Buddha] began to contemplate the twenty-four universal causal relations of condition and so on, his omniscience certainly found its opportunity therein.... Rays of six colours—indigo, golden, red, white, tawny, and dazzling—issued from the Teacher's [the Buddha's] body.... The indigo rays issued from his hair and the blue portions of his eyes. Owing to them the surface of the sky appeared as though besprinkled with collyrium powder, or covered with flax and blue lotus-flowers...

> The golden rays issued from his skin and the golden portions of his eyes. Owing to them the different quarters of the globe shone as though besprinkled with some golden liquid, or overlaid with sheets of gold, or bestrewn with saffron powder. . . . The red rays issued from his flesh and blood and the red portions of his eyes. Owing to them the quarters of the globe were coloured as if painted with red-lead powder, or besprinkled with the liquid of molten lac, . . . The white rays issued from his bones, teeth, and the white portions of his eyes. Owing to them the quarters of the globe were bright as though overflowing with streams of milk poured out of silver pots, or overspread with a canopy of silver plates . . . The tawny and dazzling rays issued from the different parts of his body. Thus the six-coloured rays came forth and caught the great mass of earth. . . . The rays penetrated the earth and caught the water below. . . . They penetrated the water and caught the atmosphere . . . they sprang forth into the open space beyond. . . . into the open space across to the infinite world-systems. . . . Even Great Brahmā, able to diffuse light throughout a billion world-systems, became like a glow-worm at sunrise.[40]

Conclusion

This chapter has explored how Theravada Buddhist meditation relates to Abhidhamma, the Theravada analysis of causality that provides the blueprint for spiritual transformation. We set out by identifying distinctive features of *borān kammaṭṭhāna*. We then compared *borān kammaṭṭhāna* with two systems of more widely recognized types of meditation: the system found in the *Visuddhimagga* and that found in Vipassanā, the nineteenth–twentieth century meditation revival stemming mainly from Burma. We found significant correspondences between them.

While all three systems relate to Abhidhamma, *borān*

kammaṭṭhāna takes the realization of Abhidhamma a stage further. It considers not only the transformation of consciousness, *citta*, and aspects of consciousness, *cetasika*, the objective of all Theravada meditations, but how these also affect materiality, *rūpa*, the body of the practitioner. This makes *borān kammaṭṭhāna* a somatic practice in which the body is not just the object of meditation, but its subject. The body is the locus of personal transformation. We therefore considered the process whereby *borān kammaṭṭhāna* seeks to harness changes in consciousness to bring about physical change in the body by drawing the achieved meditative attainments into the body, centered in the "womb" of the practitioner, and embedding them there.

Key to this process is the manipulation of the meditation attainments, usually represented by their corresponding eidetic experiences, *nimitta*. While *nimitta* are explained in the *Visuddhimagga*, their use in *borān kammaṭṭhāna* is far more extensive and the delivery methods unique to the practice. This led us to the question of whether the pervasive Abhidhamma of *borān kammaṭṭhāna* is fundamental to it or a superimposition on an earlier, non-Theravada system of practice. We concluded that modernity has obscured rather than emphasized the Abhidhamma foundations of this practice, and that *borān kammaṭṭhāna* is the literal, detailed enactment of the Abhidhamma path. This enactment takes the physical transformation of enlightenment seriously, a transformation recognized in colorful accounts of the Buddha's own enlightenment journey in late canonical and early commentarial texts.

While this chapter has identified the Abhidhamma elements of *borān kammaṭṭhāna*, we also noted other methods it employs for bringing about transformation, methods that are not found in the authoritative literature of Theravada. Before turning to examine these other features in more detail, the next chapter summarizes the evidentiary basis for our understanding of *borān kammaṭṭhāna*. How extensive is the evidence, and can it provide a timeline for the practice?

3

Documenting the Esoteric

The Production and Survival of Evidence for Borān Kammaṭṭhāna *Meditation*

The princess cowers within the *sāl* tree, still shifting anxiously between its five branches. Every day now the five giants who have protected her grow weaker even though she continues to care for them. The three warrior queens have persistently attacked her in her refuge. She has resisted but is tired, and now the most insidious of the queens has infected the tree with termites. As the infestation takes hold it grows ever more doubtful that the tree can continue to support the princess and her giants. The three spiteful queens have sent ingratiating messages to the king, informing him of the next strategy he should employ: "Send a snarling tiger, your majesty, or a rampaging elephant; otherwise a wild bear or a fearsome man brandishing a sword. If she sees them coming to get her she'll weigh her options quickly and rush to you to escape." The king comes in person and stands quietly watching. Then as the princess drops out of the tree, hoping to find a new one nearby, the king snatches her. He rapes her. Afterward she escapes from him to a new tree. The king cannot see her, but stands there waiting, knowing that at some point she will have to leave her new sanctuary too.

—Abridged, adapted translation from
the non-canonical *Maraṇañānasutta*, Sinhala
redaction by Varañāṇa Mahāthera, c. 1759[1]

In the previous chapter, I gave an account of *borān kammaṭṭhāna* practice and how, despite the shared underpinnings of Abhidhamma, it differed from the Theravada meditation systems most well known in the modern period. In this chapter, I want to look at the evidence on which that account was based. Given that *borān* meditation is an esoteric practice, and one close to extinction, what evidence for the practice is there? Also, while the practices indicate an Abhidhamma worldview in place by the fifth century C.E., this only establishes the *terminus post quem*, the period during or after which these practices arose. What does concrete evidence for the practice tell us about the *terminus ante quem*, the date by which these practices were in circulation?

This chapter will provide a broad description of the genres of textual evidence available for *borān kammaṭṭhāna* and an account of where we find this evidence. By way of background we will discuss the material culture of Theravada manuscripts. We shall examine the effect and politics of the adoption of printing, as well as resistance to it. In this context, we start to see how modernity began to affect the nature of Theravada Buddhism and the place of *borān kammaṭṭhāna* within it. This leads us to examine how the material evidence that we do have came to be produced and how it survived, as well as how it relates to both extinct and surviving, living lineages. At the end we shall examine what the existing evidence tells us about the dating of this tradition. A summary of this evidence and the timeline it provides is found at the end of the chapter, in Figure 3.

Genres of *Borān Kammaṭṭhāna* Texts

First, let us look at the textual evidence for *borān kammaṭṭhāna* in terms of content. What genres of text provide evidence for it? Since *borān kammaṭṭhāna* was part of a broader culture, there is no clear cutoff for this, but I shall focus on the two main genres pertinent to meditation. At the end of this section I shall touch briefly on a few other types of text that indicate either the conceptual framework for *borān* practice or ways in which it is applied to other areas. The main two genres are narratives that provide allegories and explain the broader context and manuals directly related to instructions for meditation.

Exoteric and Esoteric Narratives

Not all material related to *borān kammaṭṭhāna* is esoteric. The opening excerpt above is from a narrative text redacted for one of the queens of the Kandyan kingdom of Sri Lanka by one of the meditation masters from Siam. The text is an allegory. The princess hiding in the trees is called Princess Mind or Consciousness, *citta*. The king who lusts after her, determined to dominate and control her, is Māra, king of the realm of death and rebirth, samsara. The five-branched tree is her body in this life, the five giants her inner strengths. There are five birds of prey in the tree, which guard the gems within. These birds are the senses, and one must overcome them to realize the gems, the truths, of Buddhism. The three warrior queens constantly on the attack are called Birth, Old Age, and Sickness, the most insidious being the last. The termites represent the diseases that in life gradually weaken our body. The entire story is an allegory for the inevitability of death and rebirth, unless one can find the gems that are the Four Truths, or four stages of spiritual progress, hidden within oneself. This timeless story, the story of each and every one of us, was recounted by the Siamese monk Varañāṇa Mahāthera to the chief queen of Kandy in Sri Lanka at some point in the late 1750s.[2]

Such allegories are used to convey both the doctrine and the experience of medical and existential crisis. Using narrative to teach doctrine adds the experiential, emotional dimension not represented in a dry treatise or textbook. The story conveys the anxiety of daily life and the inevitability and horror of death, which one needs to acknowledge and accept at a fundamental level if one is to make the life-changing effort to find a way out of samsara. It is the horror of this experience that sends Princess Cittā, or Prince

Citto in the versions for men, in search of the Buddha and the truths he taught.

Here, I have abridged the story of Princess Cittā; in full it includes interlinear commentary that draws out the allegorical meaning much as I have just done.[3] It explains the psychology of death, that even when people survive other onslaughts, shock and fear may still kill them: hence the final shock tactics suggested by the three queens to the king whom they serve. Asides in the text add further information on how to interpret the signs that people begin to see shortly before death as prognostications of their imminent rebirth.

The text about Princess Cittā typifies one of two genres prevalent in the evidence for traditional meditation: narratives and meditation manuals. Each narrative provides an explanation of doctrine in an accessible, memorable, and motivational form, conveying complex concepts and emotions. The concepts explained are the Buddhist theories of death, rebirth, life, and salvation. Another such narrative text, which appears to be connected with *borān kammaṭṭhāna*, is the non-canonical *Nibbāna Sutta*. It also opens with a tree, this time representative of our defilements, which hold us back from nibbana, and must be cut down. The text goes on to describe the otherwise intangible state of nibbana as a beautiful city, thronging with birds and bees, each component a metaphor for some aspect of the Buddhist path, an image found beautifully depicted in eighteenth-century Thai manuscripts.[4]

While these two apocryphal *suttas* are exoteric texts, some narratives reveal a hidden symbolism. For example, the well-known Indian epic the Rāmāyaṇa, in which Prince Rāma must rescue his abducted wife Sītā, is recast in *borān* Theravada as an allegory for the path to nibbana. Prince Rāma is the *citta*, the mind of the practitioner. His devoted servant, the monkey god Hanumān, is the internal breath of the practitioner. Sītā is the internal gem or sphere of light that the practitioner must realize within him- or herself. The gem represents the *nimitta* that mark the stages of successful meditation culminating in nibbana—just as Rāma progressively comes closer to finding and releasing Sītā, so the practitioner must undertake the progressive stages to find and realize nibbana. The island of Laṅkā on which Sītā is imprisoned is the maternal womb. The crossing of the ocean is the initiation that the practitioner undertakes with the meditation master. The army of monkeys that help Rāma are the meritorious actions of the practitioner. The villain Rāvaṇa and his twelve brothers are the negative qualities that the practitioner must overcome. Sītā's banishment is the death of the practitioner, and the final reunion of Rāma and Sītā is entry into nibbana.[5] Such narratives can be extensive. The narration of the Rāmāyaṇa was recorded by François Bizot in Cambodia in 1969. It was related to him by a traditional storyteller over the course of several days.[6] Anne Hansen observes that earlier generations of Cambodians had been very wary of revealing this and other esoteric material to outsiders. In 1903, one of the first outsiders to document *borān* material, Louis Finot (1864–1935), then director of the École française d'Extrême-Orient, repeatedly requested a copy of this very text but was declined.[7]

Practice Manuals

In contrast to this rich imagery, the manuals of *borān kammaṭṭhāna* tend to be technical and minimalist rather than evocative and discursive. They are extremely terse, often in the form of mnemonics and semi-encoded. These features reflect the esoteric nature of the practice, the fact that the manuals are prompts rather than complete set of instructions. In the longer manuals, the aspiration appears to be to contain the entire path to liberation, as detailed in the Abhidhamma, in a single set of instructions. While lengthy, they are still tightly composed and technical. So laconic are these manuals that, without the evidence of living practice lineages—many of which came to an end in the mid-to-late twentieth century—the guidance they provide for meditation practice would be impossible to follow. It may well be this that confounded early textual scholars and led outsiders to dismiss the practices. The living practices recorded by Bizot and others in Cambodia before they died out and the few remaining adapted living traditions, which are detailed below, have been crucial in understanding how the practices are to be performed. For the higher level practices, some elements are a matter of speculation, since I am unaware of a living tradition that pursues the unmodernized practices at the highest level documented in some of the early modern manuscripts.

Manuals vary in length from a few pages to thousands of verses. Traditional meditation teachers (*achar/grū*) in Cambodia would carry one on their person, sometimes tucked inside their shirt. Such manuals tend to consist of around ten short-length palm-leaf folios and provide diagnostics for the teacher to check when listening to the experience of his pupils. They simply list meditation subjects and the possible physical and visual phenomena, the *nimitta*, that the meditator might experience at different stages of practice. They therefore remind the teacher of the order of practice and what to expect at each stage, so that he can keep track when dealing with the regular reports of multiple meditators, all at different stages of the practice. Fuller manuals provide the *nimitta*, the places that these should be moved to in the body, and the patterns and combinations of movements to be made. They may break down the entire path from ordinary mortal, *puthujjana*, to arhat into cumulative stages of bringing the *nimitta*, representing the desired *cetasika*, aspect of consciousness, into the body, in combination with the desired *citta*, state of consciousness, and the physical elements. The Sri Lankan manual that we drew on in the previous chapter, the *Amatākaravaṇṇanā*, is terse and uses a variety of abbreviation techniques. Nonetheless, it takes up 100 full-length palm-leaf folios.[8]

Some manuals also provide litanies for the rituals of devotion and offerings to the Buddha and the teacher, to be performed by the practitioner, as well as the requests to the meditation experiences, which, as we have seen in the previous chapter, must be invited to appear as if autonomous, external entities. Litanies may be embedded in meditation manuals or freestanding. The litany that accompanies the *Amatākaravaṇṇanā* is presented separately and, on its own, takes up a further 50 folios, making the complete set of instructions 150 folios in length. Bearing in mind that these 150 folios are an abbreviated form of the practice, we can see that the complete practice entails an extensive period of meditation, and progression is envisaged as taking place over months if not years. Even the first stage undertaken in Cambodia today takes place over the course of the three months rainy season and is not necessarily completed in a single year.

Other than manuals for meditation and preparatory devotional practice, there are instructions for how to apply the meditation, for example to healing or protection.

Other Topics in Borān Kammaṭṭhāna *Texts*

While these two broad textual genres, the narrative and the technical manual, are the most common texts available to date, other texts touch on aspects pertinent to *borān kammaṭṭhāna* or its worldview. These include texts on language and cosmogony, the origin of the world, and even texts for consecrating Buddha images. Also, narrative and manual texts are not always exclusive: occasionally they intertwine. Each might include additional information in the form of numerology in association with language, alchemy and embryology, explanations of symbolism, or signs relevant to prognostication.

Material Evidence

Having looked at the *borān* texts in terms of content, I now turn to the material evidence: in what form are these texts preserved? The material evidence provides us with piecemeal information that will allow us to draw up a timeline for the most recent centuries of *borān* practice traditions.

Inscriptions

As we shall see, few manuscripts in the Theravada world date back more than two to three centuries, with the earliest—other than those inscribed on more durable materials such as stone or metal—dating to the sixteenth century. It is therefore tantalizing that an inscription discovered at Wat Suea, Changwat Phitsanukok, the "Phitsanulok inscription," dated to 1549, contains a text that in versions preserved at later dates in manuscript form have a connection with *borān kammaṭṭhāna*. Now housed in the National Museum in Bangkok, the text equates parts of the Buddha's body with different components of the attributes of the Buddha and the doctrines of Abhidhamma.[9] The text continues to circulate and is used, as seems appropriate, in the consecration and empowerment of Buddha images. In addition to the use of drawing parallels between the physical and the spiritual attributes, slightly longer versions of this text also guide the meditator to recognize these parallels. This and the conscious construction of a Buddha body within the practitioner as a composite body of spiritual attributes suggest that the inscription is related to the *borān kammaṭṭhāna* tradition. However, the brevity of the inscription prevents us from using it as a source of dating for *borān kammaṭṭhāna*, even though, as we will see, a text associated with the Lao Supreme Patriarch Sivisuddhisom in the early sixteenth century confirms the contemporary presence of *borān kammaṭṭhāna* in the region.[10]

Some other inscriptions from the Sukhothai cultural region, centered to the west of Phitsanulok, may also be of relevance, not as direct evidence of *borān kammaṭṭhāna*, but of the attitude to language as a potent force. Dated to around the fifteenth century, they contain Pali formulae of the qualities of the Buddha and the contents of Abhidhamma, condensed down to representative syllables. In the middle of the sixteenth century, Ayutthaya was sacked by the Burmese. Traditional Southeast Asian warfare involved the capture and relocation of large numbers of war slaves, so with Ayutthaya depopulated, people from the Sukhothai region were forced to migrate to Ayutthaya to restore its numbers. Peter Skilling, in his study of these inscriptions, suggests that the culture of letter alchemy represented by these inscriptions, also found in shorter form on images from the region, may have been taken to Ayutthaya with them.[11] Given the contemporary presence of *borān kammaṭṭhāna* in the region, it is possible that this mass relocation influenced the subsequent development of Ayutthaya as a hub of *borān kammaṭṭhāna*. As we shall see below, Ayutthaya's influence in the transmission of *borān kammaṭṭhāna* reached its height in the eighteenth century, until it was again sacked by the Burmese in 1767. At this point Ayutthaya's direct influence ended, but it continued indirectly through those who moved with the capital to Thonburi.

The Physical Manuscript

Manuscripts in Sri Lanka and Southeast Asia were mainly written on two kinds of material: the stacked palm leaf, following the traditional Indian format; and the much softer local paper formed in long, folded sheets. Both are vulnerable to insects and animals, to rotting if damp, and to becoming brittle, cracking, and turning to powder if they dry out. Most extant manuscripts therefore only date back to the past few centuries. A small number of manuscripts date back to the sixteenth and seventeenth centuries, but these are the minority. Texts from before the eighteenth century were therefore usually only preserved for as long as they were used, because these would be recopied. This means that we cannot look to manuscripts to provide physical evidence to offer a full timeline for Theravada meditation, be it *borān kammaṭṭhāna* or other practice lineages. On the other hand, the importance of reproducing texts to ensure the survival of the Buddhist religion, the *sāsana*, meant that manuscript copying was highly meritorious in its own right. This, and the ready availability of the most commonly used materials, means that hundreds of thousands of manuscripts have survived from the eighteenth and twentieth centuries. These were produced throughout the Theravada world by Buddhist monks and laypeople, who for the most part received their training in literacy at the monastery, often during temporary ordination. The number of these that relate to *borān kammaṭṭhāna* is at least in the hundreds, and possibly more.

Palm-Leaf Manuscripts

Palm-leaf manuscripts are made mostly from the Talipot palm, *Corypha umbraculifera Linn*. They are usually preserved flat, two inches in height and twelve to eighteen inches in length. They are bound together by rods or strings passed through one central or two proportionately spaced holes, depending on the length of the leaf, and clamped between two rigid wooden cover boards. Those *borān*-related texts that were treated as literary compositions, such as the story of Princess Cittā and the *Amatākaravaṇṇanā*, both mentioned above, are found in this form. Manuals appropriate for carrying about on the person tend to use shorter leaf sections, perhaps eight inches in length. This is the form taken by some of the meditation manuals of *borān kammaṭṭhāna* still circulating in Cambodia today, retained by teachers on their person for quick consultation, containing just key terms and descriptions of *nimitta*. Shorter texts, such as those used for astrological records, may also be rolled along their length, the palm leaf remaining highly flexible for a number of years. I have not come across any *borān kammaṭṭhāna*–related texts in this form.

The lettering on palm-leaf manuscripts is cut into the leaves with a sharp stylus, after which soot is rubbed over the leaf, catching in the incisions so as to make the letters stand out black against the creamy yellow of the leaf. A single manuscript may contain a few leaves or several hundred, and may contain only part of a text, a single text, or several texts.

Since palm leaf splits easily and the available surface space is relatively small, illustrations on them are rare, although their covers may be highly decorated. Despite the rarity of illustrations within the body of palm-leaf manuscripts overall, both medical manuals and *borān kammaṭṭhāna* meditation manuals contain line drawings that illustrate instructions. The diagrams in the meditation manuals mostly indicate the correct placing of *nimitta*, signs of meditation experiences, on or in the body. These are often in the form of concentric circles, perhaps with lines coming from them indicating patterns of movement for manipulating the *nimitta*.

Paper Manuscripts

In Southeast Asia, there are paper manuscripts with a larger format, with the writing surface of each opening measuring as much as ten to twelve inches by fifteen to twenty-four inches, made of two different trees belonging to the family Moraceae. One is mulberry paper, made from the paper mulberry tree, *Broussonetia papyrifera* (Moraceae). The other paper is called *khoi* (Thai) and is made from *Streblus asper* (Moraceae), common in central Thailand.[12] Although *Streblus asper* is also grown in Sri Lanka for its medical properties, the paper is not found there. The pulp made from the bark of either plant is set in long strips, which are glued together to form a continuous *leporello*, or folded book. The larger format allows for painted illustrations and detailed depictions of medical diagrams and narrative scenes. The softer mulberry paper is also used for protective diagrams, *yantra*. *Yantra* on mulberry paper may be pulverized and drunk mixed in a liquid, such as water or milk. Other types of surface may also be used for *yantra*, such as cloth, so that it may be worn; lead, so they can be inserted under the skin; and the body itself, with the diagrams drawn on the skin through tattooing.

Ink, Secrecy, and Printing

The ink used on paper manuscripts is also traditionally made of soot, in this case made liquid by being dissolved in animal bile and other substances. Secrecy surrounds the additional ingredients used in such ink when the syllables to be written are medical or protective. Because of the furor in 1920s Cambodia over the printing of a Buddhist text (below), the significance assigned by traditionalists to all aspects of manuscript production is well documented. Not only the paper, the ink, and the script, but also other aspects of the manuscript including the wrappings were regarded as sacred and also richly symbolic of matters considered fundamental to esoteric Theravada practice, such as fetal development.[13] However, by the second half of the twentieth century, partly as a result of the gradual erosion of manuscript culture after the arrival of the printing press, partly for convenience, modern European-style school notebooks also began to be used for the writing down of Buddhist texts. Cambodian *borān kammaṭṭhāna* manuscripts in closed teacher-pupil lineages from the 1960s–'70s are often in this form.

Since *borān* practice was still widespread when manuscript culture gave way to printing in the twentieth century, we can still hope to find a substantial amount of evidence of pre-modern Theravada Buddhist thought and practices. The challenge for identifying material on *borān kammaṭṭhāna* is the esoteric nature of the tradition and the lack of distinguishing terminology. This means that cataloguers may not recognize the lineage to which a meditation manual belongs. The identification of related materials is also hindered by the lack of accessibility of some national collections in Theravada countries.

The Production and Survival of *Borān Kammaṭṭhāna* Manuscripts

The esotericism of *borān* meditation and symbolism was retained until recently and explanations were not to be passed on to any but initiated students. As such, manuscripts were made to support such esoteric teachings and not for general circulation. This limited the number of manuscripts that circulated as well as the content.[14] As noted above, meditation manuals created in the context of disciple-pupil transmission were for the most part straightforward lists of key terms intended as supporting documents to an oral tradition. They focused on providing lists of *nimitta*, diagnostic checklists for teachers to assess the level of attainment reached by their students. On their own, they tell little about the practice, and this meant that those seeking to revive or understand meditation solely on the basis of texts found the sophistication and rationale of the practice hard to detect or appreciate.

The inclusion of such texts and more extensive manuals in personal and temple library collections seems to have come about largely when they ceased to be used as a support for practice. This lack of use made them vulnerable to being recycled or given away without new copies being made. One form of recycling of manuscripts in mainland Southeast Asia is to pulverize them as powerful ingredients for protective amulets. This has been the fate of some of the manuscripts at Wat Hong in Thonburi, once an important center of *borān kammaṭṭhāna* associated with King Taksin in the late eighteenth century and still home to a historically significant collection. Nonetheless, a significant number of *borān* manuscripts have survived into the modern period, becoming part of bigger collections once they had ceased to be used by the practice tradition. Individual *borān kammaṭṭhāna* manuscripts also turn up in temple collections in Laos, Cambodia, Thailand, and Sri Lanka.

More extensive *borān kammaṭṭhāna* manuscripts seem to have been produced at specific periods in response to a crisis or some kind of insecurity: the need to secure for posterity what had previously been transmitted orally from teacher to pupil outweighed the concern for secrecy. The high concentration of manuscripts at Wat Hong and at other temples in Thonburi such as Wat Ratchasittharam may be a reflection of the status of these temples as the homes to lineages transmitted from Ayutthaya, the old capital of Siam (Thailand), in the aftermath of the Burmese destruction of Ayutthaya in 1767. We shall discuss the history of these lineages and others in later chapters.

The in-depth nature of *borān kammaṭṭhāna* manuscripts that circulated in Sri Lanka from earlier in the same century also reflects the feared fragility of the transmission. Three missions of monks and texts were sent from Ayutthaya a decade before its sack to help revive Buddhism in Sri Lanka. The second mission, in 1756, brought *borān* meditation masters. The Sinhalese monks they trained knew they would not have the luxury of being able to consult their teachers for long. After eight years, their Siamese teachers returned home, and many of the local monks were dispersed to provincial monasteries throughout Sri Lanka. Anticipating this disruption, the students wrote manuals to support their continued long-term practice once they were without a teacher, and it is thanks to their foresight that we are able to relate *borān* practice to a detailed expertise in Abhidhamma. These manuals tell us little about the initial stages of the meditation, but a great deal about the advanced practice.

Since the importation of the tradition to Sri Lanka in the mid-eighteenth century was part of an attempt to revive Buddhism on the island, it coincided with an escalation of Pali and Sinhala literary production. Narratives and commentaries relevant to the tradition were also written down, such as the allegory of Princess Cittā cited above. Some meditation manuals were also ornamented with literary flourishes such as poetic openings to the sections and the inclusion of *paritta* newly composed by Välivița Saraṇaṃkara, the supreme patriarch who led the revival.[15]

The resulting texts related to *borān* meditation were produced within these practice lineages after the arrival of the meditation masters from Siam, and as such were not part of the prestigious, well-documented consignment of texts that was also sent from Siam at this time, which were housed in important temples of the period. If we studied only the latter texts, we would learn nothing of the meditation practices that were part of the revival. As the lineages of pupils from these initial practitioners died out, their manuscripts passed into local temple libraries, and that is how we have access to them today. Several were still circulating in Sri Lanka when two monks, Ratnajoti and Ratnapāla (below), consulted them in the early 1960s. Individual manuscripts are found in temple libraries in Sri Lanka and in the Colombo Museum. They also found their way into European collections, such as the Museum für Indische Kunst in Berlin,[16] and the British Library.

Another crisis that led to the writing down of this otherwise primarily oral tradition took place in the 1970s in Cambodia, in the lead-up to the Democratic Kampuchea period, in which the Marxist-Leninist Khmer Rouge under the leadership of Pol Pot oversaw the suppression of religion, economic policies that led to mass starvation, and mass genocide. To prevent the tradition from being lost, Cambodian practitioners wrote down what they could recall. These modern manuscripts were important for the research of French scholars working for the École française d'Extrême-Orient (EFEO), primarily François Bizot and Olivier de Bernon. After the Pol Pot period, when EFEO returned to Cambodia in 1990, Olivier de Bernon and local staff based at Wat Uṇṇalom began to organize the collection, documentation, and storage of Cambodian manuscripts that had survived the devastation of the civil war. They estimated that over 90% of Cambodia's literary heritage had been destroyed in a period of just fifteen years. Nonetheless, at least five *borān kammaṭṭhāna* manuals (the *Mūlakammaṭṭhāna*) are recorded in their catalogue, the FEMC, launched in 2011.[17] Meanwhile, some practitioners within the tradition had also done their best to keep as many texts as possible safe. One such practitioner was Achar Oun of Kampong Cham Province, who gathered a collection of approximately seventy traditional manuscripts, including some from the families of fellow practitioners who had died in the civil war. Five of them are specifically *borān* meditation manuals, and there are also about a dozen modern-style notebooks on the subject.[18] These have also been copied by staff at the École française d'Extrême-Orient.

In Laos the Marxist revolution of the 1970s appears to have done less damage to manuscripts than in Cambodia. Although the tradition was not revived in Laos, some *borān kammaṭṭhāna* manuscripts have been identified by researchers, and at least nine *borān kammatthāna* manuals appear in the catalogue of the

Digital Library of Lao Manuscripts (DLLM) launched in 2009.[19] Individual copies from Laos also occasionally appear in European collections.[20]

The Difficulty of Identifying *Borān Kammaṭṭhāna* Manuscripts

Many temple and library manuscript collections are yet to be fully catalogued, and more *borān kammaṭṭhāna* texts seem likely to emerge when they are. Because of the shared Abhidhamma basis of meditation terminology, distinguishing between different systems of practice when cataloguing a manuscript can be difficult. Also, cataloguers may be unaware that there are such differences. When the *borān* affiliation of a manuscript is recognized, it is often a result of its resemblance to the *Yogāvacara's Manual* published by Rhys Davids in 1896 or its similarity to works published by François Bizot and Olivier de Bernon. The presence of the unusual circular diagrams peculiar to these meditation manuals is of additional assistance in identification. Of the nine manuscripts identified in the DLLM, two have the distinctive diagrams; the remaining were recognized by the title of *Mūlakammaṭṭhāna*, "fundaments of meditation" or "fundamental/original meditation," the subject of the PhD thesis of Olivier de Bernon and of work by Bizot.[21] *Mūlakammaṭṭhāna* is the usual Southeast Asian name for the manual that in Sri Lanka circulates as the *Amatākaravaṇṇanā*, drawn on in our examination of the more complex aspects of the practice. However, the term *Mūlakammaṭṭhāna* is found elsewhere in Theravada meditation literature and does not necessarily indicate that a text belongs to this tradition.[22]

The Formation of Large Manuscript Collections

There are large collections of Sri Lankan and Southeast Asian manuscripts in Europe, Calcutta, and Bangkok that were formed by a process of laying claim to the material and knowledge cultures of the newly colonized, or, in the case of Bangkok, newly centralized territories in the late nineteenth and early twentieth centuries. Although British, Thai, and French dominance of the region is reflected in the collections of the British Library in London, the National Library of Thailand in Bangkok, and the Bibliothèque Nationale in Paris, at this time other European countries, such as Russia and Germany, were also adding to their manuscript collections.[23] The Nevill collection at the British Library, put together by the British colonial officer Hugh Nevill in Sri Lanka, contains a particularly high concentration of *borān* manuscripts, consisting of at least seventeen separate texts across eleven manuscripts.

During the period when Nevill was building his collection, meditation appears to have been pursued primarily by members of the newly introduced Rāmañña Nikāya monastic lineage. Monks of the Rāmañña Nikāya were influenced by canonical text-based meditation and the beginnings of Vipassanā meditation that were being developed in Burma. The manuscripts related to *borān kammaṭṭhāna* had largely been discarded. One century on from the Siamese mission that had introduced them, they were now to be found, unused, in monastic libraries around the country. Nevill, with his eye for the unusual, acquired them, even though knowledge about Buddhist meditation among Europeans at the time was minimal, as we have seen. The manuscripts are particularly interesting because of their extensive detail. They also represent the single branch that arrived from Ayutthaya in 1756, allowing us to form a relatively complete picture of a single system of practice. For while there is overlap between the different texts, none is completely the same, each adding more details of the instructions. The collection was bought by the British Library in 1897 after Nevill's early retirement and death, ultimately believed to have come about from his injury in a riot against the British six years earlier.[24]

An as yet little-explored collection of manuscripts that already looks set to contain a significant number of *borān kammaṭṭhāna* manuscripts is held in the National Library in Bangkok. It was formed during the first decades of the twentieth century when the policy in Thailand was to gather up and—in public—destroy the nation's regional manuscripts. Some manuscript collections survived, some by favor, some by subterfuge. Others were overlooked, and some survived because the manuscripts were in the personal possession of monks and laypeople rather than in the temple libraries. However, hundreds of thousands of vernacular and Pali-vernacular mixed language texts were removed from monasteries and villages throughout the country.

This destruction or removal of vernacular, local materials took place in parallel with the government-sponsored publication of normative materials in high numbers. Normative texts were those now regarded as representing orthodoxy or orthopraxy by the hierarchy of the Thammayut (Pali *Dhammayutika*) monastic lineage, a minority, reform wing of the Sangha established by the future King Mongkut (Rāma IV) in 1833 when he was himself a monk. Although the lineage was in a minority, it was given precedence and power over the majority Mahanikay (Pali *Mahānikāya*) "large monastic lineage" under King Mongkut and his successors. The normative publications they produced in Pali and Bangkok Thai languages were distributed nationally. One set of texts was the entire Pali canon. This was the Chulachomklao Tipiṭaka of 1893, the first-ever printed edition of the Pali canon, compiled in twenty-eight volumes under the patronage of King Chulalongkorn, Rāma V, the son and successor of King Mongkut. Other printings circulated included works on meditation and monastic discipline on the model of the new textbooks produced to roll out the educational reforms of another of Mongkut's sons and Chulalongkorn's half-brother, the scholar-monk Wachirayan. We shall look at the effect of these reforms on meditation practice later.

An additional reason behind the removal of manuscripts across the country may have been the ongoing belief in the knowledge and supernatural power contained within them, knowledge mastered in traditional training. We can see a parallel in the European treatment of Buddha relics. Whereas the Protestant British and

Americans were merely dismissive of the tooth relic of Sri Lanka, the Portuguese Catholics went to great lengths in their attempts to acquire and destroy the tooth relic in ways specifically designed to destroy its inherent power—indicating the extent to which they accepted the power of relics as real.[25] Similarly, in the 1890s–1910s, Thai authorities burnt many manuscripts to destroy their inherent power. However, they also wanted to retain that power for themselves. So, many—perhaps the majority—of the manuscripts were not in fact destroyed but transported to Bangkok. Several hundred thousand manuscripts collected by the authorities over a period of two decades now lie in the National Library in Bangkok, an institution that was set up in the midst of this process in 1905 by the merging of royal libraries. For the most part the extent of this wealth of manuscripts was not public knowledge until very recently, although a fraction of the collection began to be digitized and catalogued in the 2000s. Among many other subjects covered are writings relating to *borān kammaṭṭhāna* and to the transmission of the Ayutthaya tradition of *borān* meditation to Sri Lanka.[26]

A collection based on interest in meditation was made by the monk Jan, abbot of Wat Baromnivat in Bangkok, in the 1890s. His collection included our earliest datable text, a seventeenth-century manuscript that recorded a text that had once belonged to the early sixteenth-century Lao Supreme Patriarch Sivisuddhisom, giving us the earliest conclusive date for *borān kammaṭṭhāna*. We shall discuss this collection more in the context of publications made in the 1930s.

A collection of manuscripts dating back to the Ayutthaya period has been recently reassembled in *khana* 5, the meditation section of Wat Ratchasittharam, former home to the late eighteenth-century Supreme Patriarch Suk Kaitheun. These texts were dispersed within the monastery under the tenure of the section head prior to the present incumbent, Phrakhrusangkharak Veera Thanaveero, who is his son. According to Veera Thanaveero, other section heads borrowed interesting or important manuscripts, including personal manuscripts that had previously belonged to Suk, and did not return them. Veera Thanaveero has spent the last forty years trying to reassemble and protect the collection. It is not yet clear to me whether this implies that the living practice lineage also underwent duress, although the temple has a continuous, named teacher lineage. In 2012, Veera Thanaveero set up a foundation dedicated to its preservation, the "Foundation Institution Kammatthan Majjhima Baablumdup." Another Thonburi temple with a significant number of relevant manuscripts is Wat Hong, associated with King Taksin, who is known to have practiced this form of meditation.

As noted above, even though palm-leaf manuscripts contain little room for illustrations, diagrams were drawn on them to show the positioning of *nimitta* in the body. Some of the larger format folding manuscripts from the Ayutthaya and Thonburi periods, which permit fuller illustration, attempt to show the final stages of the path by showing the arhat, fully enlightened practitioner, realizing the gem at his navel. One such illustration, depicting the final four of eight supramundane states into which the culmination of the spiritual path are categorized in Theravada, is shown on the cover of this book. The eight stages are the path to, and realization of, these four stages: stream entrant (one who has a maximum of seven lifetimes left in samsara), once-returner, non-returner (who, not quite becoming an arhat in this life, matures to that status in a particular heaven), and arhat, the liberated, awakening individual. The cover illustration is of the non-returner and arhat.[27]

The Introduction of Printing to the Theravada World

The printing press acted as a catalyst both in the expression of new ideas developed in the response to colonialism, and in the imposition of centralized reform on the former diversity and relative autonomy of Theravada teaching lineages in Southeast Asia. Here we shall show how print both marginalized *borān kammaṭṭhāna* and provides us with some of our most extensive, informative, and earliest evidence.

Printing had its origins in East Asia at the end of the seventh century. A contributing factor was the desire to stem the decline of Buddhism by preserving the Dhamma, combined with the idea that the written word was representative of the presence of the Buddha.[28] Although the same beliefs were also found in Southeast Asia, and the related technology of seals in the creation of Buddhist sealings was employed in the region, the printing press was not adopted in Southeast Asia prior to European influence. Rather, beliefs about the protective power of the Dhamma and the importance of ensuring the ongoing presence of the Buddha's teachings informed and sustained the long tradition of manuscript sponsoring and copying, with the production of manuscripts being an integral part of the culture of merit-making that lay at the heart of Theravada practice.[29] When the printing press did arrive in the modern period, it was not immediately adopted by Buddhists. Even once it was, some traditionalists continued to resist it.

It had taken several centuries for printing technology from East and Central Asia to reach Europe.[30] When European presses such as that of the German printer Johannes Gutenberg were developed in the fifteenth century, they had a significant impact on the transmission of new religious ideas, and were instrumental in the spread of the Reformation.[31] Similarly, the mechanical high-speed printing press, first designed by Friedrich Gottlob Koenig for *The Times* in London, led in the early 1800s to a rapid increase in the transmission of ideas and new scientific discoveries, as well as to the development of the Press as an institution. Mindful of printing's initial impact during the Reformation and its subsequent usefulness in cheaply producing tracts in debates between Christian groups, Christian missionaries of the colonial period introduced printing to Southeast Asia and Sri Lanka in the mid-nineteenth century.[32] Their intention was to spread "the Word" and thereby displace Buddhist and other beliefs.

The activities of the missionaries awoke Buddhist reformers and revivalists in the region to the potential of printing to spread new ideas and help prolong the now-imperiled teaching of the Buddha.

They were inspired to acquire presses of their own both to try to stem the encroachment of Western ideas and Christianity, and also to influence fellow Buddhists. Prince Mongkut of Thailand acquired a printing press at Wat Bovornnivet shortly after the American missionary Dan Beach Bradley introduced the printing press from Singapore in 1835.[33] In 1862 the Sri Lankan Buddhist monk Mohoṭṭivattē Gunananda, who went on to win a decisive and influential debate between Buddhists and Christians at Pānadura in 1873, acquired a press that had been imported by Christian missionaries.[34] Both Mongkut and Gunananda were influential in the development of modernized, rationalized Buddhism with claims to its civilizational superiority and its congruence with modern science. Located as these presses initially were in the hands of those ready to adopt new technology, it was not the more conservative, the supporters of *borān kammaṭṭhāna*, who used them to express their worldview.

The Impact of Printing on *Borān Kammaṭṭhāna*

A noted impact of the printing press is to "democratize" literacy and access to literature, including newly introduced or freshly written literature, beyond the circles of the literati—as the Catholic Church had found to its cost during the Reformation. The printing press can free people up from the set canons of their traditional sources of learning. It allows individual writers and small organizations to reproduce and distribute any texts they choose, and to have their name associated with them. It can encourage diversity and support subversion. On the other hand, when publication is in the hands of a centralized authority or works are printed by a prestigious, powerful individual or group, or if the distribution of books is accompanied by a rhetoric of state-building or of defending against the decline of Buddhism, it can have the opposite effect. We see both effects in the Theravada world of the nineteenth and early twentieth centuries.

Among Theravada Buddhists, once they too adopted the printing press, the former effect was more pronounced in countries such as Burma and Sri Lanka where the king had been deposed, leaving the Sangha without royal patronage and in need of popular support. The printing press empowered those engaging in a response to Christians and colonialism, such as the lowland Buddhists in Sri Lanka. It enabled the rise to prominence of individual writers such as Ledi Sayadaw, mentioned in the previous chapter as one of the key promulgators of the newly honed Vipassanā meditation.

On the other hand, the second phenomenon, of imposing uniformity, was more pronounced in countries where a Buddhist royal court and Sangha hierarchy still represented the central locus of power, namely Thailand and Cambodia. There, printing was adopted in response to colonial encroachment, to promote modernizing Buddhist teachings, and to undermine the existing hierarchies in local competitions for power, as elsewhere, but it was also used to further enhance central state control over the periphery. While in Burma and Sri Lanka colonial power represented the center, in Thailand it was at the periphery that colonial encroachment was most feared. Combined with the centralization of education and reorganization of the Sangha under a single, centralized hierarchy with the backing of the court, and the imposition of Thai language in education and administration, the impact of printing was to suppress diversity.[35] This was especially true after the publication of normative Pali canonical and commentarial works, noted above, and their translation into the vernaculars of the political center, namely Bangkok Thai and, later, under Thai influence, modernized Khmer. These printed editions could then be used as a yardstick against which to judge national religion, not only among an elite as had been the case in previous textual reforms, but among the population as a whole. Authoritative writers at the time with the backing of the palace, such as the Thai monk-scholar Prince Wachirayan (1860–1921), who was appointed as supreme patriarch of Siam, now had their dominant voices amplified by the technology of the press. A similar development occurred in Burma after Independence, with the printing of the Pali canon following the Sixth Council in 1956.[36]

Initially printing was not adopted in Cambodia for Buddhist materials even by the more modernized members of the Sangha hierarchy. There was a strong belief in the sanctity of all aspects of Buddhist writing and manuscript production. Internal reform in the majority wing of the Sangha, the Mahanikay, was taking place with Thai and later French colonial support. It was modeled on the Thai reformist wing of the Sangha, the Thammayut ordination lineage founded by Prince Mongkut when he had been a monk. At the same time, within the Mahanikay there were also more traditionalist monks who sought to preserve pre-reform Buddhism, including *borān kammaṭṭhāna*. With the Thammayut representing Thai and globalized Buddhism, pre-reform Buddhism in Cambodia increasingly seemed to characterize a distinctively national, Cambodian tradition. The developing international networks between Buddhist countries from the end of the nineteenth century onward brought together those at the reformist end of the spectrum, while those preserving the traditional forms of Buddhism became increasingly isolated from one another, and this also encouraged the growing tendency to identify *borān* tradition with the local. Over a timespan of three or four generations the pan-Theravada presence of *borān* Buddhism was forgotten. Cambodians familiar with the practice, interviewed in 2012, were surprised to learn of Thai branches.[37]

While the power of language as a catalyst for change was motivating missionaries, reformers, and modernists alike to use printing technology, an alternative view of the power of language as a catalyst for change saw traditionalists in Cambodia actively preventing the printing of *borān* materials. There, practitioners of the *borān* tradition sought to protect traditional knowledge and to contain the power of *borān* writings in the safe hands of those within the esoteric teaching lineages empowered to receive and transmit it. They prevented the printing and publication (i.e., making public) of all Cambodian Buddhist texts, retaining their reproduction within the hands of skilled manual copyists.

This protectiveness was seen as reactionary, elitist, and backward by younger, modernist monks within the Mahanikay camp, and ironically the unwillingness to allow traditional teachings to be committed to print eventually led to the loss of the very thing it sought to preserve. In 1920, three reform-minded monks within the Mahanikay, based at the supreme patriarch's headquarters at Wat Uṇṇalom in Phnom Penh, deliberately flouted the Sangha hierarchy by using a printing press to publish and disseminate an accessible work on monastic rules, Vinaya, composed by one of the three.[38] In the eyes of traditionalists, this not only desecrated the teaching of the Buddha, but also, by making the contents of a religious book accessible to anyone regardless of whether they had a teacher's permission and guidance, broke the emphasis on teacher-pupil transmission and flouted a law enacted just two years earlier to prevent such a development.

The three reformists were defended by the Cambodian royal family and later supported by the French colonial administration then governing Cambodia including by Louis Finot, head of the École française d'Extrême-Orient in Hanoi. This abrogated the privilege of the supreme patriarch to discipline his junior monks' insubordination, and ultimately ushered in a further phase of the marginalization of *borān kammaṭṭhāna*. *Borān kammaṭṭhāna* was just one aspect of the traditional Buddhism being criticized by the young, modernizing monks, but it was expertise in this that gave the then supreme patriarch his authority. The modernizers, in contrast, promoted knowledge of the canonical texts as a higher source of authority. The response of the temporal powers undermined moderate traditionalists within the Mahanikay hierarchy. As a result, the three younger, more radical modernists—to whom we shall return when considering the decline of *borān kammaṭṭhāna*—rose in power and were instrumental in introducing Western and Thammayut-inspired Pali scholarship and the printing of Buddhist texts to Cambodia, extending this approach beyond the direct influence of the Thammayut. They were also involved in the translation into Khmer of the Pali canon, which appears not to have formed part of Cambodia's repertoire of religious literature until that point, although decades of devastating warfare prior to the arrival of the French complicate an assessment of the historical state of Cambodian religious literature.[39]

The First Printed Sources

As a result of this convergence between the acceptance of the printing press and the espousal of reformist, Pali-canon-based Buddhism, we do not find *borān* materials (including meditation texts) being published in the early days of the printing press in Cambodia. In fact, throughout the entire region, it was only after the disruption of the living tradition that *borān kammaṭṭhāna* materials began to appear in print, and it first happened in those areas where familiarity with it had first faded from memory. The Sri Lankan meditation manual published in Britain as *The Yogāvacara's Manual* at the end of the nineteenth century, through collaboration between British Pali text scholars and the Buddhist revivalist Anagarika Dharmapala, was done on the basis of a single manuscript and no practitioner input.[40] Around the same time, this being the period that saw the creation of French Indochina, two French scholars published snippets or descriptions of *borān* materials from Southeast Asia. The first was a passage relating the origin of the universe from Pali syllables from a text called the *Dhammaviṅsun* included in a book on Cambodian Buddhism by Adhémard Leclère. Leclère spent a considerable time in Cambodia, holding various official posts there between 1886 and 1911.[41] The second was published by Louis Finot, the director of the newly established École française d'Extrême-Orient, who later taught two and helped the careers of all three of the above-mentioned modernists. In 1917 Finot published a survey of traditional Lao literature, which offered the most detailed coverage of *borān* works until work began over half a century later by successor generations of scholars at EFEO, from the late 1970s to the early 2000s, notably François Bizot, François Lagirarde, and Olivier de Bernon.

Interest in Publication of Meditation Materials in the 1930s

The next bout of publication of *borān* materials took place in the 1930s, among those interested in using textual studies to promote meditation and Buddhist revival.[42] Senior members of the Thai Sangha hierarchy, after a crisis in their ranks caused by the pro-democracy coup of 1932, sought to promote meditation, the practice of which had been undermined even within their own lineage, the Thammayut, which had been established by Prince Mongkut a century earlier. A likely motivation contributing to this greater interest in meditation is that the pro-democracy change in government also altered the structure of the Thai Sangha. Members of the Thammayut no longer had automatic authority over monks of the majority Mahanikay lineage. The association with meditating monks provided an alternative source of authority for the Thammayut as they now needed to enhance their popularity in the absence of the security that royal endorsement had provided.[43]

The loss of endorsement for the Thammayut administrative hierarchy in itself gave greater freedom to those who had maintained an interest in meditation. These two factors enabled the publication of books containing *borān kammaṭṭhāna* meditation manuals, the most significant being the anthology by Yasothararat in 1936. Some of the manuals it contains had been gathered in the northeast of the country where the Thammayut forest tradition had adapted their meditation practice to ensure conformity with the Pali-normative reform, making traditional *borān* materials redundant. The similarly important and partially overlapping anthology by Darunnakon in 1935 was additionally informed by the continuous living tradition at Wat Ratchasittharam, discussed above, even though this is not immediately apparent in the volume. (The temple maintains to this day the policy of nondisclosure of practice details until one has reached the appropriate stage of training in one's apprenticeship to an established, authorized teacher.)

These publications by Yasothararat and Darunnakon are extremely important for the study and dating of *borān kammaṭṭhāna*. They provide the most extensive published documentation of the tradition, including both meditation instructions and manuals on the application of the methods to healing. These publications identify the former owners of some of the manuscript manuals they used, allowing us to establish that the court-sponsored Sangha hierarchies of Siam and Laos, and the supreme patriarchs and meditation lineages of Ayutthaya and Vientiane, were advocating *borān* practices as far back as at least the sixteenth century.[44] It was a branch of the Ayutthaya lineage recorded in these manuals that found its way to Sri Lanka in the mid-eighteenth century, through the missions of royal monks authorized by the supreme patriarchs and by the kings of the two realms, Ayutthaya and Kandy. Thus the text published by T. W. Rhys Davids on the basis of a Sri Lankan manuscript also represents this transmission.

Publications in Thailand in the 1930s would go on to inform the first doctoral dissertations on the subject of *borān kammaṭṭhāna* at Western universities. The first, defended at Hamburg University in 1999, was based on Yasothararat 1936. It was written by the then-monk Mettanando Bhikkhu, who had recently left Wat Phra Dhammakaya (the headquarters of the Dhammakaya movement, to which we shall return below), which maintains a later branch of this transmission.[45] Olivier de Bernon, in his PhD, defended in 2000, describes two other publications from 1930s Thailand. Both are editions of a short manual called the *Mūlakammaṭṭhāna*, mentioned above, both based on a late eighteenth-century manuscript that may now be lost.[46] One of these refers to a manuscript of 1661 as the basis for the eighteenth-century version.[47]

It was also in the 1930s that the two monks in Sri Lanka, Ratnajoti and Ratnapāla, began working toward the publication of a pair of *borān kammaṭṭhāna* manuals, one a mixed Sinhala-Pali work related to the text published by T. W. Rhys Davids, the other a version of the Pali *Amatākaravaṇṇanā*, the text we examined in the previous chapter. In other words, both texts represented the mid-eighteenth-century transmission from Ayutthaya. The interest in meditation and in Buddhism's past reflects the ethos of revivalism in Sri Lanka in the interwar period, as Buddhism continued to be viewed as a source of inspiration and national pride in the independence movement. However, Ratnajoti and Ratnapāla's endeavor was interrupted by World War II, which also led to the loss of the source manuscript on which they had based their initial editions. In the introduction to their published version they report that the manuscript they had worked from had been discovered in the storage chest of a monk who had died. It bore a label identifying it as deriving from the Asgiriya temple in Kandy, but they explain that it was moved and lost during the war.

Post–World War II Independence-Period Publications

Ratnajoti and Ratnapāla were able to make a renewed effort to publish the material they had been working on some time later when, in post-independence Sri Lanka, Buddhism and Buddhist publications were promoted by the Bandaranaike government as part of their quest for a majority mandate in the late 1950s–1960s. The two monks were able to find a number of related manuscripts in Sri Lankan libraries to confirm their earlier work, and they eventually published the pair of texts—alongside a third unrelated text—in 1963, twenty-five years after they had begun.[48] The titles of other *borān* manuscripts that they report consulting during the revision of their pre-war work are confirmed by the colophons of related, extant manuscripts collected by Hugh Nevill in the preceding century and now in the above-mentioned Nevill collection of the British Library.

Following World War II, with independence for the region's nations came a resurgence of Buddhism. Helped by the Buddha Jayanti celebrations marking 2,500 years of the Buddha's *sāsana* (religion) in the mid-1950s, particularly by the Sixth Council held in Burma, meditation practices inspired by looking afresh at the early Pali canonical and commentarial texts came to the fore. Burmese Vipassanā began to move into a dominant position in Southeast Asian meditation teaching. Nonetheless, in Thailand a diversity of practices included a modernized branch of *borān kammaṭṭhāna* called *vijjā dhammakāya*. Developed and popularized by the monk Candasaro Sot (1884–1959), the abbot of Wat Paknam in Bangkok, this system included practices available in a nonesoteric form, more openly available.

This period saw the stirrings of the Western interest in Buddhist mind-culture, which from the 1970s onward would radically transform global access to and adaptations of Buddhist teachings. In these early days Sot's method was well represented among pioneering Westerners. Summaries of his practice made by his disciples began to appear, including the first-hand account, cited in the previous chapter, of Kapilavaḍḍho, ordained by Sot in the early 1950s. He was the first British monk from the English Sangha Trust to be ordained in Thailand, and he wrote his account when back in England and convalescing from a severe illness, now disrobed and under the assumed name of Richard Randall. Considered insufficiently sensational for the publishers approached at the time, it only appeared in 1990. Another British devotee, Terence Magness, began to write English accounts of Candasaro Sot and his teachings from the 1960s onward.[49] The earlier branch of *borān kammaṭṭhāna* that Sot's *vijjā dhammakāya* method most resembles has been identified by Phibul Choompolpaisal as that taught by fifty-six meditation masters at Ayutthaya in the eighteenth century.[50]

Publications in Laos and Cambodia from the 1970s

From the mid-1970s onward in Cambodia, at a point when *borān kammaṭṭhāna* had largely been suppressed and on the eve of communist revolution, François Bizot, an archaeologist working under the auspices of EFEO, began to document the remains of the textual and living traditions there. His access to both was the result of a chance connection with the living tradition through the Khmer family into which he had married.[51] He recognized the vulnerability and unique nature of the practice. The first book he published on the subject centered on the story of Princess Cittā / Prince Citto in the five-branched tree, published as *Le Figuier à cinq branches.* This is the story also retold for one of the queens of Kandy in Sri Lanka by one of the Siamese meditation masters who took *borān kammaṭṭhāna* there in the mid-eighteenth century, with which this chapter opened. The combination of textual and anthropological work makes Bizot's the most significant academic portrayal of *borān* Buddhism and *borān kammaṭṭhāna*. He ensured the documentation of aspects unrecorded in texts and largely discontinued after the Marxist revolution. We shall return to a discussion of this period later in this work.

In 1975, a Marxist government was also established in Laos by the Pathet Lao. This saw the initial suppression and ongoing government control of Buddhism and the abolishment of the rank of supreme patriarch (Sangharāja). Just the year before, however, the government had published an authorized account of meditation practice in Laos entitled *Samatha-kammatthan lae Vipassana-kammatthan Chabab Boran (Muang Vientiane-Luang Prabang)* [*Samatha and Vipassana Meditation, Traditional Version (Vientiane-Luang Prabang City)*]. This contains a number of *borān kammaṭṭhāna* texts also found in Yasothararat's work (above). As pointed out by Phibul Choompolpaisal, who has written on this Lao text, it is extremely important for two reasons. First, it indicates that *borān kammaṭṭhāna* was still authorized by the Lao Sangha hierarchy as representing orthodox Lao practice as late as 1974. Second, it provides dates and names high-ranking authors or owners for the manuals it contains, including our earliest date yet for a *borān kammaṭṭhāna* text, that of Supreme Patriarch Rachathibbadee Sivisuddhisom, who recorded his text in 1501. Choompolpaisal's recent study of this work alongside those from Thailand in the 1930s provides the most detailed study to date of the diversity and historical extent of *borān kammaṭṭhāna* in Southeast Asia.[52]

Publications from the 1990s Onward

While François Bizot and colleagues in EFEO continued to publish work on materials from Cambodia, Laos, and Thailand, the next phase of publications in Thailand itself came in the 1990s with Thai practitioners beginning to publish on the subject. Ven. Sermchai Jayamangalo, abbot of Wat Luang Pho Sot Dhammakayaram in Ratchaburi, which follows Sot's *vijjā dhammakāya* method, began publishing material in both Thai and English.[53] Also inspired by Sot's teaching is the network of Dhammakaya temples with their headquarters at Wat Phra Dhammakaya in Pathumthani. This movement has taken Sot's internationalizing mission further and produced a range of paper and online publications, including videos to teach entrance-level practices.[54] More recently, in 2015, Niras Ruangsan has provided an analysis and translations of five texts of Sot's teachings directly related to his meditation practice and its applications.

Supreme Patriarch Suk Kaitheun (1733–1822) forms a key bridge between the pre-modern period, before the sack of Ayutthaya, and the early modern, colonial period, after the capital was moved first to Thonburi, then Bangkok. Two living traditions in Thailand can trace their lineage back to Suk Kaitheun. One is the lineage at Wat Pradusongtham in Ayutthaya, recently identified by Phibul Choompolpaisal.[55] The other is at Wat Ratchasittharam, in Thonburi. It was this lineage that Darunnakon consulted in the early 1930s when working on his anthology of *borān* texts. The monk who now heads the meditation section at Wat Ratchasittharam, Veera Thanaveero, whom we met above, has been publishing on it since the mid-1990s using both his practice experience and the collection of manuscripts there.[56] Some of the academic scholarship conducted since the 1990s has benefited from the input of Veera Thanaveero, who has also collaborated with a group of researchers based at the Bodleian Library to document the manuscript collections housed in his section and at nearby temples.[57] The Dhammakaya Foundation, noted above as following Sot's *vijjā dhammakāya*, has also inspired academic research in this area, searching for the precursors to Sot and the early origins of the method. In addition to the research by Mettanando Bhikkhu on Suk's medicine manual, noted above, an important contribution is the survey of Southeast Asian evidence for *borān kammaṭṭhāna* by Kitchai Urkasame.[58] Among the additional evidence provided by Urkasame are two important texts, the *Buddhanorakan* and *Phra Ñāṇakasiṇa*, which he edits on the basis of manuscripts discovered in northeast Thailand.

Oral Tradition

Despite *borān kammaṭṭhāna* being an esoteric tradition, then, substantial manuscript and printed evidence is available. In fact, collections of Theravada manuscripts often contain texts relating to meditation, and these have been little explored. The diversity and practice of meditation in pre-modern Theravada await discovery.[59] Nevertheless, the substantial disappearance of the living lineages of the tradition in the twentieth century means that our access to the oral teachings necessary to understand how these traditions work in practice is very limited and in some areas entirely lost.

In Thailand, we noted the living lineages of Wat Pradusongtham and Wat Ratchasittharam and the importance of the latter in producing materials of its own as well as informing studies of the subject. We also noted the importance of various modernized transmissions through Candasaro Sot. In Cambodia, significant oral history was recorded before the Democratic Kampuchea (Khmer Rouge) period by François Bizot, as noted above. After the Democratic Kampuchea period, some elderly practitioners who remembered early practice were interviewed by Olivier de Bernon. He also recorded a few still extant practice lineages in the late 1990s. Information from interviews and practice that I have undertaken at a few temples in Cambodia since 2012 informs some of the material in this book. Other possible living traditions have been reported to me from elsewhere, but I have not been able to verify these.

Timeline

The above evidence gives us the following broad timeline for *borān kammaṭṭhāna* (Figure 3). The earliest date comes from the 1501 text from Laos recorded in the publications of 1936 and 1974 noted above. The 1936 publication was based on manuscripts collected from the northeast by Jan in the late nineteenth century. Later, we shall return to Jan and why, though based in Bangkok, he had both interest in and access to this material. The 1974 book was published in Laos reflecting practices still current just prior to the Marxist revolution there. Both works also contain additional material from Laos from after the sixteenth century.[60] The practice flourished most recently in Cambodia and Laos, but the longest sequence and greatest range of evidence comes from Thailand. This is in large part thanks to the publications in the early twentieth century. Thailand is where the active marginalization and suppression of *borān* meditation first began, but also the source of adaptations that enabled the practice to survive as a living tradition in modified forms. The fact that Cambodian, *khom*, script was used in central Thai manuscripts until the modern period, and is still used in Thai *yantra* and tattoos, confuses this picture in that some of the manuscripts referred to in early twentieth-century publications may in fact have come from Cambodia. Not all of them have a provenance or an associated owner, author, or date.

In addition to the 1501 date from the Lao Sangharāja's text, we also have the suggestive Phitsanulok inscription dated to 1549. This means that, despite its esoteric nature, sufficient evidence is available to confirm a pre-sixteenth-century origin for *borān kammaṭṭhāna*. This is three centuries earlier than any other living meditation lineage documented as still extant in the contemporary

Theravada world. For all other lineages, we have to look to more recent, modern origins, even if they drew on the early Pali canonical and commentarial sources. In other words, other practices may at first sight seem more genuine and closer to the teaching of the Buddha, because they are recognizable in the early texts on meditation in the Sutta Piṭaka of the Pali canon, and their fifth-century commentaries. However, this conceals a rupture in the tradition.

As indicated in the previous chapter, we can also recognize in *borān kammaṭṭhāna* the worldview of the fifth-century commentarial period, but in the Abhidhamma material, not in the more familiar Sutta material that provides the discursive doctrinal teachings. We cannot for now know whether *borān kammaṭṭhāna* dates back to that period, or was even formed alongside it. Abhidhamma learning became de-emphasized in Thailand in the late nineteenth and twentieth centuries, and this may have contributed to the misunderstanding of the practice. Additionally, we also noted that its approach to language and to the body ceased to be recognized in the modern period.

Conclusion

This chapter examined the evidence for *borān kammaṭṭhāna*, from inscriptions to manuscripts, printed texts, and oral tradition. We noted the two broad genres of texts, narratives and manuals. Then we considered the fragile nature of Theravada manuscripts and how they are made. We observed that the recording of *borān* manuscripts often reflected some kind of crisis in Theravada history, a fear that the transmission might not survive or that there might be rupture to a teaching lineage.

The esoteric nature of *borān kammaṭṭhāna* prevented printing of its materials, with the printing press in its early days more often used by modernizers. One result of this is that the first printed works relating to the tradition were published by complete outsiders, Europeans from the end of the nineteenth century. The next phase of publications was in Thailand in the early twentieth century

Figure 3
Summary of Evidence for *Borān Kammaṭṭhāna*

Pan-Theravada fifth-century Abhidhamma commentaries and manuals	Thailand	Cambodia	Laos	Sri Lanka
	The correspondence between *borān kammaṭṭhāna* and the understanding of causality and the physical body in Abhidhamma-based manuals such as the *Visuddhimagga* and Abhidhamma commentarial material suggests that *borān kammaṭṭhāna* could have originated in the early commentarial period. Clear physical evidence based on dated manuscripts, texts, or inscriptions, however, is only available from a millennium later.			
16th century	Provisionally, Phitsanulok inscription		Manual of Supreme Patriarch Rachathibbadee Sivisuddhisom mentioned in later publication	
17th century	Manuscript from 1661 mentioned in later publication		Manual of Somdet Phramaha Vichaithat Ratchamahamuni mentioned in later publication	
18th century	Manuscripts from Ayutthaya period mentioned in later publication		Manuscripts from Ayutthaya period mentioned in later publication	Manuscripts from 1756 transmission from Ayutthaya

19th century	Manuscripts in use	Manuscripts in use. First publication of related texts in 1899 by Adhémard Leclère	Manuscripts in use	Manuscripts from 1756 transmission begin to fall out of use, collected by Nevill. First publication of a Sinhala manual, 1896
20th century	Manuscripts housed in large collections. Publications in 1920s and 1930s. Beginnings of publications of modified practice 1960s. Beginning of academic and practitioner publications in 1990s.	Manuscripts documented by Bizot in 1970s, pre-revolution, again by Bernon post-revolution. Academic publications from late 1970s.	First publication describing related text by Louis Finot, 1917. 1974 publication of texts confirming practice current. From 1975 disruption to practice, manuscript and text.	1904 Nevill Collection in British Library. 1916 first translation of a manual into English. Further manuals published in 1960s.
21st century	Practice continues in various degrees of modification. Academic publications in relation to practice.	Manuscripts kept safe in revolution by individuals emerge. Practitioners partially discard esotericism to safeguard continuity. Academic publications in relation to practice.		

after decades of suppression and reform had already marginalized these practices. Fortunately, even though the genres of *borān* materials, as narratives and manuals, are not subsumed within the more easily datable commentarial lineages, these publications, in combination with those manuscripts that have come to light, allow us to trace *borān kammaṭṭhāna* back to the early sixteenth century, longer than any other living tradition of Theravada meditation. Interpreting such evidence is made easier by the documentation of living traditions that survived in Laos and Cambodia until the Marxist revolutions of the 1970s, as well as by simplified practice lineages that have continued to this day.

Now that we have established the evidentiary basis for our knowledge of pre-modern esoteric Theravada Buddhism, we return to the processes involved in its practice. In the previous chapter we had looked at how *borān kammaṭṭhāna* enacts the process of transformation explained in Abhidhamma. Thus aligned with Theravada orthodoxy, it nonetheless extends the Abhidhamma approach beyond that seen in other, more well-known systems of Theravada meditation, in seeking to exact a somatic transformation by internalizing and embedding meditation experience in the practitioner's body.

In the next two chapters, we shall look at approaches to the physical realm and body that were marginalized in the modern period and see how *borān kammaṭṭhāna* relates to them. These approaches are language in the form of generative grammar, medicine, especially ayurvedic obstetrics, and chemistry or alchemy, particularly the purification of mercury used in turn in the purification of gold. Relevant is also the type of mathematics and models of change underlying these sciences. It is possible that closer examination of the parallels between *borān kammaṭṭhāna* and these resonating technologies will eventually provide us with more concrete, earlier dating. They will for now help us understand its disappearance. We shall first examine the *borān* approach to language.

4

Technologies of Transformation

Grammar, Mathematics, and the Significance of Substitution

The Buddha proclaimed,

"Meaning is understood through phonemes. The sense of all speech is understood only through the phonemes. When there is a mistake in the phonemes, there is confusion as to the meaning. Therefore, skillfulness regarding phonemes is very helpful in relation to the Sutta-teachings."[1]

On hearing the Buddha, Venerable Mahākaccāyana said,

"Lord, please permit me to compose a book on phonemes that would henceforth protect the teaching contained in the *Tipiṭaka*, with its 84,000 portions. It would enable living beings to refer to the constituents of materiality, *rūpa-dhamma*, the constituents of mentality, *nāma-dhamma*, all the volitional formations, *sabba-saṅkhāra-dhamma*, and functional consciousness as conditioning states, *kiriya-citta-paccaya-dhamma*, in conformity with the phonemes (*sadda*) that make up the entire collection of texts."[2]

The Buddha replied, "Excellent! Proceed, Mahākaccāyana."

At these words, the venerable Mahākaccāyana composed the book of phonemes in its entirety. He began,

"Now the phonemes beginning with the letter *a* are forty-one in number, namely, *a ā i ī u ū e o* | *ka kha ga gha ṅa | ca cha ja jha ña | ṭa ṭha ḍa ḍha ṇa | ta tha da dha na | pa pha ba bha ma | ya ra la va | sa ha ḷa aṃ.*

"These forty-one become the constituents of materiality and the constituents of consciousness. The vowels become materiality. The three vowels of light measure are the short vowels *a i u*. They are the articulation of the two ankles, the two knees, and the two elbows. The others are called long vowels *ā ī ū e o*. They divide into five branches. The phoneme *ā* becomes the left leg. The phoneme *ī* becomes the right leg. The phoneme *ū* becomes the left arm. The phoneme *e* becomes the right arm. The phoneme *o* becomes the torso. This is why the vowels are called 'constituents of materiality.' The thirty-two consonants become the thirty-two physical constituents of the body beginning with the hair. The single phoneme *aṃ* produces the 52 aspects of consciousness (*cetasika*), comprising the 13 neutral *cetasika*, the 14 unskillful *cetasika* and the 25 beautiful *cetasika*. The five sets of plosives (*ka-ma*) form the five aggregates that make up the psychosomatic being (*khandha*). The remaining eight consonants (*ya . . . aṃ*) become the eight factors of the noble eightfold path, beginning with correct view."

—Adapted and translated from the translation of Bizot and Lagirarde, *Saddavimala*[3]

In this passage from the *borān kammaṭṭhāna* text, the *Saddavimala*, "The Purity of Sound," we first see the standard opening of the Pali grammar composed by the sixth-century-C.E. scholar-monk Kaccāyana. It is a treatise within the Indic system of generative grammar. The opening explains the importance of grammar for understanding Pali canonical texts. It then anachronously attributes the origins of both Pali grammar in general and Kaccāyana's grammar in particular to the Buddha and his close disciple Mahākaccāyana respectively. When this version from the *Saddavimala* goes on to explain the phonemes that make up the Pali language, there is an unexpected twist. The phonemes morph into the creation of the individual, including all aspects of the Abhidhamma analysis of what makes up the psychosomatic person: their physicality and consciousness with all the possible attributes, good and bad, that can attend them. The noble eightfold path, the traditional summary of Buddhist practice, and—later—the creation and periodization of the cosmos are all said to develop from the phonemes of the Pali alphabet, with generative grammar literally acting as the source of all creation.

We have already seen that *borān* practitioners had a distinctive attitude to language, one that allowed Pali phonemes to represent meditational states, and at the same time initially prohibited the representation of the esoteric tradition in print for public distribution. In *borān* culture, the oral and physical representations of the Dhamma, the Buddha's teaching, have two functions. They make the Dhamma semantically available, accessible for its meaning, and they make it potently present, accessible for its creative and protective power. The first is a linguistic approach in which grammar is the branch of learning that describes the correct formation of the language for conveying semantic meaning. The other approach is to see grammar as a creative, potent—one might say "magical"—event, which captures the power of the Dhamma.

In chapter 2, we recognized that *borān* meditation was an enactment of the Abhidhamma path to enlightenment, but that this did not account for all of its features. In this chapter, we turn to one of those features, the harnessing of language, found both in its meditation and in related protective practices. The treatment of language as a creative principle has more in common with traditional Indic grammar systems and Abhidhamma analysis than at first apparent. The Abhidhamma understanding of language as a two-way link between consciousness and physicality in the process of communication, in which meaning moves from the intention of the speaker through the physicality of the sound to the comprehension of the listener, may have informed these connections. What I want to show here is that the underlying conception of how change comes about, and the mathematics that facilitate predicting and enacting change, are shared across Abhidhamma, classical Indic grammar, and the use of language as a creative force. We will then find, in the following chapter, that the same conceptualization of change and use of mathematics also inform traditional medicine and chemistry.

Important across all of these methods for bringing about change is the principle of substitution in carrying forward transitions from one state to another, so some attention will be given to a consideration of how substitution was theorized and applied across these technologies. Examining the shared principles and processes of these at-first-sight-unrelated sciences or technologies—generative grammar, mathematics, and medicine including pharmacy, chemistry, and Abhidhamma—allows us to understand the models of transformation that underlie *borān kammaṭṭhāna*.

Since the discussion in this chapter pertains to technology, it naturally becomes quite technical in places. A description of the applications of *borān* practice to worldly (*lokiya*) ends comes toward the end of the chapter, while a summary of the implications of the discussion is provided in the conclusion.

Contrasting Attitudes to Grammar

Although authoritative texts in non-reform Theravada tended to be in vernacular languages, Pali, the language of the Theravada scriptural canon, was retained for important and powerful terminology, such as words for sacred entities including the Buddha, and the technical words of Abhidhamma and meditation. The potency ascribed to Pali language was greater and its range of applications wider in traditional Theravada than in modern reform Theravada. The clash between reform and tradition over language was not about Pali per se. Both groups accepted its significance and were purists in their own way. The clash was, rather, between their different approaches to grammar. For the traditionalists it might be better to speak of these as modes of grammar that they did not regard as mutually exclusive. As Catherine Becchetti explains in her study of the *yantra*, the potent geometric patterns used in the Theravada of mainland Southeast Asia, the use of Pali letters in the potent sense transcends their linguistic value without doing away with that value: the linguistic value supports the creative potency.[4] The concepts underlying generative grammar, the type of grammar used in Indic culture since the first millennium B.C.E. to teach correct language use, which we explore below, support both types of application, and the full implications of generative grammar are drawn out in traditional Theravada.

In the modern period reform scholars began to be influenced by Western philology, sometimes directly, sometimes through changes in attitudes to textual study in Thailand. For example, the three influential monks involved in the printing of the first Buddhist text in Cambodia discussed in the previous chapter were influenced by new approaches to Pali studies in Thailand, and two of them went on to study at the École française d'Extrême-Orient in Hanoi (now the National Museum of Vietnamese History) under the French archaeologist and orientalist Louis Finot.

Western learning of Asian classical languages such as Sanskrit and Pali was modeled on European training in Greek and Latin. It focused on the understanding of literal meaning and the prestige performance of perfect grammar. It was also informed by comparative philology, a subject that had developed in the nineteenth century. This had itself been strongly influenced by the discovery of the relationship of Sanskrit with other languages—especially Persian, Classical Greek, and Latin—leading to the definition of the "Indo-European" language family in the early nineteenth century by Thomas Young.[5] Etymology in the European context was about analyzing the linguistic components of words, drawing out their historical evolution, and recognizing lexical and morphological connections between different languages.

Throughout Theravada history the study of Pali and Sanskrit

had also been used for the public display of knowledge and prestige learning, in addition to understanding the literal meaning. In the pre-modern period, correct grammatical usage had been a weapon employed in political rivalries and the competition for patronage. High-level debates about Pali grammar and phonetics had resulted in the change of royal patronage to the victors and the introduction of new ordination lineages. These debates were informed by a concern with correct grammar to ensure the validity of Vinaya rituals, including ordination.[6] If the Pali wording of a legal act was not enunciated or performed in a grammatically correct fashion, then doubts could be raised over its legitimacy. Perfect grammar was thus a legal necessity within the monastic institution. Such considerations had grown stronger by the middle of the second millennium C.E., perhaps in relation to millenarian anxiety, and have continued in the modern period.[7] The importance of preserving the texts and correct grammar went hand in hand with a philosophy of language that took into consideration developments of the subject in India. According to Mabel Bode, over 90% of the Pali literature composed in Pagan (Burma) from the tenth to the fourteenth centuries was dedicated to "grammar," under which should be included works on the philosophy of language drawing on Abhidhamma analysis.[8]

The traditional grammars on which Sanskrit and Pali learning had been based were generative grammars, in which the entire language can be generated from a set of roots and formulae. We shall explore the systematic, logically unfurling nature of generative grammar as a means of teaching correct language use below. Generative grammar was not, at that time, used in European language study, where descriptive conjugations and declensions were used to build up a prescriptive grammar. Indic generative grammar existed within a grammatical culture, with philosophical and practical resonances. Traditional practices applied the philosophy and creative potency of generative grammar to a number of ends. It was these creative aspects that informed the production of *yantras* from Pali syllables, and the use of Pali phrases and syllables in the meditation practices of *borān kammaṭṭhāna*. Reformers and outsiders rejected as "magical" the practical applications of these creative aspects of language.

To reject this creative aspect of language was in accordance with the Protestant, secularist, and reformist agendas of colonial and modernizing governments and monks. For them, it reflected irrational beliefs and was one of the *hocus pocus* accretions in European negative assessments of traditional Theravada religion, echoing critiques of Catholicism. By discarding this creative aspect, however, Theravada reformists also lost a fundamental branch of their traditional learning. This loss led to a divergence between reform and traditional learning at the elite level, even while the application of generative grammar to practical ends continued at the popular level. This created a fundamental rift between reformist and traditional ways of thinking. It also created a rift between Buddhism for *lokuttara* (supramundane, soteriological) purposes and Buddhism for *lokiya* (this-worldly, mundane, including apotropaic) purposes, a rift not present in pre-reform Theravada.[9]

Generative Grammar in Indic Cultures

European descriptive grammar offers paradigms and rules that can be used to predict and prescribe the formation of "correct" language. Generative grammar also prescribes correct language formation and use, but through the application of algorithms and codes. The Indic form of generative grammar was originally designed for Sanskrit. Such is the similarity between Sanskrit and Pali that it was adapted for the correct formation of the latter when it too became a prestige language.

The seminal work of Indic generative grammar is the *Aṣṭadhyāyī* of Pāṇini (c. fourth century B.C.E.). This extraordinary text in 3,959 very tersely enunciated rules—some consisting of just a single syllable—uses code letters alongside linguistic items such as suffixes, all defined within the text itself, to guide a series of substitutions that generates the entire Sanskrit language, its morphology, syntax, and semantics, all out of a discrete set of monosyllabic verbal "roots." The root is a theoretical original word or language element (*dhātu*) from which all other related word forms are derived. Thus one may begin with the theoretical root *bhū*, "to become," and through the application of the appropriate transformations, suffixes, and endings arrive, via the present stem *bhava*, at the form *bhavāmi*, "I become." In this sense, the end result is the same as Western prescriptive grammar—in this case the first person singular present active of a verb. However, instead of teaching paradigms and sets of endings, the generative grammar uses codes that trigger discrete processes involving meta-rules, recursion, and transformation, that link *bhū* to *bhavāmi*, and that can be applied universally to lead every other theorized verbal root to its correct range of semantically related forms for use in the real world. It is as if, in English, we change the root "go" to "I went," not by learning that pattern, but by learning some algorithms and applying them to the root "go," algorithms that can also be applied to every other verbal root to arrive at every other verbal statement in real language.

Pāṇini's *Aṣṭadhyāyī* is the foundational text of a highly developed system of grammar that pervades Sanskritic culture. Until the modern period, training in the generative grammar of Pāṇini or later grammarians was considered fundamental to elite education in all regions strongly influenced by that culture, including Sri Lanka and Southeast Asia. The work of Pāṇini and other South Asian generative grammarians became familiar to European linguistics in the nineteenth century, eventually influencing the development of generative grammar in Western linguistics by Zellig Harris and Noam Chomsky in the 1950s.[10] In the nineteenth and early twentieth centuries, European grammatical science was primitive in comparison with that found in Indic and Indic-influenced cultures for over two millennia.[11]

The methods used in generative grammar also had broader cultural implications. The motivation for the development of such sophisticated grammatical expertise in South Asian culture is one that we would now deem religious. In brahmanical Hinduism correct language use was one of the crucial technologies employed to control and maintain the universe. Language was believed to be a creative force, fundamental to the effective performance of Vedic sacrificial rites. Originally a medium of communication with the gods, by the beginning of the first millennium B.C.E. the Sanskrit hymns and sacrificial language expressions of the Vedas of early Hinduism—the earliest of which can be dated to around 1500 B.C.E.—came to be regarded as themselves potent in ensuring the efficacy of religious ritual. Language therefore held power over the universe, and thus the usage of language needed to be precise and accurate. The emphasis on correct Sanskrit led to an advanced science of language (grammar), including phonetics, morphology, and semantics. In parallel, we also see the development of geometry, the branch of mathematics used in the technology of constructing the sacrificial enclosures and fires necessary for the performance of Vedic rites.[12] The development of grammar and mathematics of various kinds went hand in hand.

Mathematics, Memorization, and Sequencing

The emphasis on accurate language use led to sophisticated memorization techniques in brahmanical Hindu culture. While this was designed primarily to ensure pinpoint accuracy in the recitation of Vedic hymns, the culture of memorization was not only applied to rote recitation of sacred text but to other sources of knowledge. To this day traditional Sanskrit scholars routinely retain by memory and with accuracy large amounts of analytically retrievable and semantically applicable textual material. Another branch of mathematics, group theory mathematics, which deals with permutations and combinations, is relevant to both generative grammar and the method of memorization applied to learning Vedic hymns. Recitation of Vedic verses to ensure correct memorization, pronunciation, and understanding involved the repetition of the words of each line in increasingly complex sets of permutations. For example, a line reading [word A] [word B] [word C] might be repeated, without altering the meaning, in the form [word B] [word A] [word C], and then again as [word C] [word B] [word A].[13] Each line of the verse would undergo the same set of permutations, and thus as the recitation progressed the text would be rehearsed over and again. This process facilitated greater phonetic and semantic accuracy than the simple recollecting of single strings of sound could achieve. The permutations ranged from simple rearrangements of words to complex permutations, so-called *ghana-pāṭha*, "compact recitation": AB, BA, ABC, CBA, ABC, BC, CB, BCD, DCB, BCD, et cetera.[14] The recitations back and forth in these various permutations, although performed orally, can also be represented visually. When this is done, the different permutations, through interweaving the syllables, create different geometric shapes, such as those found in *yantra* made of Pali syllables in traditional Theravada.[15] These mathematical methods of memorization were applied not just to religious texts but to mathematical texts too, confirming the sharing of techniques across these two fields.[16]

While useful in memorization, an understanding of permutation was also crucial in the development of Indic generative grammar. It allowed the totality of alternative options to be encoded in the grammar. In other words, the aim was to represent the entire language with the minimum number of rules possible, and permutation was harnessed to the task of working out the minimum number of rules necessary to enable all the necessary number of combinations. A single code could then be used to activate a set of rules in the correct sequence ultimately to generate each linguistic feature of the language. Through this mechanism a limited number of rules could represent the immeasurable totality of language. To develop this system, grammarians analyzed the language in search of the minimum number of processes that could combine to create the total range of linguistic features actually in occurrence. They also worked out the optimal sequencing of the generative procedures needed to bring them about.

Group Theory Mathematics in Abhidhamma and *Borān Kammaṭṭhāna*

At this stage in our consideration of grammar, it is worth pointing out that this use of sequencing is also found in Abhidhamma and *borān* meditation. In Abhidhamma, group theory mathematics was used in calculating and representing the totality of possible combinations of, and causal connections between, the constituents of reality, *dhammas*. These are the *dhammas* that make up the individual and their experience, namely materiality, *rūpa*, aspects of consciousness, *cetasika*, and states of consciousness, *citta*.

We will recall that the analysis of mental states into skillful and unskillful was an elaboration of the fundamental Buddhist analysis of the cause of our entrapment in samsara (the realm of rebirth and suffering) in terms of the three "fires" of greed (*lobha*), hatred (*dosa*), and delusion (*moha*). Unskillful states were those based on greed, hatred, and delusion, while skillful states were those based on non-greed, non-hatred, and non-delusion. There are also resultant (*vipāka*) mental states arising from these and so-called inoperative or functional (*kiriya*) mental states that have no karmic effect.

Our experienced psychophysical state results from the totality of the three fundamental causes of soteriological imbalance, greed (*lobha*), hatred (*dosa*), and delusion (*moha*), combined in varying degrees and different circumstances. Abhidhamma therefore harnessed the mathematical knowledge of permutation to consider the most efficient manner to develop the positive attributes that lead one out of samsara to enlightenment.[17] Commentarial Abhidhamma takes this further by expanding on the canonical teaching of impermanence to formulate the doctrine of momentariness, in which physicality and mentality are constantly replaced, and only appear to continue because of the quick succession with which one *dhamma* is replaced by another.[18] This constant replacement offers the possibility of change: if one interrupts the sequence of replacements by substituting a different kind of *dhamma* from the one that precedes, one can move ultimately from negative to increasingly positive mental states.[19] The substitution of one *dhamma* by another happens naturally, but now it can be directed. We saw, when looking at *borān kammaṭṭhāna* meditation practice in chapter 2, how the *borān* system of meditation sought to enact such substitution.

The first Theravada text to try to represent the totality of these causal combinations is the *Paṭṭhāna*, "Conditional Relations," the seventh book of the Abhidhamma Piṭaka, which constitutes the third division of the Pali canon.[20] The *Paṭṭhāna* was compiled at a point—between 200–100 B.C.E.[21]—when group theory mathematics had not yet reached that stage of development whereby the full number of possibilities of a particular permutation could be calculated by an algorithm and represented by an arithmetical, algebraic formula. Instead, the *Paṭṭhāna* gives examples of the calculations, using iterative listing. This process is also found in early ayurvedic medical works, to which we shall turn in the next chapter, until algorithms were developed to represent all the options. Whereas some early ayurvedic texts list all the possible permutations, the early Abhidhamma tradition recognized that presenting every possible permutation of causal factors, in other words, all the possible ways in which *dhammas* can relate to each other, was not viable, so examples modeling the possibilities were provided instead. Although the magnitude of the total number of combinations made full writing out of the *Paṭṭhāna* impossible—commentators described the totality of combinations as being as vast as the ocean—successive generations of commentaries did make attempts to calculate exactly how many that total was, with results ranging from 388,778,713,344 to 404,948,533,288.[22]

The *borān kammaṭṭhāna* meditation manuals similarly first provide examples of how to combine skillful and other beautiful *citta* and their attendant *cetasika* into the body, similar to the kind of iterative listing found in medical texts and the *Paṭṭhāna*. Then, in order to avoid the problem of creating extremely long texts, the meditation manuals use shortened formulae, which trigger the process that the practitioner has learned in the preceding stages.

A single word can then trigger an entire meditation process, even though that process is quite complex and cumulative. The mid-eighteenth-century manual, the *Amatākaravaṇṇanā*, explored in chapter 2, despite heavy abbreviation through this process of triggering with single words, is an extensive 3,818 verses long. The practitioner brings down processes learned earlier on in the technique throughout the entire system contained in those 3,818 verses.[23]

Phonemes as Productive Symbols

This bringing down of processes from previous stages in the manual is reminiscent of Sanskritic generative grammar. Moreover, while the *Paṭṭhāna* does not use code words as symbols of quantities or processes to assist in the management of its combinations, generative grammar does. It also uses letters as symbols. Here I want to look at its use of such letters to represent components of language and transformative grammatical processes, since this will help us with understanding both *borān* language use and the principles underlying the processes of change employed in *borān* practice. I will use Pāṇini's *Aṣṭadhyāyī* from around the fourth century B.C.E. to explore Indic generative grammar in the following paragraphs because it is the most influential.[24]

An example of its use of language symbols is the combination of an element of language *ti* (the third-person singular ending of a verb) and the code letter P to make the artificial code word ***tiP***, which stands for all the verbal endings that indicate person and number. Similarly, the combination of an element of language *lu* (part of the verb "to elide") and the letter K creates ***luK***, a code word that only applies in grammar and specifies a type of elision (*lopa*), that causes phonemes to disappear in the process of generating a word.

An important instance of this symbolic use of letters is found in Pāṇini's treatment of the Sanskrit alphabet. The standard Sanskrit alphabet order is structured around the place of articulation of the sounds in the mouth. It consists of vowels, diphthongs, two non-consonants that alter the sound of a preceding vowel, followed by the consonants. The plosive consonants are ordered according to five of the six positions of articulation (*sthāna* in Sanskrit). These are (1) throat/velar; (2) the back of the palate; (3) the head/roof of the palate; (4) the teeth; and (5) lips.[25] (The sixth *sthāna* is the nose.)[26] These are followed by the semi-vowels or liquids, and the fricatives, i.e. the sibilants and the final consonant *h*. The standard Sanskrit alphabet order is as follows. Note that the consonants are listed with an inherent vowel *a* that eases their pronunciation, so *ka* not k:

> (vowels)
> a ā i ī u ū ṛ ṝ ḷ ḹ e o ai au | ṃ ḥ |
> (plosives)
> (1) ka kha ga gha ṅa |
> (2) ca cha ja jha ña |
> (3) ṭa ṭha ḍa ḍha ṇa |
> (4) ta tha da dha na |
> (5) pa pha ba bha ma |
> (liquids)
> ya ra la va |
> (fricatives)
> śa ṣa sa ha

For the purposes of generative grammar, however, the alphabet is re-ordered and has code letters or "tags," *anubandha*, inserted into it.[27] The alphabet, with code letters at intervals (below), is re-ordered in such a way that different subsets of vowels or consonants can be referred to in a single syllable, *pratyāhāra*, made up of the first phoneme in the set or subset and the code letter that ends that set or subset. The entire set or subset can thereby be referred to without the need to list it in full. The significance of the re-arrangement is that the new sets and subsets consist of groups of sounds that, at different points in the *Aṣṭadhyāyī*, are subject to a shared generative process, rather than sharing a common place of articulation. The alphabet so re-arranged is called the *Śiva sūtras*, with reference to the Hindu myth that grammar has its divine origin with the god Śiva (a myth recalled differently by Theravada Buddhists, who, as we have seen, locate its origins with the Buddha and his disciple Mahākaccāyana). The *Śiva sūtras* read as follows:

> a i u **Ṇ** ṛ ḷ **K** e o **Ṅ** ai au **C** ha ya va ra **Ṭ** la **Ṇ** ña ma ṅa ṇa na **M** jha bha **Ñ** gha ḍha dha **Ṣ** ja ba ga ḍa da **Ś** kha pha cha ṭha tha ca ṭa ta **V** ka pa **Y** śa ṣa sa **R** ha **L**

The actual phonemes of the Sanskrit language included in the *Śiva sūtras*, with the exception of the vowels themselves, all include an inherent *a* vowel, whereas the code letters, marked in bold above, lack an inherent vowel: they are all final consonants.[28] In other words, the sound for the letter *k* as an ordinary member of the alphabet is "ka," but where the letter *k* is used as a code, the sound is "-k." This allows one to distinguish between phoneme and code letter. Thus in Pāṇini the syllable "aK" refers to the sequence of simple vowels (a i u ṛ ḷ), but "aC" to all vowels (a i u ṛ ḷ o e ai au). On the same principle, "aL" refers to the entire alphabet, "haṬ" to the sequence "ha ya va ra," and "haL" to all consonants, and so on. The code letters or tags, *anubandha*, are substitutes for real sounds and carry their distinct qualities forward into a new discussion. We shall look more at this principle of substitution below.

The Pali grammars adapted from this system were simpler, with far fewer rules, because the range of Pali word forms (morphology) is smaller than the range in Sanskrit. There are also fewer phonemes in the Pali alphabet, as given in the passage cited at the start of this chapter:

> a ā i ī u ū e o |
> ka kha ga gha ṅa |
> ca cha ja jha ña |
> ṭa ṭha ḍa ḍha ṇa |
> ta tha da dha na |

pa pha ba bha ma |
ya ra la va |
sa ha ḷa aṃ

The Principle of Substitution

The use of code letters in this way, just as in algebra, requires an act of substitution, the mechanism that we have also noted underlies momentariness and change in Abhidhamma. Here in grammar, one substitutes a given language element or type—a list, series, or process—with a tag made up of a syllable or letter in order to make a calculation or apply a process. For example, the code syllables using the *Śiva sūtras* are substitutes for sequences of sounds. This is just one kind of substitution that takes place in the *Aṣṭadhyāyī*. One also substitutes one item with another in procedures or a series of procedures in generative grammar. Thus the root of a verb is replaced by a functional entity, a verb stem. The verb stem is another theorized representative that is only "real" or functional within the grammatical system, but takes us a step closer to the real language item. One may then in turn substitute the whole or a part of that representative form with a further substitute in turn. Eventually one resolves the procedure to arrive at a specific result, a word, in the real world by substituting a real word element in place of the last theoretical substitute in the series. Pāṇini's grammar relies on the process of substitution. We have the substitution of theoretical suffixes and codes by other theoretical items then real suffixes, and of theoretical endings or codes by real word endings. Each substitution lasts for as long as is necessary—which means for as long as the particular substitution is useful in the series of procedures that take us from root to verb stem to the actual derived word. It is only when one has taken the root—and the suffixes plus the endings that each triggers in turn—through the minimum number of substitutions necessary to create the real word that one can release the process and discard all substitution.[29]

Underpinning this process of substitution is a crucial principle that maintains the continuity from start to finish of the process: the substitute is treated like the original, the real thing. In other words, the qualities of the original are transferred into the item that represents it—in our example of the *Śiva sūtras*, the qualities of various sets of sounds are transferred into the substitute letter codes. Similarly, qualities that begin in a verbal root (including the meaning) are enhanced as additional qualities are cumulatively added, and they all continue to be carried forward during the process even where they are the subject of substitution. As a result, the final output contains the entire process within it, without losing the value of the original item, such as the semantic meaning of the original root. If I take our example from English, if we start off with the root "to go" and form the first-person past tense of the verb "I went," the meaning of "go" is still present in the form "went," even though the form "go" has been lost through substitution, in the course of which loss it has additionally acquired the meaning of happening in the past.

This crucial principle is taught in a fundamental grammatical rule in the *Aṣṭadhyāyī*. We will also see how it reflects a principle understood more broadly in Indic culture in the first millennium B.C.E. with world-changing consequences. The principle is stated in rule 1.1.56, which reads,

> *sthānivad ādeśo 'nalvidhau.*
> The substitute (*ādeśa*) is like (*-vat*) the original placeholder (*sthāni-*) with the exception (*'n* = *an-*) of procedures (*-vidhau*) that apply to the phonemes (*-aL-*).

I shall explain what this rule means in a moment. First, let's note that this rule governs all substitutions except those that relate to phonemes. "Phonemes" here are represented by the code *aL*. It refers to all the phonemes of the alphabet in the order given in the *Śiva sūtras*, as identified above, beginning with first vowel *a* and ending with the final code letter *L*. (In itself, *aL* is an example of substitution in action, as L substitutes for and carries forward into the rule all the sounds of the alphabet after *a*.)

The purpose of the rule is that it allows the transference of meaning and applications from one stage of the grammatical process to another through the process of substitution: "The substitute is like the original place-holder." It is this rule that facilitates the generative process. This principle of substitution allows, for example, the meaning of a verbal root (*dhātu*, e.g., "to go" in our English example), to continue even if it is replaced by a different one in the process of grammatical generation (e.g., "went" in our English example). The rule also explains that there is a limitation to this process of substitution. It does not apply when dealing with "procedures that apply to phonemes," *aL*. For example, rules that apply to the phonemes include rules about *sandhi* or "euphony" between real phonemes juxtaposed in real-life sentences. Here the specific individual qualities of the phoneme are relevant, not those of the substituted item.[30] This restriction implies that the substituted item, the *sthānin*, retains its individual characteristics, despite being substituted by something else or transforming into a new form, while allowing that new sound form to replace the old one. Some aspects of substitution are temporary. Pāṇini teaches the elision of the code letters (rule 1.3.9 *tasya lopaḥ*), for example, discarded once they have served their purpose, but other elements in the series of substitution remain present in the final language item. Nonetheless, the *sthānin*, the original place-holder, is not lost in the *ādeśa*, the process of substitution, even when elided (below).

This principle of transferring the qualities of the original to the substitute is also applied in the brahmanical Hindu ritual context that had given rise to the close concern with grammar. This need to transfer qualities arose from the consideration of sometimes needing to use a substitute in place of the originally specified substance (e.g., the sacrificial offering), implement (e.g., a type of vessel for holding a substance), or agent (e.g., the sacrificer's wife). Eivind Kahrs cites two brahmanical ritual texts dating to around

500 B.C.E., so within about a century of both Pāṇini (400 B.C.E.) and the Buddha (sixth–fifth centuries B.C.E.), that explain this principle in order to confirm that a ritual can still be valid when a substitute is used:

> When someone teaches a modification to occur in the place of a sacrificial requisite pertaining to the prototype, it takes on the characteristics of the latter. For example . . . a vessel that of potsherds, and boiled rice that of a cake . . .

and

> When the prescribed [sacrificial requisite] is lacking, a substitute . . . [must be used] on the basis of similarity. And [this substitute] would possess the characteristics of that [which it replaces].[31]

Here, an additional component of substitution is referred to, that of "similarity."

The theorization of a principle of substitution in early Indic culture had many ramifications beyond grammar and ritual. For example, it lay behind the conceptualization of the mathematical value zero (*śūnya*, "empty") in Pāṇini itself. How so? On occasion a word element or code is deleted in the process of grammatical formation, but it still exerts its influence on the word being formed, even though we can no longer see it. In the *Aṣṭadhyāyī*, deletion (*lopa*) of an item is theorized as the substitution of the substituend by zero (i.e., an empty place or place-holder, a crucial function performed by zero in mathematics), a substitution necessary for processes to continue despite the apparent absence through deletion of what has been substituted. As already explained, the substitute, here zero, takes on the qualities of what has been substituted and carries them forward. So in the deletion, *lopa*, of a verbal root, for example, even though it becomes invisible, its meaning continues.

Thanks to the zero, the qualities of the original place-holder, *sthānin*, and subsequent place-holders in the series of procedures, continue through the process even if nothing is visible. Thus the qualities can even transfer after a place-holder has been erased or—as Pāṇini defines it—replaced by zero. This concept of a place-holder that is empty (*śūnya*), in other words "zero," is believed to have originated in the context of generative grammar. It was used by Pāṇini for the process of substitution in the generative process. This use then inspired the broader applications of zero in other fields in Indic culture including mathematics.[32]

Substitution in Abhidhamma and *Borān Kammaṭṭhāna*

We have already seen when looking at Abhidhamma in the context of meditation that the notion of substitution is crucial to explain both apparent continuity in the light of momentariness and the possibility of generating positive change. The concept of zero as a place-holder may also have informed the Abhidhamma understanding of continuity in the process of consciousness. States of consciousness are momentary and, according to Theravada Buddhism, consciousness is always consciousness of an object. There is no permanent consciousness that just exists; it only arises because of a process. The problem then is what happens between moments of consciousness that allows for an individual's mind to transition between unconscious and conscious moments. The *Paṭṭhāna*, the final book of the Abhidhamma Piṭaka, appears to be the first text to mention the *bhavaṅga*, literally "factor of becoming."[33] This is developed in the Abhidhamma commentaries as the momentary resting state of consciousness that provides continuity between phases of active cognition, a kind of default process in which nothing seems to be happening but which carries forward the continuity of the karmic process between moments of consciousness, like a zero place-holder. The *bhavaṅga* also provides the connection between the last moment of consciousness in one life and the moment of rebirth in the next.

If we turn to *borān kammaṭṭhāna* practices, we have also seen that the principle of substitution is crucial for the method of delivering the meditation objects and their results such as positive, resultant, and functional mental states (*kusala*, *vipāka*, and *kiriya citta*) and concomitant mental factors (*cetasika*) into the body in order to internalize them. *Borān kammaṭṭhāna* combines the *Abhidhamma* understanding of substitution with processes related to those found in grammatical transformation. The visual representations such as the *nimitta* or code letters of attained *cetasika* and *citta* used in *borān* practice vary according to the branch, stage, specific topic of meditation, and the individual. That variety aside, they all act as substitutes for the qualities the practitioner should acquire, and these are progressively substituted in turn during the meditation. Finally they are embedded in the *khandha*, the mental and physical make-up of the practitioner, and create the practitioner's *cittaja rūpa*, materiality born of consciousness. In this way these qualities are progressively incorporated, forming the new, increasingly supramundane body.

The use of substitution in the representation of *cetasika* by *nimitta* or letter symbols might draw on a certain similarity between substitute and substituend, as in the case of the principle of ritual substitution noted above. However, that similarity might be mathematical: the similarity of place in a group or series. Thus, as noted previously, the series of five joys, *pīti*, mental factors, *cetasika*, that form part of the first *jhāna*, can be represented by a series of five sacred syllables, such as the series *na*, *mo*, *bu*, *(d)dhā*, *ya*. Exoterically these syllables mean "Homage to the Buddha," *namo buddhāya*, a phrase used to show reverence to the Buddha when initiating Buddhist ceremonies. Esoterically they substitute for a chosen series of five concepts, in this case the five *pīti*.[34]

Regardless of whether or not the term *sthānin* was ever used for the original place-holder qualities, the same process of substitution is applied. In the sequence, the substituend brings new attributes while retaining attributes of the substituted item. The application of these substitutions in series employs the type of group theory mathematics we have outlined above, for the purpose of seeking the optimal number of combinations. This contributes to our understanding of the high level of permutations and apparent repetitiveness of the meditation instructions found in the fuller manuals of the *borān kammaṭṭhāna* tradition. We shall return to this use of substitution, language, and mathematics in *borān kammaṭṭhāna* below.

Pali as a Sacred Language

The use of letter syllables in the substitution of *citta* and *cetasika* in *borān kammaṭṭhāna* harnesses a unique aspect of language. While the state of mind and intention to speak are aspects of consciousness, language itself is an aspect of materiality, formed by the wind element (breath) moving from, against, or through various places of articulation from the larynx to the nose, all aspects of materiality, and this being comprehended by hitting against the ear, before comprehension and aspects of consciousness take place in response. Thus materiality can transfer meaning and affect consciousness. Language is therefore a material product of consciousness, *cittaja rūpa*, and can also act as a material bridge between consciousnesses.[35]

The use of letter syllables in *borān* practice only uses Pali language and this reflects an understanding of the Pali language as potent in a way that is different from ordinary languages. All language is potent in that it has the power to convey meaning. When someone speaks, meaning is conveyed; when writing is applied to a surface, it suddenly bears meaning, referring to a dynamic world beyond itself. We might therefore regard all language as inherently potent and magical. But Theravada Buddhists attributed uniquely to Pali the same attributes that in the brahmanical world had been uniquely attributed to Sanskrit as a powerful, creative, and transformative agent. While early Buddhism may have emphasized meaning over form, the Theravada tradition came to believe that Pali was the language spoken by the Buddha. They further believed that it was uniquely appropriate for the encapsulation of the Dhamma, the transformative truth taught by the Buddha, because its expression was innate rather than derived. The reformers of the modern period, in contrast, were influenced by comparative philology in which all languages are historically derived. Indeed, in the Western discipline of Indology, Pali is treated as "derived from," or at least closely related and secondary to, Sanskrit. Whereas modernists and traditionalists shared an understanding of etymology that examined the derivation of words from roots and stems, modernists also saw etymology in terms of historical derivation of one language or linguistic form from historical precursors. In contrast, etymology for the traditionalists was about understanding the power held within Pali phonemes, a power that could be harnessed through the principle of substitution and the application of mathematics. This type of etymology, understanding broader concepts represented by sets of Pali syllables and the possibility of their metamorphosing into something else, is a distinctive feature of the explanations found in *borān kammaṭṭhāna* manuals.

The difference, in the modern period, between traditionalist and reformist beliefs about language is not a difference found in earlier reforms. The treatment of Pali as a sacred language for Buddhism, on a par with the similar conceptualization of Sanskrit in brahmanical Hinduism, can be traced with certainty to the fifth-century commentaries attributed to Buddhaghosa, which Theravada monastic scholarship has taken as representative of orthodoxy.[36]

Buddhaghosa identifies Pali as the "primary language of all creatures," one that a child left untutored in the vernaculars of his parents will automatically start speaking[37] and one that is universally understood: "in hell, in the realm of animals, in the realm of ghosts, in the world of mankind, and the world of the gods."[38] Buddhaghosa, the most "orthodox" representative of Theravada, credits Pali with being innate, universal, pure, uniquely pleasing and the sole language appropriate for the words of the Buddha and for this reason undertakes the translation of the commentaries from the vernacular into Pali.

Borān kammaṭṭhāna narratives take the significance of Pali a stage further. Cosmogonic texts such as the *Dhammajhān* or *Dhammaviṅsun* from Cambodia describe how the universe and the Dhamma originate from the mantras of *borān kammaṭṭhāna* using significant groupings of the syllables of the Pali alphabet such as *na mo bu ddhā ya*; *ma a u*; *ku sa lā a ku sa lā*; or *a ā i ī u ū e o*.) These phonemes are produced by "Divine Ear." Having a divine ear or divine hearing is one of the attributes of the Buddha in canonical texts, but here it is personified as a creative principle. Another creative principle is embodied as the qualities of the Buddha, *buddhaguṇ*, which uses the phonemes provided by Divine Ear to create the elements, the first boy and girl, the components of the Dhamma, et cetera.[39] A variation of this account, in which this cosmogony is explained as being made possible by grammar, and which extends the creativity that unfolds from the phonemes further, is seen in the excerpt from the *Saddavimala* that opened this chapter.

Application of Potent Language to Worldly Ends

I mentioned above that the divergence between reform and traditional understandings of grammar led to a rift between *lokuttara* (supramundane, soteriological) and *lokiya* (this-worldly, mundane, including apotropaic) applications of Buddhism in reform Theravada that is not found in traditional Theravada. In traditional Theravada the right-hand and left-hand paths use the same procedures to deliver transformation, whether salvific (right-hand) or practical (left-hand). The following summary account of a practitioner making *yantra* using sacred powder is taken from a study of *borān* practice by François Bizot and Oskar von Hinüber. It documents the explicit use of grammatical substitution in relation to Buddhist qualities and Buddhist sacred phrases in a left-hand application. To their description I have added explanations of how this relates to rules of substitution within Pali generative grammar.

The *grū* (lay master) is using protective powder to make *yantra*, geometric designs made up of Pali syllables. The word *yantra* means "mechanism for restraining, controlling, or subduing," and these designs offer protection from harm and control over others.[40] The *grū* uses the powder to write Pali syllables on a slate. He writes five Pali words: *idha cetaso daḷhaṃ gaṇhāhi thāmasā*. The exoteric meaning of this phrase is "In this connection grasp it firmly with perseverance of the mind."[41] The Cambodian esoteric meaning given to the phrase is "Young girl, come here and love me forcefully with the strength of the love in your heart." However, the Pali phrase is taken from Kaccāyana's grammar. It comes at the end of the section that teaches *sandhi* (phonetic change or euphony when phonemes are juxtaposed). It occurs at the end of a rule that teaches the substitution of a single voiced or unvoiced consonant with a double consonant after a vowel—for example, *ca* + *jhā* = *cajjhā*. It also teaches that the first consonant of the two should be the unaspirated version of the second. Aspiration is indicated in the transcription of Sanskrit and Pali phonemes by *h*, so *ca* + *jhā* becomes *cajjhā* not *cajhjhā*. It gives as an example *ca* + *jhāna* + *phalo*, which becomes *cajjhānapphalo*. The phrase *idha cetaso daḷhaṃ gaṇhāhi thāmasā* is offered, however, as a counterexample, not for its semantic meaning but because of its form: these are forms of words where the rule does not apply and the consonants are not duplicated after the vowels.

It is possible that this line is chosen because the rule is about the substitution of sets of five. If we think back to the Sanskrit and Pali alphabet, the main consonants form a set of five fives. Phonemes in the same horizontal row are all pronounced in the same place in the mouth, from velar *k*, *kha*, et cetera down to labial *pa*, *pha*, et cetera.

The phonemes in the same vertical column are all pronounced with the same effort, from unaspirated, unvoiced *k*, *ca*, et cetera to nasal *ṅa*, *ña*, et cetera:

ka kha ga gha ṅa
ca cha ja jha ña
ṭa ṭha ḍa ḍha ṇa
ta tha da dha na
pa pha ba bha ma

The non-aspiration of the first consonant in the pair of phonemes created by duplication after a short vowel means that when *jha* from the fourth column is duplicated, *ja* from the third column takes its place. Likewise duplications of any of the five consonants in column four, the column of voiced aspirated consonants (*gha*, *jha*, *ḍha*, *dha*, *bha*) will be replaced by its corresponding consonant among the five consonants in column three (*ga*, *ja*, *ḍa*, *da*, *ba*), resulting in the conjunct consonants *ggha*, *jjha*, *ḍḍha*, *ddha*, *bbha*. The same applies to the second and first columns respectively. The *grū's* activity is not about word formation in the grammatical sense, but about the formation of potent syllables, and will culminate with the substitution of sets of five by sets of five.

The *grū* erases the five words of the initial phrase *idha cetaso daḷhaṃ gaṇhāhi thāmasā* and then reorders it, using substitutions nominally based on Kaccāyana's generative grammar. The result is twelve "word stems" consisting of a total of twenty-four syllables as follows: *ida iti iti assā udaṃ ahaṃ aggaṃ ahaṃ ahaṃ ithaṃ amma assā*. He erases it again with a new set of substitutions. In each transition he has in mind specific substitution rules from Kaccāyana's grammar, as he cycles through several more sets of substitutions, until finally he arrives back to the phrase *idha cetaso daḷhaṃ gaṇhāhi thāmasā*. All the while he is repeating in a high voice the grammatical rules that name the vowels and different consonant groups (short, long, voiced, unvoiced, et cetera). The *grū* then explicitly employs the grammatical principle of *lopa*, elision, to remove the five words and replace them with the five syllables *na mo bu ddhā ya* "homage to the Buddha":

> *paṭhamaṃ* ***idha*** *lopo ca* ***na****-kāro hoti sambhavo*
> *duṭiyaṃ* ***cetaso*** *lopo ca* ***mo****-kāro hoti sambhavo*
> *ṭatiyaṃ* ***daḷhaṃ*** *lopo ca* ***bu****-kāro hoti sambhavo*
> *catutthaṃ* ***gaṇhāhi*** *lopo ca* ***dhā****-kāro hoti sambhavo*
> *pañcamaṃ* ***thāmasā*** *lopo ca* ***ya****-kāro hoti sambhavo*

> First elision of *idha*, then the phoneme *na* comes into being.
> Second elision of *cetaso*, then the phoneme *mo* comes into being.
> Third elision of *daḷhaṃ*, then the phoneme *bu* comes into being.
> Fourth elision of *gaṇhāhi*, then the phoneme *dhā* comes into being.
> Fifth elision of *thāmasā*, then the phoneme *ya* comes into being.[42]

Here there is elision of the five original Pali words. They are substituted by nothing, zero. As a result, the five sacred syllables arise—as if from nothing, but in fact as another stage in the substitution process. From these five syllables further aspects of creation, of the path, or of the qualities of the Buddha may be created through further substitution, as the text goes on to elaborate. Bizot and von Hinüber proceed to show how this kind of substitution process, particularly to the stanzas listing the qualities of the Buddha, Dhamma, and Sangha, a set of stanzas beginning with the phrase *itipiso* commonly used in Theravada litanies, can be rearranged in these ways. Complex *yantra*, the geometrical representations of the substitution process, are thus formed and complex permutations employed in their creation.[43] The greater the number of repeated substitutions, the more "dense" the *yantra*, making it more powerful and more impervious to attack. It thereby increases in terms of its impenetrability and protective power.

The Grammar of Kaccāyana in *Borān Kammaṭṭhāna*

Kaccāyana's grammar is the earliest extant Pali grammar, in part based on two Sanskrit precursors, Pāṇini's *Aṣṭadhyāyī* and the *Kātantra*, which is in turn a simplified grammar based on the *Aṣṭadhyāyī*.[44] It continues to be taught throughout Southeast Asia to this day and, as we have seen, is referenced in *borān kammaṭṭhāna* and related practices. Kaccāyana is dated to around the sixth century C.E. as a historical author. However, in the origin narrative for the teaching of grammar, he is identified with the Buddha's personal disciple Mahākaccāyana, "The Great Kaccāyana." This conflation of the two Kaccāyanas allows the origin of grammar to be presented as occurring in response to an intervention by the Buddha, as related at the opening of this chapter. In that story, the first words of Kaccāyana's grammar, *attho akkharasaññāto*, are spoken not by Kaccāyana but by the Buddha himself, making grammar the sacred word of the Buddha, *buddhavacana*. There are a number of versions of the story, all of which occur in the context of *kammaṭṭhāna*, the practice of meditation. The crux of the story lies in the phrase that monks use while meditating, called the "aid," *parikamma*, in *borān kammaṭṭhāna*, but equivalent to a mantra in other Buddhist traditions. While some of the key *parikamma* have symbolic meanings beyond their literal meaning, such as "*a ra haṃ*" and "*na mo bu ddhā ya*," the literal meaning of others is directly relevant to the practice. For example, the phrase *sukhī homi*, "May I be happy," is recited as the aid to the first stage of the loving kindness (*mettā*) practice. The basic origin story for the need to teach grammar relates to the practice of using such aids to meditation and runs along the following lines—I have conflated it from various sources to give the gist:

> An elderly monk sits at the edge of a lake, his mind composed. "Arising and fleeting, arising and fleeting. *Udayavaya, udayavaya*," he murmurs to himself, accepting the

> transient nature of all in his purview. Across his field of vision moves a heron, hunting in the shallows. "Heron in the water, heron in the water. *Udakabaka, udakabaka*," murmurs the old monk. The Buddha senses the change in the monk and intervenes. Kaccāyana volunteers to provide a grammar to prevent errors of this kind.

This tale is reminiscent of a story that introduces the error behind the divine origin of Sanskrit grammar told in the *Kathāsaritsāgara*, a collection of tales composed in eleventh-century Kashmir, and thought to trace back to a second-century-B.C.E. precursor. When King Sātavāhana is playing at the edge of a lake with the women of his harem and the queen says, "Stop splashing me with water, sire! *m'odakair deva paritāḍaya mām*!" the king hears, "Throw sweets at me, sire! *modakair deva paritāḍaya mām*!" Humiliated by her ensuing scorn, he seeks to learn the secrets of grammar.[45]

The protagonists in these two stories, both set in ancient India, have fallen foul of the transformative power of language. A mere syllable misconstrued (or undisambiguated as we might now say) or out of place spells the difference between victory and humiliation. In the second case, it is the confusion over meaning that causes the problem. The king, not knowing the laws of euphony (*sandhi* in Sanskrit) fails to realize that what sounds like "sweets" *modaka* can also mean "not water" *mā* + *udaka* = *m'odaka*. In the first case, the confusion is over form, as the old monk, losing focus, allows the sound *y* to switch to *k* and the sound *v* to *b*. "Arising," *udaya*, becomes "water," *udaka*, and "fleeting," *vaya*, becomes "heron," *baka*. While it seems strange to confuse *y* and *k*, the mistake makes sense in an Indic rather than a Southeast Asian context: someone is confusing their Pali with their Prakrit, another of the languages close to both Sanskrit and Pali, in which *k* can be replaced by *y*, and *v* by *b*.[46] The question is whether the change in form will affect the quality of the practitioner's meditation. On the one hand, because of the innate relationship between Pali and its meaning, a *parikamma*/mantra recited will take effect even if the reciter is unfamiliar with its semantics. According to Veera Thanaveero of Wat Ratchasittharam, head of the *borān kammaṭṭhāna* lineage there, knowing the semantic meaning can even be a hindrance as the practitioner then projects an expected experience onto the process rather than allowing the experience to arise spontaneously from the process. Does this mean that our meditator will shift from practicing a meditation that will lead to an understanding of the truth of impermanence to being entranced by a creature killing fish, potentially a bad *kamma* for which the Buddha himself once suffered negative consequences? Or is the quality of the meditator's mind unaffected, or unaffected if still focused on the original meaning?

The Southeast Asia versions of this story are ambivalent. In the fifteenth-century commentary on Kaccāyana's grammar by the Burmese monk Chapaṭa Saddhammajotipāla of Pagan,[47] two monks are meditating using the phrase "destruction and decay," *khaya-vaya*. One sees the heron and recites "water heron," *udako bako*; the other sees a cloth in a pot and recites "in the pot a cloth," *ghaṭe paṭaṃ*. Although the Buddha, by means of a supernatural light, proclaims the sentence *attho akkharasaññāto*, "Meaning is understood through phonemes," and Kaccāyana composes his grammar in response to the Buddha's statement, the text nonetheless confirms: "Their Kammaṭṭhāna was also effectual."[48]

In the *Saddavimala*, the *borān kammaṭṭhāna* text, the elderly monk is not confused. The Buddha gives him the choice of *gantha-dhura* or *vipassanā-dhura*, the duty of book-learning or the duty of meditation leading to insight. The monk chooses the latter.

> Seeing a flock of herons feasting on the fish in the lake, the monk is profoundly moved and says, "These numerous fish live in perpetual fear of being exterminated by beings who torment them. It is just the same for people, and for me too. We are all subject to birth, aging, sickness, death, destruction, and danger, which torment us. We are destined for destruction, doomed to die." When

> he had finished this observation, he used it as the basis of his meditation and repeated without interruption, "The herons are eating the fish. The herons are eating the fish." Just then, eighty thousand monks were returning from their alms round, and hearing the elderly monk they criticized him, assuming he was speaking in error and was a fraud. They reported the matter to the Buddha. The Buddha replied, "Monks, the elderly monk is a true son of the Buddha. He is certainly no fraud. The way in which he is meditating is quite correct for he is not aware of the prescribed syllables for meditation. Moreover, he is meditating in accordance with both the semantics and the phonemes in the vernacular. Indeed, this is in no way a case of a fraud." At this the monk Anuruddha prostrated himself before the Buddha and asked, "Please, Lord, what are 'phonemes'?" Whereupon the Buddha proclaimed, "Meaning is understood through phonemes, *attho akkharasaññāto*. The sense of all speech is understood through the phonemes. When there is a mistake in the phonemes, there is confusion as to the meaning. Therefore, skillfulness regarding phonemes is very helpful in relation to the Sutta-teachings."[49]

This brings us to the textual excerpt from the *Saddavimala* with which this chapter opened. In consequence of the Buddha's further explanation of the importance of understanding phonemes, Kaccāyana then volunteers to teach his grammar.

In the *Saddavimala*, then, the meditating monk is vindicated. He does not need to know the prescribed wording to meditate successfully. Moreover, he is in fact using the correct phrasing for the meaning in the vernacular. The younger monks who insist on following the prescribed text are in error in dismissing the elderly monk as a fraud, and it is they who are in fact ignorant of the true importance of phonemes. When Kaccāyana then teaches his grammar, it is not only the semantic value of the phonemes that he teaches, but their creative potential. It is the creative potential of Pali that is emphasized in the *Saddavimala*.

The story is emblematic of the longstanding debate between experience/practice, *paṭipatti*, and textual study, *pariyatti*, but also suggests that the textualists are themselves arrogant, ignorant that they are falling short of a true understanding of the importance of grammar. In *borān kammaṭṭhāna*, generative grammar was applied not just in the learning of Pali and the generation of correct Pali sentences. It underpinned the belief in Pali as a potent, generative force. Its phonemes, specific words, and whole sentences could embody entities greater than themselves, and, through a process of substitution, were instrumental in creation itself at both a cosmic and personal level. Etymology in this context is about drawing out hidden meaning and cosmic resonances, which are timeless.

The understanding of grammar for correct sentence formation was maintained. We can see the shared concern between Vinaya specialists and at least some *borān* practitioners for correct language. The former were concerned to ensure correct grammar and pronunciation of Pali phonemes to ensure the validity of monastic rituals, particularly those that pertain to ordination. The litanies used in *borān kammaṭṭhāna* employ the same Pali wording used for ordination into the Sangha to ensure the validity of the initiation into the meditation practice.[50] At the same time, in the right-hand path, the entities that Pali phonemes represent can be employed to internalize factors and stages of spiritual development, including the positive mental states (*kusala citta*) and attendant mental factors (*cetasika*). Meanwhile, in practices of the left-hand path, they are recited or applied to a surface using the appropriate script in order to harness the power of statements of the Buddha, his *buddhavacana*, including the grammar believed to have been initiated by him, for more worldly ends.

Borān kammaṭṭhāna, being directly concerned with transformation, paid close attention to how transformation was to be achieved and the range of transformations that can be achieved by language. These include the ability of generative grammar to create language, the ability of language to convey significance beyond itself, and to carry processes from forms of consciousness to forms of materiality. Also included are the related concepts of letter alchemy, which uses phonemes to bring about change in the substratum to which they are applied.

A similar attitude to language is found in the tantric Buddhism of the Himalayas and Central Asia. It was one of the features criticized by early European observers, who detected in it echoes of Catholicism's *hocus pocus*, or superstitious accretions, just as modernizers in Cambodia regarded the *borān* use of Pali. They therefore saw such practice as counter to the specific type of rationalism that they projected onto their understanding of original Buddhism. However, in the European portrayal of Buddhism, there was no need to take seriously the issue of the actual mechanisms for transformation involved in the Buddhist path since Nibbana was not accepted as a valid or real goal of religious life.

Conclusion

In this chapter, we examined how *borān kammaṭṭhāna* participates in a worldview that valued, analyzed, and sought to harness the creative potential of language. This related to the importance of the science of generative grammar, developed in Sanskrit and Pali, the sacred language of Theravada Buddhism, a technology largely displaced in modernist Buddhism of the colonial period. This attitude to language is significant in understanding how *borān kammaṭṭhāna* understood the process of transformation in two key ways. First, in terms of potent language itself, we saw that traditional Theravada Buddhism interpreted this creative power more broadly, in terms of the creation of the universe and the *dhamma*, the Buddha's teaching and the components of reality. It harnesses this potency in its *borān kammaṭṭhāna* by using Pali syllables to represent and convey qualities attained in meditation to embed them in the body, and to protect the body, for example in creating protective powder and *yantra*, including tattoos. Second, the mathematics underlying generative grammar provides models for transformation also applied in *borān kammaṭṭhāna*. One key mathematical tool was substitution, including the use of zero as a place-holder, the substitution on the basis of similarity (numerical similarity and similarity in quality), and the transfer of qualities from the substituted into the substituend.

The other key mathematical tool was group theory mathematics, which can be used to work out which components are necessary for a particular transformation and the minimum number of changes required to complete the full range of options or processes necessary to reach the end goal. In grammar, this is used in the creation of a word, whereas in *borān kammaṭṭhāna* and *Paṭṭhāna*, the portion of Abhidhamma that analyzes the interrelationship of causal factors, the end goal is an enlightened being. Substitution and group theory mathematics allow for the replacement of successive states of consciousness and materiality, and group theory mathematics underlies the combinations and sequencing. This is then applied in relation to changes made through meditation in the states of consciousness (*citta*) and aspects of consciousness (*cetasika*), which are then internalized to transform the materiality (*rūpa*) of the embodied practitioner. The theory and processes of bringing about change are shared between generative grammar, letter alchemy, Abhidhamma, and *borān kammaṭṭhāna*. How traditionalists and modernists differ in their applications of this same background knowledge is important in understanding how *borān kammaṭṭhāna* functions and why the orthodox theoretical basis of its functionality ceased to be recognized in the modern period.

This exploration of generative grammar has helped us understand how potent language and sequential substitution are distinctive features of *borān kammaṭṭhāna*. There are three further distinctive aspects of *borān kammaṭṭhāna* still to be explained. The first is the use of specific pathways to deliver the desired aspects of consciousness into the body starting with the nasal cavity. The second is the location in which these aspects of consciousness are combined and bound into the body, primarily in the practitioner's "womb," regardless of the gender of the practitioner. The third is that the practice involves extensive repetition. In the next chapter, we shall look at two other sciences or technologies current in premodern Theravada cultures to make sense of these features.

5

Transformation of the Body

Meditation, Medicine, and Chemistry

> Here we are, in the center of the womb, where the embryo sucks water from its mother, grasping the umbilical cord. . . . Having just completed our visit inside this cave we have acquired great merit, for this is the womb of our sacred mother. The opening here is the golden gate. In going through it to practice asceticism, we have regressed into the mother's stomach. In this way we are born anew. Let us ask for forgiveness for having soiled our sacred mother.
>
> —Teaching inside the "cave of birth" at Mount Sampau near Battambang, Cambodia[1]

The above teaching was given to a group of pilgrims performing a rebirthing ritual in the womb-shaped cave at Mount Sampau, the core of which involved *borān* meditation and the chanting of the *parikamma* that attend it. François Bizot recorded this pilgrimage in 1971, just three years before the last such ritual took place in 1974, as the practice was interrupted by the Khmer Rouge period. Following his discussion of this rite, Bizot provides descriptions of other embryology-related rituals and translates Khmer texts explaining the embryological significance and symbolism of *borān* meditation practice, the use of sacred syllables, and the requisites of the monks, such as their monastic robes.

In the previous chapter we examined the use of potent language and letter alchemy in relation to Indic generative grammar. We saw the role of the underlying concepts of substitution and group theory mathematics in bringing about change. In this chapter, we will extend our consideration of technologies in the pre-modern Theravada world, so that we can further unravel the processes of transformation envisaged in *borān* meditation. The progressive substitution of lower states of consciousness and concomitant mental factors with higher ones is clearly an enactment of Abhidhamma. The infusion of those aspects of consciousness into the body in order to transform the materiality of the individual is also clearly based on the Abhidhamma understanding of *cittaja rūpa*, that some materiality is generated by consciousness. However, the process of infusion is distinctive. Here we seek to understand the process of the infusion of the body with the desired mental states. Why is it that the mental factors are brought into the body through the nasal cavity and down to an area referred to as the womb of the practitioner? And why is this process performed iteratively?

The most obvious and widespread transformative technology for improving the state of the body is medicine, and we shall look at traditional Indic medicine (Ayurveda) here. As we shall see, *borān kammaṭṭhāna* is used as a type of medicine, drawing on ayurvedic analysis of illness. But we also find medicine as a model for meditation, particularly as it applies to the creation and treatment of a new being.[2] In Buddhist meditation, the new being is the enlightened individual. In medicine, the new being is the embryo in the womb, and it is in ayurvedic obstetrics, medicine for embryos, that we will find parallels with the processes of transformation used in *borān kammaṭṭhāna*. As Bizot has extensively demonstrated, embryology pervades *borān kammaṭṭhāna*. Here we shall see that it is not only symbolic, but of practical relevance for process of transformation.

Borān kammaṭṭhāna is also about purifying the individual. It is in the technology for the purification of metals, an aspect of chemistry, that we shall find further parallels with the processes applied in *borān* meditation. Thus we find a correlation between embryology, chemistry, and spiritual transformation.

After looking at the parallels between *borān kammaṭṭhāna* and these technologies, we shall examine what happened to these technologies, particularly to medicine, during the colonial period to see if this helps us understand how the techniques applied in meditation changed during that period.

Group Theory Mathematics in Ayurvedic Medicine

Substitution and group theory mathematics, two concepts discussed in the previous chapter in relation to ritual, grammar, Abhidhamma, and *borān kammaṭṭhāna*, were also important in Indian medicine. Substitution contributed, for example, to the highly advanced development of plastic surgery for the reconstruction of noses, genitalia, and limbs lost through disease, punishment, or fighting, including rhinoplasty from the reversal of the forehead skin flap. The physical substitutes, such as the skin flap in rhinoplasty, took on the attributes of what they replaced, just like the grammatical substitutes discussed in the previous chapter. Such medical procedures are described in the seminal ayurvedic treatise the *Suśruta Saṃhitā*, thought to date back as far as 500 B.C.E., and were among the medical technologies adopted from India by neighboring cultures.[3] In the late eighteenth century Indian rhinoplasty also reached Britain, after being witnessed by British surgeons in the Third Anglo-Mysore War (1789–1792), even though at this time, as we shall see, the British were claiming superiority in medicine over local physicians.

Substitution is also important in the preparation of medicines. It is necessitated by the variable availability of herbs and other pharmaceutical substances according to region and season. In this case the pharmaceutical substance represents a particular quality that the medical practitioner wishes to inculcate in the body of the patient according to the problem being addressed. Therefore, a quality is represented by a substance that may be substituted and may undergo various procedures such as pulverization or cooking. Again the principle of substitution still applies: the substitute transmits the quality for which the original substance was selected.

Group theory mathematics is likewise important in traditional Indian medicine, in diagnostics and pharmaceuticals. In ayurvedic medicine disease and illness are understood as arising from an imbalance of the three *doṣa* (Sanskrit; *dosa* Pali). The term *doṣa* is often translated into English with the word "humor," on the basis of the pre-modern European medical analysis of biological imbalance, although the parallels are limited. The three *doṣa* are *vāta* "wind," *pitta* "bile," and *kapha* "phlegm," and they all have a role in the functioning and maintenance of the body.[4]

Ayurveda used group theory mathematics to understand the possible permutations of each of the three *doṣa* in combination with the bodily tissues (*dhātu*) and other variables. Blood was also considered in addition to these three in the case of wounds.[5] How many combinations of humor imbalances this could lead to according to strength and combination was worked out in ayurvedic texts. According to how they assessed the variation of humors and whether blood was added, the options varied from fifty to sixty-two. Armed with this knowledge, ayurvedic physicians could then apply the appropriate combination and proportions of pharmaceutical substances, such as specific herbs, to counter the specific imbalance identified by the physician in relation to their flavors, potency, et cetera.[6] How many combinations of these items were then possible was differently calculated by different medical treatises, with the number sixty-three reached by *Caraka Saṃhitā,* the other key foundational text of Ayurveda, which dates from before 300 C.E. and had reached its current form by 500 C.E.[7]

Although algorithms for working out combinations came to be used in other sciences such as astronomy from the sixth century C.E. onward, in early ayurvedic medical texts, iterative listing was still required.[8] We similarly find such iterative listing in the *Paṭṭhāna*, the seventh book of the Abhidhamma that deals with combinations of causes and effects, and in *borān kammaṭṭhāna* manuals. The calculations in both medicine and Abhidhamma are about progressive substitutions, whether to replace a humor imbalance (medicine) or change from one mental or ethical state to another (*Paṭṭhāna* and meditation). Thus two important mechanisms for understanding and generating change that we found in generative grammar, namely substitution and group theory mathematics, are also found in medicine. Moreover, they are also found in Abhidhamma and in *borān kammaṭṭhāna*, which, like early Ayurveda, uses iterative listing to work through the possibilities.

The Involvement of Theravada Monks in Medicine

Training in grammatical expertise was provided to Buddhist monks as a way to ensure the correct transmission of the Dhamma and the correct performance of ecclesiastical rites. Hence a correlation between meditation and generative grammar is understandable within a monastic context. Before looking in greater depth at the correlation between medicine and *borān* meditation, we should establish the extent to which Theravada Buddhist monks were exposed to medical expertise. Was medical training a part of monastic culture?

Reformers of Buddhism sought to prohibit monks from practicing medicine. These included the kings of Burma, following the eighteenth-century Thudhamma reform, the monk Väliviṭa Saraṇaṃkara, who led the eighteenth-century reform in Sri Lanka, and Mongkut, who initiated the reform of Thai Buddhism in the nineteenth century. They applied more restrictive interpretations of monastic conduct. This in itself suggests the practice of medicine by monks was sufficiently widespread to warrant their disapprobation. For Buddhists, the most famous medical practitioner in history is Jīvaka, not a monk but a lay devotee who tended to the Buddha. He is credited with using such techniques as surgery, including cranial surgery, the treatment of humor (*doṣa/dosa*) imbalance, and intranasal applications of medicine, a point to which we shall return below, using wax as the medium of delivery. Several Buddhist medical traditions, including the royal Thai ayurvedic tradition, claim to trace their origins to him.[9]

While Jīvaka was a layman, the long history of monks also having medical expertise is nonetheless confirmed by the range of medical literature authored and transmitted by them since the early centuries of Buddhism.[10] The earliest Buddhist medical text for which we have evidence is contained in the Buddhist canon itself. Ironically it is in the division of the canon dedicated to monastic regulations, the Vinaya Piṭaka, on the basis of which reformers sought to prohibit monastic medical practice. In the Pali canon of Theravada Buddhism the relevant text is the *Bhesajja-khandha*, "Medical Section." Vernacular versions of the *Bhesajja-khandha* were still being composed in Burma in the nineteenth century.[11] The canonical version includes a list of implements to deliver medicine, such as those to deliver substances to the eyes and nose to avoid infection from application with the hands. The reason these utensils are included in a work on monastic regulations is that the Vinaya as a whole delineates what monks may or may not do, and what they may or may not own, beyond the permitted eight "requisites" allowed to all monks.[12] The utensils listed in the *Bhesajja-khandha* are indicated as medical items that may be personally owned by monks.[13] These utensils tell us that the delivery pathways used for applying medicine include, again, the intranasal cavity.

While such utensils may have been owned by monks so that they could treat themselves and fellow monks, a range of evidence including archaeological remains of hospitals excavated in close correspondence with monastic sites in ancient India and Sri Lanka suggests that provision of medical care outside the Sangha had long been a recognized element of monastic life.[14] It is possible that Buddhist missionaries recognized medical care as a technology of conversion, just as it was for Christian medical missionaries in the early modern period. On the other hand, both medicine and other technologies of transformation employed by Buddhist monks, such as meditation, share an optimistic worldview: one can and should use knowledge and the treatments based on that knowledge to intervene in the psychophysical given. One's physical body and attendant consciousness should be treated to ameliorate one's experience, reduce suffering, and transform one's condition.

In the case of a newborn baby, for example, the character and physicality are the products of a number of factors including karma (actions) in previous lifetimes, the qualities of its parent, its experience and nutrition in the womb, and the relative balance of humors (*dosa*). The individual at any point in his or her life may suffer or improve according to the maturing of the cumulative effect of such factors and others. Since some of these factors are susceptible to intervention, whether by religious practice or medical action, Buddhist monks, as technicians of transformation, naturally drew on whatever technologies were available to treat individuals in order to alleviate suffering and guide people to a better state.

This holistic approach was later disrupted by the mind-body and science-religion dichotomies that informed Buddhist reform movements of the colonial period, and later still by the specialization of religious and medical vocations. Until such time medical expertise was one strand of knowledge to be gained through ordination, which until the modern period was the primary means of gaining literacy and other types of education that built upon literacy. Former monks were also among the foremost native medical practitioners and authors in Burma and elsewhere in Southeast Asia. While on the whole socially conservative, monks were also often pioneers in taking up new knowledge.[15]

Medicine and *Borān Kammaṭṭhana*

Having established that expertise in medicine circulated among Theravada monks, meaning that medicine and meditation were two technologies found alongside each other, let us now look at the different ways in which this juxtaposition or relationship is manifest in *borān* meditation.

Borān kammaṭṭhāna is associated with medicine in two main ways: first, it is applied to medical ends, and second, it shares with medicine the same underlying model of transformation. First, let us look at the application of *borān kammaṭṭhāna* to medical ends. Those who have attained the advanced stages of *borān kammaṭṭhāna* are believed to be able to benefit others medically with their acquired power. The texts of Suk Kaitheun, the supreme patriarch of Siam (Thailand) from the end of the eighteenth century (1794–1816), include detailed instructions for the application of meditation to treat medical ailments. A detailed knowledge of ayurvedic medicine, including the issue of imbalance of the *doṣa/dosa* in relation to the different bodily tissues, *dhātu*, pervades his work. What the *borān kammaṭṭhāna* medical system adds to Ayurveda is a way of using the *nimitta* experienced in meditation to address medical problems in specific bodily areas. The method utilizes the combining of qualities, represented by the *nimitta*, and the ability to move the *nimitta* around the body and embed them in the chosen area.

> The meditator who has mastered the technique of... *samatha* and *vipassanā* can transfer a well-established visualized image [*nimitta*] which he has cultivated, or any member of the five joys (*pīti*) which he has well cultivated, or the visualized image of the relic of the Buddha to one of the nine Bases [locations within the body] and work according to the specific purpose, for example, for warding off pain and curing diseases.
>
> Before knowing the arts of healing, the meditator must know thoroughly the following fourteen evils [*akusala*, unskillful mental states/factors]...
>
> For the [=to] cure element aggravation, the meditator is to move the visualized image right down to the lower space surface, and then make a resolution: drawing together all the four elements, the five faculties for enlightenment together with the seven constituents of

> wisdom. Having got them all stabilized at the Base, he is to suppress all the entities at the Base with a number of repeated resolution[s]. He must keep them all together there at one place and not to allow any of the constituents to move up from the Base. While doing this, even breathing, he is to keep them all there suppressed with his consciousness until the symptom subsides.[16]

Here the positive aspects of consciousness, mental factors that can counteract the unskillful aspects and states of consciousness, are combined with the elements at the relevant part of the body. So whereas in ayurvedic medicine a pharmaceutical element of the correct combination and strength should be applied to the imbalance in the *dosa* in combination with the elements, in the *borān kammaṭṭhāna* medical system, the positive, purifying aspects of consciousness are used in place of, or as, the pharmaceutical elements. This makes sense given two aspects of the Abhidhamma understanding of the psychophysical being. First, pain is an aspect of consciousness, *cetasika*, coming under the category of sensation *vedanā*, one of the five aggregates that make up each individual. *Vedanā* can be pleasant, painful/unpleasant, or neutral. A painful *vedanā* can therefore be dealt with by replacing it with different types of *cetasika*. Second, according to the Abhidhamma analysis of causality, some materiality, or aspects of physicality, are "consciousness-born," *citta-ja*. This means that mental states directly affect the body and can be used to treat it.

The treatise of another supreme patriarch, Vichay That Mahamuni, who was the head of the Sangha in Laos at some date between the sixteenth and eighteenth centuries, also attests to the use of *borān kammaṭṭhāna* in treating medical disorders. The manual indicates that the facility acquired by the meditator to switch back and forth between different meditation experiences and to hold multiple experiences at the same time is applied to sort out disorders of the wind element and restore physical balance and health.[17]

Overall the parallel between ayurvedic medicine and *borān kammaṭṭhāna* medicine is that both treat imbalances in the *dosa* (humors) in combination with the physical elements (*dhātu*, i.e., earth, water, fire, wind, and space), by applying pharmaceutical agents or medicine and manipulation. In Ayurveda those medicines are made up of herbal and mineral extractions, each providing the qualities which need to be combined to combat the three types of *dosa* imbalance. In *borān* medicine, the medicines are created from positive mental states, combining elements of non-greed, non-hatred, and non-delusion with the physical elements to treat three types of *dosa* imbalance. Movement of these states are used to free up blockages just as movement of water, or another liquid, might be used to free up blockages in medicine.

This application of positive mental states, combining elements of non-greed, non-hatred, and non-delusion to treat medical imbalances might relate to the three roots of imbalance in the individual, namely greed, hatred, and delusion, the cause of us being trapped in samsara. Our embodiment is the combination of the elements (*dhātu*), earth, water, fire, wind, and space, with our states of consciousness and their concomitants (*citta* and *cetasika*), which are either based in the three unskillful roots (greed, hatred, and delusion) or their opposite: the mental and the physical are interrelated. Being able to replace the negative with the positive, as in medicine, is what is needed to change the unenlightened individual (*puthujjana*) into an enlightened one, an arhat.

This aim helps us understand the second connection between *borān kammaṭṭhāna* and medicine, namely that there is a medical model underlying *borān kammaṭṭhāna* that shapes its distinctive somatic practices. To deliver desired changes in the meditator's mind and body, *borān kammaṭṭhāna* uses a delivery process that corresponds with delivery of pharmaceutical substances in Ayurveda. The meditation brings *nimitta*, which represent the qualities of mind achieved in meditation, into the body based on the idea that one is recreating oneself as a Buddha or arhat from within. This process will transform the individual into an enlightened being by drawing in the qualities that will progressively substitute any weaknesses with the desired qualities. Perhaps because of the idea that one is creating a new individual, the model of transformation is the creation of a new child, a fetus. Just as a mother nurtures the new child-to-be in her womb, the locus to which these desired qualities are directed is the "womb" of the practitioner, whether male or female. Corresponding to this imagery, the delivery system used in *borān* meditation parallels that for the medication of the fetus in ayurvedic obstetrics, as will be explained below.

The model of transformation in ayurvedic obstetrics is so fundamental to *borān kammaṭṭhāna* that extensive references to embryology pervade every aspect of the tradition across the entire spectrum of applications. These include the rebirthing ritual alluded to at the start of this chapter, longevity rituals, the symbolism of manuscripts and monastic robes, correlations made between the development of the embryo, Pali sacred formulae, and aspects of the Dhamma.[18]

The pervasive references to embryological development in *borān kammaṭṭhāna* are understandable as a metaphor for the creation of a new being within, but it is also more than a metaphor. It underpins the technology of transformation in a completely literal sense. The methods for treating the unborn fetus in Ayurveda are applied in inducing change in the meditation practitioner as they generate a Buddha within themselves. The delivery methods are applied with the help of the techniques of substitution and combination in both *borān kammaṭṭhāna* and ayurvedic medicine. In *borān kammaṭṭhāna* the pharmaceutical substances are replaced by the *nimitta* that arise in meditation or by the Pali syllables that represent them.

Ayurvedic Obstetrics

To understand the pathways for delivering medicine and meditative states to baby and practitioner respectively, and thereby understand the relationship between *borān kammaṭṭhāna* and ayurvedic obstetrics, this section looks at the treatment of a real embryo during pregnancy. As noted above, ayurvedic medicine and Buddhism both accept that intervention can ameliorate or enhance one's inherited condition. The belief that current *karma/kamma* can affect the psychophysical organism in fact encourages intervention. Like Buddhism, ayurvedic medicine accepts *karma* as one cause of one's current condition, but it also looks to other factors, such as imbalances of the *doṣa*, astrology, and the intervention of supernatural beings, that may be addressed through a variety of means to cure illness. As continued to be the case in ayurvedic practice in Thailand in the nineteenth century, we therefore see multiple methods of treatment being used to treat and prevent disease in the unborn embryo/fetus.[19]

Ayurveda and Buddhism both assume that the stay in the womb for the fetus is precarious, uncomfortable, and painful.[20] A developed theory on how to treat the fetus is found in the *Caraka Saṃhitā*, one of the two seminal works of ayurvedic medicine mentioned above. The treatment was not only to ensure safe gestation and delivery, but also to influence the baby's character and gender. The right side of the body is associated with a male fetus and the left side of the body with a female fetus. In order to change the gender to a male child, one should apply medicine to the right nostril of the pregnant mother. Male gender could also be achieved by using a small metallic model of a man to infuse milk for the mother-to-be to drink, or by wearing the metallic model hung to the right of the mother's navel.[21] Both methods parallel the way in which *nimitta* of light and of a visualized Buddha are used in *borān kammaṭṭhāna*. The treatment of the fetus by application of pharmaceutical substances through both intranasal and oral pathways, requiring fine pulverization or liquid in the case of the former, continued throughout the history of Ayurveda, as can be seen in the nineteenth-century prescription of "snuff" in Thai ayurvedic medicine.[22]

Mitchell Weiss explains,

> The *garbha* [fetus] is made up of the four elements (*prabhava, bhūta*)—namely, wind, fire, earth, and water—and six types of nourishment (*rasa*). These are also constituents of maternal blood, paternal semen, food, and one's own deeds, which in turn contribute the components of the *garbha*. Contributions from karma and the parents thus have a physical basis.[23]

In the *Caraka Saṃhitā* the physical components of the body are divided according to whether they come from the mother or the father. There is a general tendency for bloody and softer components such as the flesh, fat, and heart to come from the mother, and harder substances, such as nails, teeth, and bones, to come from the father,[24] a division also found throughout *borān kammaṭṭhāna*. The heart is the place where the fetus experiences feelings. Its heart is linked to the mother's heart. Nutrients pass from the mother's heart to the fetus's heart through connecting channels.[25]

The three *doṣa/dosa* (Sanskrit/Pali) are further associated with three strands or qualities, *guṇa*, that make up the material realm: *suddha* "pure," *rajas* "impulsive," and *tamas* "lethargic."[26] The *Caraka Saṃhitā* understands that the character of the fetus and future child relate to the relative predominance of each of these. It also equates the character of the fetus with different cosmological realms. Fetuses in which the pure (*suddha*) quality predominates are equated with different deities, and the character of the child-to-be will match the qualities of the relevant gods. The Brahmā-god fetus will be truthful and wise, the Indra type powerful, et cetera.[27] Buddhism similarly equates different mental states, based on the three roots of *akusala* (greed, hatred, and delusion) and the three roots of the beautiful mental states (non-greed, non-hatred, and non-delusion), which are present in such meditative attainments as the *jhāna*, with different cosmological realms.[28] Both traditional medicine and Buddhism therefore correlate the character of an individual with their constitution and with cosmological realms.

Monastic Knowledge of Obstetrics

Before taking this similarity between obstetrics and esoteric Theravada meditation further, we might ask how this might be possible when the Theravada Sangha is a celibate monastic order, with monks forbidden from having physical contact with women. Obstetrics treats the unborn child from conception to birth, so is associated with reproduction and entails physical contact with women. While the involvement of monks in medicine throughout the history of Theravada is well attested,[29] it might be reasonable to assume that monks were not involved in obstetrics.

However, Leslie (R.A.L.H.) Gunawardana has demonstrated that the composers and compilers of Theravada texts, from the first-century-B.C.E. *Milindapañha* through to the fifth-century commentaries attributed to Buddhaghosa onward, maintained a detailed and up-to-date knowledge of the subject.[30] Not only did their knowledge reflect developments in ayurvedic learning, according to Gunawardana they developed improvements on the knowledge to be found in the two seminal ayurvedic works, the *Suśruta Saṃhitā* and *Caraka Saṃhitā*, mentioned above. While such interest may in part reflect the Abhidhamma focus on analyzing the human condition and causality, attention is also paid to medical details. These include the factors leading to conception, which developed from the early Indic assumption that conception occurred during menstruation (presumably on the model of animals in season), to an understanding that menstruation was the least likely time for conception to take place, and the understanding that nutrition was transmitted through the umbilical cord/navel rather than from the heart of the mother to that of the fetus.[31] This familiarity does not mean that monks treated women. Throughout Theravada history, most ordinations have been undertaken only temporarily, so medical education within the Sangha may have been for use after disrobing, and it is also possible that some medical knowledge displayed by monks was acquired before the period of monkhood.[32]

Obstetrics as a Model for Creating the Buddha Within

Let us now see the extent to which the shared interest between ayurvedic obstetrics and *borān kammaṭṭhāna* in the creation of an ideal, healthy new being leads to shared technology of transformation. In ayurvedic obstetrics, with the goal of creating a healthy human being of good character, a range of treatments are applied to the mother, among which are alchemy and the application of pharmaceutical substances either orally or within the intranasal cavity, as noted above. Once applied intranasally or orally the substances then pass down the energy channels and centers of ayurvedic anatomy. In *borān kammaṭṭhāna*, with the goal of creating a being that is higher than human, visual alchemy may be used to apply the attributes of the stages of the path to the embryonic Buddha in the practitioner's "womb." In other words, the *nimitta* that represent the desired factors of consciousness, or Pali letters in their place, are moved from the nostril to the "womb" of the practitioner where the new enlightened being is constructed. The meditation technique uses the same channels of delivery, particularly the intranasal route.

Multiple aspects of the ayurvedic treatment of the embryo find parallels in *borān kammaṭṭhāna*: the assignment of the right- and left-hand sides of the body to male and female respectively, the terminology for the stages of the embryo, and the terms for the implantation by the father/practitioner of his semen/the attributes in the "womb."[33] The division of physical substances into male and female in *borān kammaṭṭhāna* extends earlier Buddhist analysis of the body into thirty-two components by aligning them with male and female.[34] As we have seen, the male-female division pervades other aspects of symbolism in *borān kammaṭṭhāna* and traditional Theravada in general.[35]

The pharmaceutical elements in the case of *borān kammaṭṭhāna* are not physical substances, but the stages of the meditative path to enlightenment, broken down into elements and typically represented by their *nimitta*, or adapted *nimitta* including letters or a visualized image of the Buddha. Just as Ayurveda uses group theory mathematics to match the pharmaceutical constituents to the desired rebalancing of the three *doṣa*, so *borān kammaṭṭhāna* uses group theory mathematics to ensure all the positive attributes of the path are thoroughly bound into the body of the practitioner. We could analyze this more specifically to the overcoming of the three roots of negative/unskillful attributes, *akusala dhamma*, since the early meditative exercises displace the *akusala*, unskillful, negative, with *kusala dhamma*, positive/skillful attributes, and their resultant states (*vipāka*). At the higher levels these are then replaced with the functional (*kiriya*) states that in the enlightened individual replace and are the equivalent of the *kusala* states of those lower on the path, but have no karmic consequences. The substitution of negative/unskillful attributes with positive attributes and the generation of components of materiality, the physical body, from consciousness, fits with Abhidhamma understandings of causality. Moreover, in the Indic model, consciousness is mobile. However, the pathways used in *borān kammaṭṭhāna*, from the nostril to the womb, can only be understood by seeing the correlation between this form of meditation and ayurvedic obstetrics.

While the medicines applied in obstetrics draw on the combinatorics of ayurvedic pharmacy to address *dosa* imbalance to create a child of the right qualities, in *borān kammaṭṭhāna* we observe the use of permutation, where the order of the combination is important. In other words, the desired attributes of consciousness or their representative *nimitta* must be combined in the body in specific order, its reverse and other combinations. This is because some causes cannot lead to some results, for example, an unskillful mental state, *akusala dhamma*, cannot be directly substituted by *kiriya dhamma*, the functional mental states of those who have reached the supramundane states in becoming an arhat. The sequence is important in progressing from the starting point to the end goal. So while combinatorics applies in each moment, in that certain *cetasika*, attributes of consciousness, coexist in certain states of consciousness, permutations apply over a series of moments. In the *Paṭṭhāna*, the book of the *Abhidhamma Piṭaka* that looks at combinations and permutations in relation to causality, we find two terms: *anuloma*, "in order," and *paṭiloma*, "in reverse order." These two terms are those most frequently found for designating the order in *borān* meditation, alongside other terms for more complex types of permutations. Much space in the more extensive of the *borān* manuals is dedicated to listing the *nimitta* and elements to be combined in order, reverse order, and more complex permutations, and the details of their movements.

To sum up, the use of the intranasal cavity to bring the *nimitta*, which represent the desired attributes of mentality achieved in meditation, into the body of the meditator at his or her "womb," is based on the medical method of using the intranasal cavity of the mother to deliver pharmaceutical and alchemical substances into the body of the baby-to-be located in the mother's womb. The use of specific combinations of *cetasika* to counteract imbalances derived from the three fires of greed, hatred, and delusion, or to induce desired positive attributes, is parallel to the use of specific combinations of pharmaceutical agents in obstetrics to counteract imbalances of the *dosa* (humors) and induce desired positive attributes in the child-to-be.

Purification of Mercury and Gold: Alchemy or Traditional Chemistry

Looking at parallels with medicine has helped us to understand the combinations, the intranasal delivery pathway, and the central location of the womb in *borān* meditation. However, this does not explain the degree of repetition in *borān* meditation, with the *nimitta* repeatedly brought into and out of the practitioner's womb. To understand this process of repeatedly applying and withdrawing the transformative substance we need to turn to another technology. That technology is alchemy or, rather, traditional chemistry.

Alchemy involves the addition of mercury and sulfur to base metals to create new compounds, with the highest transmutation thought possible being the creation of gold.[36] To be used for alchemy, mercury must be extracted from its ore as quicksilver and then refined to different degrees. Its most dense form is a dense solid. To reach this stage, in which mercury's volatility has been subdued, the purification process must be repeated. David Gordon White describes the process of purification based on a twelfth-century Indian treatise on alchemy:

> The process takes place in two steps: first the mercury [seen as male] penetrates the sulphur [seen as female] and other female elements . . . , and it subsequently absorbs into itself the power residing in those female, less subtle elements. . . . The mercury then emerges from the crucible, reborn as it were, from the womb (*garbha*) of the female elements, purified and fortified, having left behind its own impurities in a useless compound (*bhasma*; ash, oxide) with the sulphur and the other female elements. At each successive "killing" [the purificatory process], the mercury enters into greater and greater quantities of sulphur . . . The purification process of mercury may be repeated over and over again, as mercury mounts the six stages of its form, and thus increases its powers of transmutation. In the end, it becomes capable of transmuting hundreds, thousands and millions of times its own weight of base metals into gold.[37]

The process of repeated penetration of the sulfur by the mercury requires the mercury first to suffuse the sulfur and then be withdrawn out of the sulfur again. In other words, the mercury is moved in order (Pali *anuloma*) and reverse order (*paṭiloma*) just as the meditation attainments suffuse the body in order and reverse order.[38]

The chemical process of Indian alchemy is also harnessed in Indian religious practices, applied internally to bring about personal transformation and immortality. White shows how this model is also used for the performance of sexual practices in Śaiva tantra. The semen is seen as the mercury and the female is seen as the crucible containing the sulfur, parallel to the blood and other female substances. The mercury (semen) and sulphur (female substances) combine in the formation of the new being. In certain Hindu sexual practices the male practitioner retains the power of his semen/mercury not by withholding it (one possibility in Indian religious practice), but by withdrawing back into his penis the "essence" of the ejaculated semen. White writes of both alchemy and Śaiva tantra, "In many ways, the Sāṅkhyan system [the earliest school of Indian philosophy for which we have evidence] from which these traditions took their structure, is based upon embryology."[39]

In the discussion of Pali as a potent creative principle in the previous chapter, letter alchemy was mentioned as one of the means to induce transformation, on a par with letter alchemy found in tantric systems. The use of the phrase "letter alchemy" appears to be literally applicable to the method of transformation here. The elements of the path to Buddhahood, the realization of the progressive desired mental states developed in meditation and represented by *nimitta* and phonemes of the Pali alphabet, penetrate the female (i.e., practitioner's) body and enter the womb. They are then withdrawn again and applied again, with the result that the body becomes more and more suffused with the elements of Buddhahood. The same embryological imagery is found in alchemy, Śaivism, and *borān kammaṭṭhāna*. *Borān kammaṭṭhāna* does not use sexual practice or identify mercury with semen, but rather identifies the substance that causes transmutation, the mercury, as the qualities achieved through meditation. In other words, *boran kammaṭṭhāna* recognizes the outcomes of meditation, represented by the corresponding *nimitta*, as transformative elements and provides a technology whereby those elements can systematically transform the individual from an ordinary mortal subject to samsara into a pure, enlightened being, an arhat. The parallels in terminology we noted between meditation and obstetrics also apply to mercury purification, including the use of terms for womb (*gabbha,* Sanskrit *garbha*) and impregnation/implantation (*ṭhapeti*).

The greater the density of the mercury resulting from the alchemical process outlined above, the greater is its impenetrability. Such impenetrability through density is a key concept in the use of alchemy for self-transformation in order to attain invincibility and immortality.[40] Once the alchemist has achieved this state, he can use his power to transmute other things and other persons. Similar notions are present in *borān kammaṭṭhāna*. The repetitions of the practice strengthen the practitioner, transforming his physicality, *rūpa,* bringing him closer to nibbana. Density is also increased by repetition in the creation of *yantra* used for protective purposes, as described in the previous chapter.

In *borān* meditation, the process of bringing the desired attributes of consciousness—or their representative *nimitta* or Pali phonemes—into the body becomes more complex at the more advanced stages. While this may replicate the process for increasing the density of mercury, there is a possibility that it also represents a further stage in the chemical process: the use of mercury to either transmute the base metal into gold or to purify gold. The chemistry of using mercury to purify gold involves the suffusion of the substratum that contains the gold with mercury. The gold dissolves in the mercury resulting in metallic beads. When heated, the mercury evaporates to leave the gold. This may explain various aspects of *borān kammaṭṭhāna* practice, such as the retention of heat in the Cambodian initiation practice and the movement of *nimitta* to suffuse the practitioner's body with qualities, in meditation, or to transform the sensations in a specific part of the patient's body, in medicine. The heating and stirring of gold without mercury, while skimming off impurities, is another method of gold purification. The history of these processes in ancient India is not yet clear, but the connection between the purification of the individual and the purification of gold and silver in a furnace or crucible is explicit in *borān kammaṭṭhāna*. Prayers that precede the different stages of the practice recorded in the litany from Sri Lanka, the *Vākkappra-karaṇa*, that accompanies the *Amatākaravaṇṇanā*, one of our most extensive meditation manuals, repeatedly beseech the Buddha:

> Lord, make me pure without blemish. When I have been made pure like silver or gold burnished in the mouth of a furnace, may I have a radiance like that of the spotless orb of the moon over Mount Yugandhara.[41]

To sum up, the iterative processes of *borān kammaṭṭhāna* practice reveal parallels with the traditional method for purifying mercury. Correlations between mercury purification, embryology, and religious practice are found in other Indic religions, such as Śaiva tantra. The complexity of the higher stages of *borān kammaṭṭhāna* practice may further reflect the use of mercury to purify gold.

Disappearing Technologies

In the previous chapter, we noted the correlation between meditation and generative grammar had become misunderstood by the early twentieth century as a new, European model of learning influenced modernizers and revivalists. In this chapter, we have observed correlations between meditation and two other technologies or sciences: medicine and chemistry.[42] The traditional forms of these technologies also began to lose ground from the end of the nineteenth century, as European colonialism introduced different knowledge systems and sought to control the extraction of minerals and the practice of meditation. Thailand followed suit and was often the primary agent in modernizing the technologies with which *borān kammaṭṭhāna* resonated. In this section we will examine how changes in hegemonic technology, particularly medicine, took place and how these would have affected practitioners of *borān kammaṭṭhāna*.

Colonial Competition

The two colonial powers that dominated the nineteenth-century heartlands of Theravada Buddhism were Britain and France, with Britain annexing Burma (Myanmar) and Ceylon (Sri Lanka) and France controlling Indochina (now Cambodia, Laos, Vietnam). Siam (Thailand) lay between them. Although the Bowring Treaty of 1855 gave Britain the advantage in central Thailand, both countries continued to compete for cultural influence there. Neither side would give up the possibility of Siam's "annexation"—to British territories in the south and to the west of the Chao Phraya (Menam) river basin, or to French territories to its east—until their Entente Cordiale was formalized in 1904. Siam's position was only guaranteed after her involvement in World War I, to which we shall return in the next chapter. Both Britain and France sought to impose their views of progress and science on their colonial subjects where this served their economic and political purposes, either directly or indirectly, for example, by way of demonstrating the beneficence of their rule.[43]

Among the benefits of progress through scientific and social advancement, the historian of religion Draper, whose views on Buddhism and "Progress" we explored in chapter 1, includes medical advances such as progress in the eradication of smallpox. Since the history of smallpox prevention is relatively well documented globally, we can follow its path to understand how medical knowledge was an arena for competition, and why the hegemony of Western medicine in the colonial period could have an impact on such an apparently unrelated matter as Buddhist meditation.

Methods of Smallpox Prevention

Before the development of vaccination, smallpox prevention was by means of inoculation, by giving the patient a weakened form of the virus. For smallpox, this was done by variolation, using the weakened form of the smallpox virus (*variola*), extracted from the smallpox scabs of those who had survived the disease. In the eighteenth century, variolation was introduced to America from Africa by slaves and to Europe from Asia via the Ottoman Empire, with officers of the East India Company also learning the technique from local medical practitioners in Bengal. It had been practiced in Asia since the first millennium C.E. through the blowing of the pulverized pock scab into the nostril.[44] Other delivery methods were trans- and subdermal. They included inserting the infected matter directly into the blood or lymph system using a sharp implement to abrase, scratch, or cut the skin; and an oral method, the consumption of the variola particles mixed with other substances, such as milk.[45] Similar delivery methods are used for a range of pharmaceutical and non-pharmaceutical treatments.

Success in the intranasal delivery of medication depends on the size of the particles or droplets administered, hence pulverizing the scab.[46] In Asia, this is documented at least as far back as the *Caraka Saṃhitā*, so the middle of the first millennium C.E.[47] We observed above its use in ayurvedic obstetrics, a method paralleled in *borān* meditation.

The second method of delivering inoculation, that of introducing the infected material under the skin, akin to intravenous, transdermal, and subdermal drug delivery in Western medicine, is similar to the traditional Asian method of tattooing.[48] Other protective practices related to tattooing in the region include the subdermal implanting of lead *yantra* (protective geometric drawings), using the same designs as tattoos, to protect the bearer against bullets. Finally, oral delivery, while universally familiar on the model of, and overlapping with, the consumption of food, was also used for ingesting substances that would not nowadays strike us as medicinal, such as powerful texts. We can therefore see a number of parallels between the delivery of medicine, including inoculation, and delivery methods used in traditional Theravada meditation and protective practices.

These methods of improving the well-being of the subject and offering protection from a range of dangers predate the division of religion and science (including medicine) into discrete enterprises. In the absence of the necessary microbiology to isolate which factors were essential, a variety of interpretations were given for their effectiveness. Atsuko Naono writes, "Smallpox, as we know from several cases in nineteenth-century Burma [as elsewhere in Asia], was often viewed as a powerful, hostile spirit, and inoculation could easily have been presented as a means not unlike a tattoo that granted some kind of special protection against it."[49] Similarly, inserting lead *yantra* under the skin to protect against bullets draws on a range of protective devices, which include the implantation of a smaller dose of the dangerous enemy (or the power of the enemy)—here a smaller "dose" of a lead bullet—both against and through whom the device offers protection. Such practice can be seen as another type of inoculation. Theories concerning the underlying reasons for the effectiveness of inoculation, then, drew on a range of religious, cultural, and scientific frameworks and sat alongside other methods of prevention, such as other medical procedures, dietary prescription, and good or meritorious works in both Asia and the West.[50]

Competing Claims to Medical Superiority

Surgeons attached to the East India Company first implemented sporadic smallpox inoculation among the military in the late 1780s, launching a wider, highly successful campaign during 1800–1802 among the civilian population. Variolation was promoted as an improved method of European innovation, and its pre-existence in India was downplayed. As routines for inoculation became standardized and universally accepted, many of the unshared cultural aspects of treatment were discarded. The weight of the risks and relative advantages of competing delivery methods were debated and disputed. While these may seem to be primarily medical issues, aspects of culture and competition also influenced the rhetoric. Intranasal and transdermal methods, popular in Asia, were dismissed by Western medical officers. From a medical perspective, Indian-style variolation may in fact have been safer. Indian variolators preferred to use dried matter (which they would moisten before application to abrasions on the arm, for example), while the British "preferred to use fresh matter taken directly from a ripe pustule."[51] This difference stemmed from British concerns about the possibility of storing variolous matter and its effectiveness if it was not fresh, but using fresh matter and the arm-to-arm technique enhanced the risk of infection with other diseases. Initially, then, claims about the superiority of Western inoculation related to the delivery method. Then, with the arrival in 1802 of vaccination using cowpox, inoculation was dismissed as an inferior, native technology in spite of its continued greater reliability for several decades in that context.[52]

Vaccination had been developed at the end of the eighteenth century by Edward Jenner (1749–1823) using the milder cowpox virus, *vaccinia*, from *vacca*, "cow," which gave its name to the new treatment. As Louis Pasteur (1822–1895) developed artificially weakened strains of other viruses for prophylaxis he extended the term's usage in Jenner's honor. Although vaccination was available in British colonial territories in Asia as early as 1802, it was often made ineffective and difficult to implement by the instability and inadequacy of the bovine lymph available in Asia. Inoculation through variolation remained the preference of the majority of local people. In the late 1910s, James Entrican, the British superintendent of vaccination in Burma, reported:

> I believe the chief cause of its [variolation's] popularity is the absence in the majority of cases of any troublesome symptoms, such as sometimes follow vaccination under insanitary conditions. The inoculated child may of course develop generalised small-pox and die, this risk is clearly recognised, but accepted, because in the majority of cases the after-effects are almost nil. A small

> pock with perhaps 2 or 3 still smaller ones round it, is the usual course of an inoculation, and the children require little if any attention.[53]

The method of delivery remained a perennial issue. Direct contact between the pocks of cowpox-infected children to cuts made in the arms of those to be vaccinated bore with it the risk of the transmission of other infectious, fatal, or disfiguring diseases such as syphilis ("the great pox").[54] Vaccination through contact with infected calves or animal lymph led to outbreaks of painful pocks, might be ineffective if the lymph was poor quality, and could lead to fatal complications from unsterile treatment. Despite his acknowledgment that Burmese preference for variolation over vaccination could be justified, Entrican still regarded variolation as a mumpsimus, the "folly of ignorant people."[55]

The American medical missionary Francis Mason (1799–1874) recognized that many monks fulfilled the role of medical practitioner, despite attempts by the final kings of Burma to prevent monks from providing this service. He therefore distributed information to monks, as a way of introducing vaccination to the broader community. His *Materia Medica*, translated into Burmese, gave a clear explanation of vaccination including its relative mortality risks and was incorporated into an important Burmese work on Western medicine in 1881.[56] In Burma, vaccination became common in urban centers such as Rangoon (Yangon), where the colonial administration could enforce policy, and popular among ethnic minorities, where Christian missionaries had more success. Otherwise variolation, which gave lifelong immunity, remained the norm. It was not until the early twentieth century that locally based doctors came up with solutions that were effective for their area and cheap enough to implement successfully.[57]

The Ban on Traditional Medicine in French Indochina and Thailand

As in Burma, so in Cambodia and Thailand, there were several competing medical systems including Chinese medicine and various branches of local systems that drew on Indian Ayurveda either directly or through Buddhist medical traditions. Resistance to Western medical developments was strong, and the preference for inoculation over vaccination continued until the early twentieth century. Vaccination was made compulsory by the French in Cochinchina (southern Vietnam) in 1871, and Louis Pasteur himself was involved in the setting up of the Institut Pasteur in Saigon in 1890. Variolation was banned in Cambodia in 1907. Nonetheless, the implementation of vaccination in rural regions, including much of Cambodia and Laos, continued to be hindered by the inaccessibility of rural areas coupled with deterioration of the lymph in transmission. Although the popularity of vaccinations generally was given a boost when King Sisowath of Cambodia received a vaccination against plague after the death of one of his favorite sons during a plague epidemic in 1908, medical officers were still reporting on the use of variolation in 1924.[58] Therefore, the impact of Western medicine was confined to the urban centers, especially Phnom Penh, leaving traditional meditation and medicine to continue unaffected in rural Cambodia.

In Thailand, King Chulalongkorn (Rāma V, r. 1868–1910) had taken an interest in traditional medicine, instigating the publication of works on the Royal Thai medical tradition that had developed at court.[59] However, his modernization of the country, in both response to and reaction against the presence of British and French colonial powers, led to the undermining of traditional medicine, particularly during the final years of his reign. Two years after his death, the ongoing resistance to vaccination collapsed following an epidemic in 1911–1912.

Around this time, Chulalongkorn's son and successor, King Vajiravudh (Rāma VI, r. 1910–1926), began to sponsor research into vaccination, setting up an institute to seek a rabies vaccination following the death of his cousin, Prince Damrong's daughter, from the disease. In 1917, following Pasteur's breakthrough discovery in relation to rabies, this institute was renamed the Pasteur Institute and was involved in the promotion of other types of vaccination. The royal promotion of vaccination meant that in February of 1914 it was possible to implement a law in Thailand making smallpox vaccination compulsory.[60] Vaccination was delivered at temporary clinics set up in Buddhist temples, hospitals, and police stations. By 1922, vaccination had become almost universal thanks to Thailand's highly centralized, organizational structures, well-funded and staged preparation, and a move to require vaccination certificates for attendance at schools and government employment. In 1923, Vajiravudh took this modernization and Westernization a stage further by banning traditional medicine.

The Effect of Undermining Traditional Medicine on *Borān Kammaṭṭhāna*

While the outlawing of traditional medicine was later reversed, the ban and the promotion of Western medicine affected *borān kammaṭṭhāna* in several ways. First, *borān kammaṭṭhāna* was in itself a form of traditional medicine, applied to healing the body as well as the psychophysical organism as a whole. Second, *borān kammaṭṭhāna* is based on the model of the human psychophysical organism that—derived from Indic Ayurveda—underlies traditional medicine. The delivery pathways in the body, beginning with the intranasal cavity, used in meditation for delivering the desired aspects of consciousness into the body, are based on those of traditional medicine. Third, while those who study *borān kammaṭṭhāna* in the traditional manner contribute to the livelihood of their meditation masters in the form of the offerings they make to them, the more reliable income for such meditation masters comes from their ability to offer rituals, blessings, protection, and healing.

With the undermining of traditional medicine and, as noted

previously, traditional attitudes to the potency of language, the methods of bringing about change found in *borān kammaṭṭhāna* began to become isolated, no longer part of a network of resonating technologies. Other resonating technologies, such as chemistry, were also disrupted by the processes of modernization and centralized control, whether on the part of European colonial powers or the Thai monarchy. In more rural areas of former French colonies, where these modernizing policies had less impact and traditional medicine would continue to be the main recourse for treatment well into the second half of the twentieth century, *borān kammaṭṭhāna* also continued to thrive.

During the thirty years or so before the outlawing of traditional medicine in Thailand in 1923, the place and practice of meditation monks in the country had been transformed beyond recognition by far-reaching changes to Buddhism, administrative structures, and education. These set the context for the rejection of *borān kammaṭṭhāna* by the elite, and for the discarding of its practices more widely, particularly after its resonating technologies were no longer recognized. We shall examine these developments in the next chapter. Here, let us briefly return to the theory put forward in the late twentieth century that *borān kammaṭṭhāna* is not orthodox Theravada at all, but a borrowing from another Buddhist tradition, such as Tibetan tantra. I countered that suggestion with the observation that *borān kammaṭṭhāna* is based on Abhidhamma and an enactment of the Abhidhamma path of transformation. Having looked at the relationship between *borān kammaṭṭhāna* and medicine, we can see a reason for the apparent similarities. While there is no evidence of borrowing between *borān kammaṭṭhāna* and Tibetan or other forms of tantra, they both use somatic practices that seek to transform both the consciousness and physicality of the practitioner. The understanding of the body that underlies the somatic practices in both cases is derived from traditional medicine, heavily influenced in both regions by Indian Ayurveda. While there are almost no Buddhist texts shared between Theravada and Tibetan tantric Buddhism, Indian medical texts such as *Suśruta Saṃhitā* were used and translated throughout the region, as far west as the Middle East, to Cambodia in the east, and to Tibet in the north.[61] We may therefore look to the spread of the mathematics, medicine, and other technologies underlying *borān kammaṭṭhāna*, rather than to a direct influence from another religious tradition, to understand similarities between them.

Conclusion

This chapter has explored the close parallels between *borān kammaṭṭhāna* and other technologies designed to bring about change, especially the obstetrics of ayurvedic medicine and the chemistry of mercury purification. It was noted that the same underlying principle of substitution as the process whereby change is brought about, and application of group theory mathematics for the effective harnessing of that process of change, were shared between these technologies, the generative grammar examined in the previous chapter, Abhidhamma, and *borān kammaṭṭhāna* itself. While the creation of a new being might be seen as a metaphor for spiritual transformation, the pervasive presence of embryology in *borān* practice and analysis, and the mirroring of obstetric practice in *borān* meditation, indicated a more literal, practical relationship. These were resonating technologies based on shared understandings of how to bring about change.

The question then arose of how these resonating technologies disappeared, leaving *borān kammaṭṭhāna* isolated. Having examined competition over ideas concerning language, and manuscript and print technology, previously, we turned here to the competition between medical systems fought throughout the colonial period. Local traditions were suppressed, even when they remained more effective. In those areas under the control of modernizing power structures, namely urban centers in the European colonies, the centralized Thai state, and groups influenced by Christian missionaries, Western knowledge systems became increasingly hegemonic. This altered the model of the body and the visible technologies of transformation. The methods to bring about change that had shaped *borān kammaṭṭhāna* ceased to be recognized.

Having explored the methods for bringing about change in *borān kammaṭṭhāna* and examined how the resonating technologies were undermined in the modern period, in the next two chapters we return to broader changes to Buddhism. We will trace the place of *borān kammaṭṭhāna* from center to periphery and adaptation. To do this, we must examine the ways in which Buddhists sought to protect their religion from decline and revitalize it to face the challenges of the modern period.

6

From Center to Periphery

The Changing Place of Borān Kammaṭṭhāna *under Thai Influence*

> King Kīrti Śri Rājasiṃha, "in his lofty desire to promote the religion of the Omniscient One, and with great loving-kindness, built a forest abode for the two venerable teachers of vidarśana meditation, Mahānāma and Brahmasvara, who were endued with manifold virtues, such as love of solitude, and entrusted to them twenty-four bhikshus [monks] who had received ordination under them to be instructed in the method of vidarśana meditation, and entreated them to train these (pupils) carefully in the practice of forty karmaṣṭhāna meditations.
>
> —*Kuśalakriyānusandeśaya*[1]

Before the late nineteenth century the "old meditation," *borān kammaṭṭhāna*, had yet to be deemed old or corrupt. It was current technology, referred to here simply by such generic names for meditation as *vidarśanā* "insight" (Sinhala; *vipassanā* in Pali) and *karmaṣṭhāna* (Sinhala; *kammaṭṭhāna* in Pali).[2] As indicated in the passage cited here, it was the dominant practice established and promoted by royalty and by the supreme patriarchs of the Buddhist Sangha in the countries that would become Cambodia, Laos,

Sri Lanka, and Thailand. As we saw in the previous two chapters, it also resonated with other technologies of cultural importance from generative grammar to medicine. Here we shall see that it was an instrument of international diplomacy, a subject of interest to members of the royal families of the region, and was sought after by the vanguard of the first major revival movement responding to the threat of European colonialism. We have already touched on how modernization in the context of Western hegemony represented a challenge to the technologies with which *borān kammaṭṭhāna* was related. In this chapter, we shall follow the further history of Theravada countries, to see how political events coupled with distinctive responses to colonialism conspired to marginalize the practice, pushing it from the center to the margins of Buddhist culture.

Esoteric Meditation at the Heart of Revival

In the mid-eighteenth century, the royal house of Ayutthaya, the capital of Siam (Thailand), responded to a request from the royal house and aristocracy of Śrīvardhanapura (Kandy), the capital of the Kandyan Kingdom in the central highlands of Ceylon (Sri Lanka). After two and a half centuries of European colonial presence, the Sinhalese embassy to Ayutthaya reported Buddhism to be in a sorry state of decline on the island, with no viable ordination lineage. King Boromakot (Pali *Paramakośa*, r. 1733–1758) responded by sending three separate missions of monks.[3]

The first monks from Ayutthaya reestablished the full ordination lineage in Kandy at the behest of Kīrti Śrī Rājasiṃha (r. 1747–1782), ruler of the Kandyan kingdom, and Välivița Saraṇaṃkara (1698–1778), the monk who would be appointed supreme patriarch and head the revitalized Sangha. In 1756 a second mission followed, specifically dedicated to reviving meditation. One of the Siamese was Varañāṇa Mahāthera, the monk who composed the Sinhalese version of the *borān* narrative of Princess Mind (Cittakumāri) for Kīrti Śrī's chief queen, recounted in chapter 3. Varañāṇa had a reputation as a scholar of grammar, which, as we have seen, was an important strand of transformative technology that runs through *borān kammaṭṭhāna*. It may have been his language skills that led him to undertake the task of presenting this text for the queen. Varañāṇa's companion, Mahāvisuddhācariya, was better known for giving meditation instruction. At least twenty-four local monks studied under two other meditation masters, Ven. Mahānāma and Ven. Brahmasvara, an event captured in the account of the second mission cited above. They or their disciples wrote down, as reminders of their instructions, the manuals still found in Sri Lankan manuscript libraries. King Kīrti Śrī's patronage was continued by his brother and successor, Śrī Rājādhi Rājasiṃha (r. 1780–1798), who issued an edict (*katikāvata*) encouraging monks to meditate.[4]

The Meditation Lineage from Siam

When the Sri Lankan monks wrote down the methods in their own personal manuals, they focused not on the preliminary phases of meditation but the details of the advanced methods. Presumably basic skills in inducing meditative states and attainments had been learned sufficiently well in the first eight years of the transmission. It was the advanced guidance that needed recording before the Siamese teachers returned home. It is this activity that has recorded for us the most in-depth representation of the full practice and allowed us to see how closely it correlates with the Abhidhamma path, as discussed in chapter 2. Mostly written in a mixture of Pali and Sinhala, these manuals were mnemonic aides to individual private practice, however, not part of the impressive literary repertoire being built up within the large monastic libraries of the eighteenth-century revival. This aspect of the Siyam Nikāya's agenda was therefore less visible than others. This low visibility, in conjunction with the demise of the tradition, has led to its receiving little attention in studies of the period, despite its relatively recent date.[5] The manuals had fallen into disuse by the end of the nineteenth century, and it was this that allowed a number of them to be acquired by the British colonial officer Hugh Nevill (1848–1897).

At least one line of the Siyam Nikāya transmission of *borān kammaṭṭhāna* continued until the end of the nineteenth century.[6] This last known case was reported in 1916 by G. Sagāris de Silva to F. L. Woodward, when he was assisting him with the translation of the Bambaragala manual that Rhys Davids had published as *The Yogāvacara's Manual* twenty years earlier. Rhys Davids had published it at the behest of Anagarika Dharmapala, who was not alone in his struggle to make sense of the text. Its mysteries so confounded the pair of erudite monks who also published the related Pali manual, the *Amatākaravaṇṇanā*, in the 1960s that they mistook the latter's mathematical permutations and fine-tuned mnemonics for bad grammar and bowdlerized it beyond use.[7]

Ratnajoti and Ratnapāla were unfortunate not to have come across one of the many living practitioners still to be found in Cambodia, Laos, and to a lesser extent Thailand in the 1960s. The recent international gatherings—the World Fellowship of Buddhism in Colombo in 1950 and the Sixth Council in Rangoon in 1954–1956—had brought together many monks from all the Theravada countries, but these representatives tended to be from reform branches of the Sangha. Those among them who knew of *borān kammaṭṭhāna* had by that time rejected it as a corruption of Buddhism, a view held by the supreme patriarchs of both the Cambodian *nikāya* (monastic lineages) by that time (below). As a result, the form of meditation that spread through the connections made at those gatherings was Burmese Vipassanā. It seems that Anagarika Dharmapala had also been unfortunate in missing a living lineage during his search in the last decades of the nineteenth century. However, Dharmapala seems mainly to have turned to outsiders, including the theosophist Madame Blavatsky and to texts, primarily the *Visuddhimagga*, despite his interest in this manual and despite the fact that he knew of the monk Doratiyāveye Atthadassī. Doratiyāveye was the last known disciple in a *borān* lineage, as Woodward found out when translating the manual in 1916, but by that time, Doratiyāveye had died.[8]

The Rupture with Ayutthaya

The disappearance of *borān* meditation practice from Sri Lanka relatively early, given that it continued to thrive in mainland Southeast Asia at this time, reflects two things: the position of the Siyam Nikāya in Sri Lanka, to which we shall return, and the dwindling influence of Ayutthaya almost immediately after the Siyam Nikāya was founded.

As mentioned above, King Boromkot authorized three missions of Siamese monks to Kandy in the mid-eighteenth century. The third mission arrived in 1759, bringing more Siamese monks, ostensibly to support the revival. Its undercover purpose was a conspiracy between the Siamese and one of the factions of the Sinhalese aristocracy to replace King Kīrti Śrī on the throne with one of the Siamese princes. The prince had even come along with the mission ordained as a monk. It may seem surprising that Välivița Saraṇaṃkara, the leading light of the reform and new supreme patriarch, whose polemics against the existing priests had included purist attacks on their unspiritual motivation, would be involved in a plot to kill the king. Yet the efforts to introduce a new ordination lineage to Sri Lanka had partly stemmed from the jostling for power among the Sinhalese aristocracy in first place, the rhetoric of decline and reform masking the power struggle.

The assassination plot was foiled, the lay conspirators were beheaded for treason, and Saraṇaṃkara was imprisoned. Hulaṃgomuvē Buddharakkhita, the monk who informed on the conspirators, was granted a substantial tract of land for his loyalty.[9] This led to a rupture with Siam, and moves on the part of Sri Lankan Buddhists to secure the protection of Buddhism on the island with help from the Siamese royal family were put on hold until the nineteenth century.

The other factor in this rupture, and one that would contribute to *borān kammaṭṭhāna* not being reintroduced at a later date, was the Burmese invasion of Siam the same year. Despite a cessation of the hostilities the following year, the fighting resumed and culminated in the sack of Ayutthaya in 1767. The king was killed, hundreds of thousands of inhabitants slaughtered, and tens of thousands taken in captivity to Burma. City buildings, religious artifacts, and many manuscript libraries were destroyed. When the Burmese had to redeploy their troops at the end of the year to combat an invading Chinese army to the north, the power vacuum in Siam following the Burmese withdrawal led to a civil war that lasted between 1767 and 1770.

Thonburi, Taksin, and the Beginnings of Modern Thailand

From the Siamese civil war, Taksin (r. 1767–1782) emerged the sole victor. He established a new capital at Thonburi (now a district absorbed by the expansion of Bangkok). Thonburi had been sufficiently remote from Ayutthaya to escape the Burmese destruction, and temples there such as Wat Hong and Wat Ratchasittharam, which were now relatively close to the new centers of power, became important centers for meditation. While at least one lineage from Suk Kaitheun, the supreme patriarch between 1794 and 1816, survived in Ayutthaya at the temple Wat Pradusongtham, Suk moved to Thonburi, basing himself at Wat Ratchasittharam. Both Wat Hong and Wat Ratchasittharam still house *borān kammaṭṭhāna* manuscripts, and the latter is still the home of a living tradition of *borān kammaṭṭhāna*.[10] Wat Hong is associated with King Taksin.

While the story of Taksin's interest in meditation and his claims to supramundane attainments are well known, specific details of his religious practices have been hard to ascertain because of the distortions of the historiography that immediately followed his execution by his own prime minister in 1782. That prime minister would become known by the names Buddha Yodfa Chulalok (Rāma I), for he was the founder of the Chakri dynasty, which replaced Taksin and continues to this day. However, a recent analysis by B. J. Terwiel of an illustrated Thai manuscript commissioned by Taksin in 1777 confirms the link. The manuscript, after describing and illustrating the City of Nibbana, presents eight Buddha-like figures in monastic dress, each representing one of the eight stages of enlightenment: the path and fruit (*maggaphala*) of stream entrant, once-returner, non-returner, and arhat. The final stage shows the arhat holding a crystal ball in front of him, at around the level of his navel, imagery that immediately associates it with the realization of crystal-like *nimitta* at the womb of the practitioner. This illustration on the manuscript commissioned by Taksin shows that the imagery of *borān kammaṭṭhāna* practice was familiar to Taksin and the artists who created these manuscripts, indicating that Taksin was practicing within one of the *borān kammaṭṭhāna* lineages that came to Thonburi after the Burmese sack of Ayutthaya.[11]

From the earlier defeat at the hands of the Burmese emerged a stronger, more militant Siam. Taksin and the Chakri dynasty exploited Burma's overstretched military capacity to regain lost territories. They also drew on Burmese models for ethnic integration, taking them much further, in part by using Buddhism and the Sangha as a unifying, centralizing institution. The new Chakri capital was established at Bangkok on the opposite bank of the Chao Phraya river from Thonburi. This allowed the new dynasty to take advantage of the large natural harbor at Bangkok to engage in international trade, which included importing the latest weaponry initially from China and then from Europe. It was the beginning of the transformation of Siam into a modern state. The engagement of the Chakri dynasty with global modernity would later have significant impact on the shape of meditation promoted as part of future reforms of Buddhism.

The success of the early Chakri dynasty with its military, weaponry, and economic reforms led to rapid modernization. There were two alterations in the organization of the Sangha during the first Chakri reign (1782–1809) that contributed to the later marginalization of *borān kammaṭṭhāna*. The first was a restriction on the movement of monks: they were now required to hold identity papers, and monasteries were required to report guest monks and check their papers. This inhibited the institution-free lifestyle of the majority of wandering forest monks, those most likely to dedicate their lives to serious meditation practice.[12] The second factor was the structural reorganization of the Sangha with the loss of the separate "forest dwelling" *āraññavāsī* section, which had formerly been represented institutionally among the highest ranks of the Sangha hierarchy and therefore at court.[13] The beginnings of modernization, centralized control, and a shift in favor of non-meditating monks would pave the way for developments under subsequent Chakri kings.

Mongkut's Establishment of the Reformist Thammayut Monastic Lineage

Prince Mongkut (1804–1868), later King Rāma IV, is the single figure most associated with the reform of Buddhism in Thailand. As a royal prince he was ordained as a monk, in line with the Thai tradition of temporary ordination for all young men, at the age of twenty in 1824. As heir-designate of Rāma II, Mongkut was expected to disrobe to become king. However, he remained a monk for twenty-seven years, until 1851, because his half-brother Nangklao, though regarded as having a lesser claim, managed to accede to the throne as Rāma III.

In 1833, while still a monk (1824–1851), Mongkut founded a new monastic lineage, the Thammayut (Pali Dhammayutika) Nikāya, on a reformist, rationalist platform. Its name means "the monastic lineage that adheres to the Buddha's teaching" and represents an explicit rejection of those practices for which he saw no canonical authorization. An example of the way in which consultation of the Pali canon influenced Mongkut is how monks in his lineage dressed. In Mongkut's new *nikāya* the traditional robes, which had symbolic significance for *borān* practitioners, were discarded and a simpler monastic dress used, based on the description found in the canon of just three robes with no accoutrements.[14]

Most of the existing Sangha lineages had already been centralized and unified to a degree under the first Chakri reign and were now given the collective term "Mahanikay" (Pali *Mahānikāya*), *mahā* meaning "great/majority" and *nikāya* meaning "monastic fraternity or ordination lineage." The Thammayut did not have the monopoly on modernization and reform. While monks within the Mahanikay were later to mirror Thammayut developments, for example by adapting monastic robes, reformist elements were already being promoted within the Mahanikay by Nangklao.

While Mongkut had received a modern, Western-style education, had good command of Pali, and was genuinely interested in modern science and reform, the political situation and rivalry with his brother acted as an additional motive. By accusing the existing Sangha of being lax and establishing the new ordination lineage with himself at the head, he could circumvent his personal subordination to the existing hierarchy within the Thai Sangha, including those loyal to King Nangklao. This ploy allowed him to establish his autonomy while still enjoying the safety of remaining a monk, thus avoiding the dangerous, sometimes deadly competition to accede to the throne. King Nangklao nonetheless sought to intervene in this strategy. In the late 1840s, still anxious about his younger half-brother's more obvious claim to the throne, Nangklao promoted the princely monk Paramanuchitchinorot (1790–1853), whom he could control, to lead the Thammayut order and the Sangha in Bangkok and the central area of Siam.[15] Nangklao also hindered the rise of the Thammayut by promoting Mahanikay monks and sending some to Cambodia as representatives of Thai royalty just as Mongkut would later send Thammayut monks.

Once king, Mongkut would use the Thammayut order to strengthen the court's hold over Thailand, using the rhetoric of a reformist, rationalist agenda. Just like the contemporary claims to scientific and civilizational knowledge on the part of European colonizers, notions of correct Buddhist behavior had become part of political rhetoric for a country defending its invasions and occupations of other lands, for a king seeking to shore up his position against foreign and local threat, for writers opining on fashionable subjects for their sponsoring readership. During Mongkut's reign as the fourth Chakri king, Rāma IV (r. 1851–1868), the external military threat switched from the Burmese to the Europeans. He and his son and successor Chulalongkorn (Rāma V) (r. 1868–1910) oversaw increased centralization and radical modernization including of administration and education. The Thammayut, now deeply loyal to the throne, became one of the Siamese state's key instruments of centralization. From 1851 until the early 1930s Thammayut monks, although a minority, were given hierarchical preferment over the monks of the Mahanikay.[16]

Mongkut's Rejection of *Borān* Meditation

Mongkut had received training in *borān kammaṭṭhāna* as a young monk in the 1820s. This had been at Wat Ratchasittharam, the temple in Thonburi that continued the lineage of the earlier Supreme Patriarch Suk Kaitheun. Mongkut was soon disaffected. It seems his natural inclination was more for study, *pariyatti*, than practice, *paṭipatti*.[17] This and his sense of personal status led Mongkut to be critical of his teachers. The explicit reason for Mongkut's criticism of the meditation was that his teachers declined to justify their instructions with reference to the Pali canon.[18]

We have already observed that *borān kammaṭṭhāna* is related to Abhidhamma commentarial material and to traditional sciences of the time. However, these connections are not apparent at the beginner stages of the practice. Also, among reform-minded Buddhists of the nineteenth to mid-twentieth centuries in Thailand, while consulting of canonical texts was important in the quest to return to the original teaching of the Buddha, the emphasis was on the Sutta Piṭaka and Vinaya Piṭaka rather than Abhidhamma. This lack of emphasis on Abhidhamma may well have confirmed the impression that *borān* methods had no authority in the canon.

Mongkut was happier with the meditation monk Thap (below), whose practice, like that of the Burmese Vipassanā tradition emerging at this time, paid close attention to the canonical sources and their commentaries. Thap used these sources in developing his insight meditation based on charnel ground observation of the decomposition of the body. To date, Mongkut is the earliest person known to have explicitly rejected the old methods of meditation, and his status lent weight to the side of study (*pariyatti*) over that of practice (*paṭipatti*) in an ongoing debate that has continued in Thailand to the present.

Study versus Experiential Practice

Mongkut's insistence that *paṭipatti* should be authorized with reference to *pariyatti* became a dominant feature of Thai Buddhist culture. It encouraged the patronage of those meditation monks who could demonstrate *pariyatti* credentials and instigated the search for texts to authorize practice.

The debate about *pariyatti* and *paṭipatti* in Thailand is mirrored elsewhere, especially in Burma. The issue is whether or not it is permissible for Buddhist teachers within a living tradition to teach on the basis of experience alone or whether their practice must be authorized with reference to textual sources, primarily those of the Pali canon. The theme is not new. In his *Visuddhimagga*, Buddhaghosa explains that if no teacher with direct personal spiritual attainment can be found, one should take as one's teacher somebody familiar with the canonical texts to avoid being led astray.[19] Therefore one can construe the debate in terms of a concern that the Dhamma taught is the true Dhamma, and not in some way misguided. Textual study therefore acts as the bottom-line guarantor of this. However, there is then the risk that, by adverting to the bottom line, direct religious experience is sidelined, even suppressed. Moreover, the canonical and commentarial sources are extensive and diverse: a *sutta*-based practice could be somewhat different from an Abhidhamma-based practice.

In the ongoing debate over the relationship between *pariyatti* and *paṭipatti* those more oriented toward institutional control and those oriented toward reform tend to advocate *pariyatti* as the priority over and prerequisite for *paṭipatti*. This position creates an external authority, potentially—and historically—controlled by centralized authorities, against which those making claims on the basis of experience may be judged.[20] On the other hand, even those who feel that they have successfully used canonical and commentarial texts as the direct basis for their meditation practice feel able, on the basis of their personal experience, to critique texts as falling short. In *borān kammaṭṭhāna* and in the Tai-Lao meditation traditions that were to be de-institutionalized by the coming reforms, textual study might be considered insufficient, irrelevant, or even counterproductive to successful practice, and some practitioners retain that position to this day.[21]

Last Moments of *Borān Kammaṭṭhāna* at the Center

In spite of his personal rejection of the *borān* meditation practice he had been taught, Mongkut did not actively suppress it. Even a century later, in 1932, one of Mongkut's own sons, Prince Vivitthavanpreecha (1860–1932), would publish a small book on meditation containing an abridged version of an eighteenth-century *borān kammaṭṭhāna* text.[22] The interest shown in *borān* meditation by one of the leading lights of the reform within the Thammayut Nikāya, Phussadeva Sa (also known as Pusso Sa and Somdet Sa) (1812–1899), is particularly telling.[23] Manuscripts of Phussadeva Sa relating to the subject are to be found in the National Library in Bangkok.[24] According to Kittivuddho (Kittiwuttho), Somdet Sa included elements of *borān kammaṭṭhāna* in his first rendering of the *Paṭhamasambodhi*, which he wrote in the 1850s during the reign of Mongkut.[25] The *Paṭhamasambodhi* is the most widely distributed biography of the Buddha in Khmer-Tai Buddhism, with versions in Pali as well as at least eight vernacular languages.[26] Sa's is the last version produced in Thailand to contain such references. Later in his career, however, Sa's position seems to have changed, reflecting the expansion of the modernizing influence of Mongkut's successors.

Sa had been ordained at Wat Bovornnivet, where Mongkut was abbot, during the 1830s. He disrobed in 1839, but secured Mongkut's permission in the 1850s—with Mongkut now king and patronizing the expansion of the Thammayut Nikāya—to reordain and return to Wat Bovornnivet. During this time he wrote his first version of the *Paṭhamasambodhi*, but in 1880, with Mongkut's son Chulalongkorn now on the throne, at a time of textual reform ahead of the first printing of the Pali canon, Sa reformed the royal chanting curriculum. Woramat Malasart has shown that in doing so, he removed from it the *Dhammakāya* verses, a text related to *borān* meditation practice that we met in chapter 1 in connection with the Phitsanulok inscription.[27] In 1890, he also produced a new version of the *Paṭhamasambodhi*, also stripped of more traditional aspects, which was later published.[28] Sa's position at the center of the modernizing Sangha hierarchy was rewarded by his appointment in 1893 as supreme patriarch, a position he held for the rest of his life. The appointment was a high honor in its own right but all the more indicative of the approval of the court and the Sangha hierarchy given that there had been no supreme patriarch appointed during the preceding forty years.[29]

The absence of a supreme patriarch throughout most of the reigns of Mongkut and Chulalongkorn had been part of their strategy to facilitate the centralized control of the Sangha throughout Siam. In the early decades of the Thammayut Nikāya its monks were insufficiently numerous to stamp its authority on the Sangha in the country as a whole.[30] The numbers of Thammayut monks increased during Mongkut's reign as a result of his patronage and the establishment of new monasteries throughout the country. Nonetheless, they remained a small minority.[31] The numbers continued to increase under Chulalongkorn as part of the policy of creating a national identity. People emulated royal patronage by donating residences to Thammayut forest monks and by providing support for rural Thammayut novices, to the degree that ordination in a Thammayut monastery offered advantageous living conditions over Mahanikay ordination.[32]

Although other Thammayut monks interested in meditation explored *borān kammaṭṭhāna* texts, this may have been an expression of personal autonomy from the modernization process as we shall see below, even as other factors at large conspired to escalate its marginalization in the early decades of the twentieth century. Active support for *borān kammaṭṭhāna* from the highest ranks of the Thai Sangha hierarchy seems to have come to an end with Somdet Sa. The policies of a new supreme patriarch and a new king combined to ensure the radical marginalization of the "old method" in Siam.

Modernization of Meditation and Education

Contemporary with Somdet Sa was the meditation monk Buddhasiri (Phutthasiri) Thap (1806–1891), mentioned above as a favorite of Mongkut's. Thap was one of the leading lights of the Thammayut reform. Thap's form of meditation focused on the ten stages of decomposition of the body known as *asubha* "unbeautiful" or "loathsome" practices. In the ordination hall at Wat Somanat where he became abbot he commissioned images of the stages of *asubha* as wall paintings. Although the *asubha* are included in the *borān kammaṭṭhāna* practices, Thap's practice seems to have been normative, based on textual studies. His text on the subject remains a standard text at Mahāmakut Buddhist University.[33] It was Thap's approach to meditation that was approved by Somdet Sa's successor as supreme patriarch, Prince Wachirayan.

Immediately after Sa's death in 1899 there was another interregnum between supreme patriarchs, of eleven years, but this is misleading: the man who would be appointed to that post, Prince Wachirayan (Vajirañāṇa) (1860–1921), was already the most powerful monk in the country. He had taken over as head of the Thammayut Nikāya in 1893, when Somdet Sa had become supreme patriarch. It was on the accession of his nephew Vajiravudh to the throne that Wachirayan—a good match for the new king in terms of enthusiasm for centralization and reform—was appointed to the vacant post of supreme patriarch.

Wachirayan combined his modern, liberal, English-medium education in the palace and his knowledge of Pali to write many works on Buddhism, especially on Vinaya, and his writings reflect the reformist modernizing approach of his father, King Mongkut. He continued the emphasis on the Sutta and Vinaya Piṭaka texts of canon as the primary authority, discarding where he saw fit the views of both the commentarial and the living traditions, as well as sections of the canon itself. We can see their approach to textual authorities in their attitude to interpretations of the *sīmā*, the sacred monastic boundary used for such important rites as ordination, which lies at the heart of monastic validity. The importance placed on the validity of *sīmā* had caused decade-long disputes and much close investigation of commentaries in Burma and Sri Lanka over the centuries. However, rather than insisting on pursuing the legal developments found in commentarial guidance and the extensive literature resulting from these disputes, Wachirayan felt comfortable taking a "commonsense" approach.[34] We can see how, within this context, expertise in commentarial exegesis as well as in Abhidhamma diminished.

Alongside his productivity in writings on the Pali Vinaya, Wachirayan was highly influential in political and educational reform. He led and designed the reform and centralization not only of monastic education but also secular education throughout the country.[35] With the support of his brother King Chulalongkorn, who had patronized the first printing of the Pali canon a decade earlier, Wachirayan pushed through the 1902 Sangha Reform Act.[36] This created a single, national hierarchical system that incorporated all monks and a centralized system of monastic education and examination. In the early decades of the twentieth century, as Siam's government sought to increase control over its outlying areas, partially in response to having lost territories to the British and French, those monks seen as representing a threat to this process were persecuted.[37] Resisting the "reformist" agenda became dangerous. Parallel political developments under the guise of purification and reform would also take place in Cambodia to undermine the authority of rural monks.

The higher-ranking monks of the Thammayut Nikāya in the main period of centralization from the very end of the nineteenth into the first decades of twentieth century were—like Wachirayan himself—closely associated with administration and *pariyatti*, textual education. Although they admired meditation monks such as Thap, who could align their practice with textual scholarship, meditation was not, then, a primary concern of the powerful administrative monks of this period. The conferment of rank and status was now granted by the central authorities, in part on the basis of a centralized exam system. The position of supreme patriarch was no longer a position associated with meditation at all but entirely with administration and textual scholarship. In this period other posts traditionally associated with meditation, such as the headship of Wat Sangwet in Bangkok, were given to administrative monks who had passed the central Pali exams made possible by the preceding printing project.[38] As Andrew Skilton has pointed out, this context sheds some light on the views of Thai meditation expressed by the British vice-consul Henry Alabaster in 1871, whom we met in chapter 1. Alabaster had arrived in Thailand in 1851, the year of Mongkut's accession to the throne, and the work was published in the early years of King Chulalongkorn's reign, based on a book written by Chao Phya Thipakon, the former foreign minister for Siam. While one might initially expect a Thai source to be more sympathetic to local meditation, Thipakon was writing from the perspective of the modernizing elite of this time.[39]

Preferment through administrative ranks meant that even monks with the Thammayut lineage who pursued meditation were rarely promoted, despite the important role Thammayut forest meditation monks played in the increasing numbers of Thammayut temples and monks in the northeast from the 1890s onward under King Chulalongkorn's patronage. The Tai-Lao forest meditation tradition that had preceded this was largely displaced by the Thammayut forest tradition, which developed text-compatible practices and were dismissive of practice within the Mahanikay.[40] Chulalongkorn was interested in supporting this development because this remote area was considered both resistant to Bangkok control and vulnerable to French annexation. Kamala Tiyavanich in her study of the wandering forest monks in the early twentieth century paints a picture of a divided Sangha in which power lay in the hands of the Bangkok-based Thammayut monks while rural, non-administrative meditation monks, even those within the Thammayut Nikāya by this time, struggled to maintain their religious pursuits.[41]

Revolt, Resistance, and Textual Interest in *Borān Kammaṭṭhāna*

This is not the complete picture, however, as some urban Thammayut monks took at least a textual interest in *borān* practices, and their efforts would be influential in securing some of the evidence for the practice that has survived to this day, discussed in chapter 3.

The senior Thammayut meditation monk Jan Sirijantho, more popularly known as Ajan Upāli/Ubali (also transcribed as Ubaalii), was a leading administrator and text-based scholar of the Thammayut reform, but also a supporter of the forest meditation monks of the northeast where his popularity remains visible to this day. As Jim Taylor explains,

> He was seemingly caught in the middle between 'theory' and 'practice', and because of his continuing concern for improving education (Pali and Thai studies) and related administrative matters pertaining to the promotion of the Thammayut, he was closer to the centre than the periphery. Nevertheless because of his confidence in Man [Man Bhūridatto, the most famous northern Thai forest monk (1870–1949)] and the latter's respect for

> Ubaalii [Jan] (shared also by Man's early teacher Ajaan Sao Kantasiilo [1859–1941]), he was seen as the senior patron and father figure of the northeastern forest tradition. Importantly, Ubaalii had helped Man and his wandering pupils gain normative credence and acceptability by many *sangha* administrators.[42]

Jan (Ubali) was born into a farming family in the region of Ubonratchathani (Ubon), relatively close to the Lao and Cambodian borders, one of the main areas targeted by the Thammayut under the centralization policy. He was promoted on the basis of his scholarly, teaching, and organizational ability. In 1888 he was the first to establish the Thammayut in Laos, although his criticism of a popular Lao monk for drunkenness combined with the French expansion in the region from 1893 onward minimized Thammayut influence there.

From the 1890s onward Jan made repeated journeys between the northeast and Bangkok, where he became abbot of the influential temple Wat Baromnivat, which had been set up by Mongkut as a forest-dwelling (*āraññavāsī*) counterpart to Wat Bovornnivet.[43] He brought with him promising young monks from Ubon to study in Bangkok. Throughout his life he felt torn between his administrative and educational roles and a hankering to pursue meditation, as seen in his resignation in 1899 from a senior, prestigious administrative role. He also showed a readiness to flout authority.

In 1915 Jan published an anti-war pamphlet *Thammavitjayanusat* "Instruction on the Conquest through Dhamma." This was seen as an attack on the decision by King Vajiravudh, Chulalongkorn's son and successor as Rāma VI, to take Siam into World War I in an alliance with the British and French. This alliance was successful in its aim of securing Siam's ongoing sovereignty, but the modernization Vajiravudh also introduced into the Thai military, reflecting his military training and education in England, sparked resentment among the Thai military establishment. The abortive Palace Revolt of 1912 in response to militarism and Eurocentrism had left

Vajiravudh sensitive to the need to stifle dissent. In response to his publication of *Thammavitjayanusat*, Vajiravudh placed Jan under house arrest in his monastery, with the terms of his confinement stipulated by Wachirayan, now supreme patriarch. Jan appears to have been confident of his position, however. Taylor reports, "One informant mentioned that whilst under 'monastery arrest,' Ubaalii [Jan] hung a bag of potatoes or yams (*man*) outside his room . . . The word *man* can also imply determination and impenitence."[44]

It is in the figure of Jan that rank, scholarship, an interest in meditation, a sense of entitlement to criticize, and access to northeastern materials combined to preserve for us the texts that reveal much about the history of *borān kammaṭṭhāna* in Southeast Asia. It is the texts that Jan collected that indicate the earlier practice of *borān kammaṭṭhāna* by the highest-ranking monks of Ayutthaya and at courts of the northeast such as Vientiane.[45] Between 1906 and the early 1920s Jan put together a collection of manuscripts, including some from Wat Sirijannimit (Wat Khao Phra Ngam) in Lopburi, that formed the basis for one of the most important publications on the subject, though it was not he who published it. Jan's manuscript-collecting activities are more obviously subversive when considered in the light of the policy enacted from the 1890s to 1910s, designed to destroy history, permanently undermine local loyalties, and enhance dependency on the central state.

By this point *borān kammaṭṭhāna* had already been substantially undermined by the Pali text-based reform so it is in the publications from the early twentieth century, made possible by Jan's collection, that the method starts receiving the description "*borān*," "old," "former," "traditional."[46] It is unclear whether Jan's interest in non-reform meditation texts was entirely a reflection of his meditative interests or also an expression of his distaste for the increasingly modernist agenda of the government and Sangha hierarchy. It is also unclear whether his activity in this area was, like his anti-militarism, frowned upon. After only a few months he was released from his confinement, and he went on to have renewed good relations with the king.[47]

Jan's influence on *borān kammaṭṭhāna* continued in two directions. First, his work on the collecting of manuscripts and the editing of relevant meditation materials was handed over to one of his meditation students, the Thammayut monk Jai Yasothararat of Wat Baromnivat. Yasothararat was tasked with this work by Jan's successor as abbot, Tisso Uan (Phra Phrommuni, abbot 1932–1942), and by the vice-abbot Piyatharo Rang (Phra Yan Rakkhit) at Wat Baromnivat.[48] In 1936 Yasothararat published a collection of these manuscripts. The manuscript materials he drew on also included some held in Wat Ratchasittharam, the former seat of supreme patriarch Suk Kaitheun, who had brought the tradition from Ayutthaya. It was this tradition that Mongkut had rejected as a young monk.

Second, Jan's disciples had constructive interactions concerning *borān kammaṭṭhāna* techniques with Candasaro Sot (Sot Janthasaro), a Mahanikay meditation monk who was, according to those who follow in his lineage today, also targeted by the government in the late 1910s and 1920s.[49] His followers report that he was publicly accused of exaggerating his meditation experience and of promulgating teachings that deviated from Theravada Buddhism.[50] The former is a particularly serious accusation in that it could be taken to be in breach of the fourth of the *pārājika* rules, contravention of which can lead to permanent expulsion from the Sangha. Sot had studied at a number of meditation temples, including Wat Ratchasittharam, where the *borān* method of Suk Kaitheun was still being taught. In 1917, he became abbot at Wat Paknam where he taught an accessible version of the practice, simplified for beginners. In the 1950s his students included foreign monks such as Terence Magness and Kapilavaḍḍho (Richard Randall), to whom we shall return. Sot's methods were also later promoted by other temples, including those in the Dhammakaya movement. As we shall see in the next chapter, Jan's influence thus not only preserved crucial evidence for *boran kammaṭṭhāna*, it also helped ensure its ongoing teaching in forms that have lasted to this day.

The Influence of Reform in Siam on Cambodia

Siam's dominance in the region meant that the patterns of reform there were reflected in Laos and Cambodia, shaping Buddhism on the east of the later Cold War divide as well. Until the end of the nineteenth century, the courts of Laos and Cambodia were heavily influenced by developments in Siam, with both monks and members of the royalty being trained there. Siam ceded some territory to France when the latter, at the end of the nineteenth century, created French Indochina by merging its territories in Cochinchina, Annam, Tonkin, Laos, and Cambodia. Both Thai and French influence led to a reform branch within Cambodia's Mahanikay, to which the French lent support as a way of extending their worldview and in rivalry with the Thai modernizing influence borne by the Thammayut.

Before the arrival of the French, King Aung Duang (r. 1841–1860) of Cambodia, placed on the throne by Thailand, accepted those of Siam's emerging reform policies that related to Buddhism. This can be seen in his request to King Mongkut in 1854 for a complete copy of the Pali canon, the *tipiṭaka*.[51] This was the *tipiṭaka* in the restricted sense familiar to Western Buddhist studies. Until and even after that point the term *tipiṭaka* was used in Cambodia in an inclusive sense to refer to Buddhist and related texts in general, most of which were in the vernacular.[52] Such traditional literature was associated with the symbolic and narrative repertoire of *borān kammaṭṭhāna* and related ritual practices alongside traditional astrology and cosmology. The broader repertoire had previously been given far more weight than the texts of the Pali canon, which were relatively rare in monastic libraries. However, over the next century, reform emphasizing the authority of the Pali canon grew in strength, associated as it came to be with both Thai and French-derived power at court. It was also an important feature of the response of a younger generation of Cambodian monks to modernization and a disillusionment with what they regarded as the corruption of the older generations of monks.[53]

In 1855, the year following Aung Duang's request for the canon, a branch of the Thammayut Nikāya was established at Aung Duang's capital in Udong. Its abbot was Mahā Pan (1824–1894), a Cambodian who had been based at Wat Bovornnivet under Mongkut. When the French built Phnom Penh as the capital for Aung Duang's son, King Norodom (r.1860–1904), who had himself spent time as a monk ordained by Mongkut, Norodom's Buddhist affiliation was reflected by the allocation of a temple in a central location close to the royal palace to the Thammayut Nikāya. The temple was renamed Wat Botum and has been the Thammayut headquarters in Cambodia ever since. In 1880 Norodom ordered the translation of the Pali canon into Khmer. He also reorganized the Sangha on the model of the Thai restructuring, but, while doing so, he gave precedence to the supreme patriarch of the Mahanikay, Samdech Tieng, rather than to Samdech Pan of the Thammayut Nikāya. Tieng (1823–1913), a Khmer who had studied as a monk in Bangkok since the age of twelve, had been a favorite of King Rāma III, who, it will be remembered, specifically promoted Mahanikay monks in order to thwart the ambitions of his younger half-brother Mongkut. Norodom's support of Tieng reflected his desire at this stage for a degree of autonomy from Mongkut, which may also have influenced his decision to sign a new treaty with the French making Cambodia a French protectorate.[54]

Reform and Centralization within the Cambodian Mahanikay

Tieng's base in the new capital of Phnom Penh was at Wat Uṇṇalom, which remains the headquarters of the Mahanikay supreme patriarch of Cambodia to this day. Tieng was fluent in Thai, Sanskrit, and Pali and conversant with those sciences important to Mongkut and Chulalongkorn: mathematics and astronomy. Like his Thammayut counterpart, Tieng was a modernist. Norodom placed his support unambiguously behind the modernists by issuing a royal ordinance in 1881. It commanded that "all Mahanikay monks should follow the precepts and methods established and observed by Samdech Tieng."[55] This left the traditionalists in the Mahanikay, initially the majority within the majority, without institutional support or representation either at court or within the Sangha hierarchy.

The political motivation influencing both the Cambodian royal family and the French colonial powers to promote extensive reform throughout the country was, as with Siam, an issue of military and economic control. The reforms and centralization were undertaken to reduce the power of the quasi-independent and often wealthy monasteries throughout the country and to ensure that new abbots were appointed with the approval of the supreme patriarchs and the relevant government ministry. This undermined the independence of abbots, and as traditionalists died they were replaced with modernists approved by the government and Sangha hierarchies. Measures designed to contain the modernists gave way to a crescendo of measures designed to undermine traditional monasteries. These culminated in the royal ordinance of December 1920, which, with reference to the Vinaya Piṭaka and the Pali canon, banned much economic activity, as well as many traditional practices. Traditional meditation and related healing practices are explicitly mentioned.

Monks were forbidden

> from making out that they had acquired attainments such as *Jhāna* [higher states of meditative absorption], *Vimokkha* [liberation], *Samādhi* [meditative concentration], *Sampat* [attainments], *Magga* [the four paths of supramundane achievements that culminate in arhatship], *Phala* [the four fruits of supramundane achievements that culminate in arhatship]; from practicing the meditation called "Angkuy Thor" to treat the sick; from diagnosing the outcome of someone's illness to them (i.e., their recovery or death); from making claims concerning the rebirth of a deceased person, that s/he is reborn at such and such a place; from making out that

they are a person of attainments and therefore powerful, strong, et cetera.

from playing games connected with money . . .

from asking for the hand in marriage of a young woman in order to wed her on disrobing

from engaging in agriculture, business, diverse employments such as wood-carver, carpenter, draughtsman, mason, jeweler, . . .

from engaging in the occupations of medicine, astrology, sorcery, tattooist, from doing tattoos, from creating numerological signs, from studying or teaching magical formulae, in a word, the whole range of Dérachchan Vichéa [*tiracchāna-vijjā*, lower/"animal" sciences]. From studying or teaching sword-fighting, boxing, wrestling, from taking medicines that supposedly render one invulnerable or from giving such medicine to another to take.

From animal husbandry, from owning carriages, carts and canoes, from keeping in the temple any kind of musical instruments except for the drums, gongs and bells required for religious services, from engaging in an entire range of games (chess, boat-racing, ball, kite-flying, etc.)

From carrying a load on the shoulders, or a double load attached to the ends of a pole, when crossing an inhabited place or a market; from going to a fish market, a meat market or alcohol stall . . .

From making use of any scents except in the case of an illness where its use is necessary; from wearing wooden clogs, slippers or embroidered slippers; from carrying a mat or a stick; from using ornaments or money; from wearing the hair long, from sporting a moustache, beard, or nails longer than permitted in the Vinaya; from dressing badly or in the manner of a layperson.[56]

This extraordinary list of prohibitions looks quite reasonable from the reformist perspective, and from that of the Western expectations of the conduct of Buddhist monks that had developed in the second half of the preceding century. However, the list actually proscribes the normal monastic conduct that had for centuries allowed monasteries to function at the heart of the village agricultural system, as centers of education and commerce. The decree also forbids many of the practices that go hand in hand with *borān kammaṭṭhāna* and those that share *borān kammaṭṭhāna* motifs, technologies, and delivery methods, such as medicine, astrology, prognostication, tattooing, and protective devices. Some of these activities were the main sources of income for *borān kammaṭṭhāna* experts as individuals as well as for institutions such as monasteries. The prohibition on medicine for the sake of healing, one of the main applications of *borān kammaṭṭhāna*, coincided with the introduction of Western medicine to the region, and came on the eve of traditional medicine being banned in Siam.

Also significant is the prohibition on claiming to have spiritual attainments. This prohibition might seem straightforward in that it is reminiscent of the monastic fourth *pārājika* offense, which prohibits *falsely* claiming supramundane powers, for transgression of which one can be expelled from the Sangha. However, in this context, the motivation was presumably to undermine rival sources of power—no monk was allowed to claim any kind of spiritual achievement, *even if true*, and thereby have any status beyond being a religious functionary. The terms employed for the prohibited claims are, as previously observed, remarkable for their orthodoxy—all the attainments listed are to be found in the *Visuddhimagga* and Abhidhamma accounts of the spiritual path, the very sources that were also authoritative for reform Buddhists. Although the reformists charged traditional practitioners and traditional meditation with being corrupt and unorthodox, the evidence signals that they could recognize that concepts used within *borān kammaṭṭhāna* were consistent with normative Theravada.

As the century progressed modernist monks within the Mahanikay further developed reformist tendencies collaborating to varying degrees with French language, education, and legal policies. The people who best exemplify the final stage of the sidelining of the old traditions are Ven. Chuon Nath (1883–1969), Ven. Huot Tath (1891–1975), and Ven. Oum Sour (1881–1939). They were friends within the reform wing of the Mahanikay based at Wat Uṇṇalom, who, while progressing smoothly through their academic studies, took on board the reform Thai and Western critical approach to the study of Buddhism and languages. Chuon Nath and Huot Tath were influenced by developments in Thai monastic education that emphasized meaning and interpretation of the canonical text. They would later study under Louis Finot at the École française d'Extrême-Orient in Hanoi. Their studies affected their stance in relation to traditional Buddhism. While still at Wat Uṇṇalom, before their period in Hanoi, the three caused a stir by claiming that the traditional texts were corruptions rather than the genuine word of the Buddha and set up a group to study canonical and commentarial Vinaya texts in secret.[57] This was the background to the first printing of a Buddhist text from within the Cambodian Mahanikay in 1920, discussed in chapter 3. The supreme patriarch of the time, Dhammalikhit Ouk, sought to defrock the group of three, all of whose names appeared on the book. The three young monks, convinced that they were reviving and protecting Buddhism, were scornful of the supreme patriarch's response. For while the supreme patriarch also saw himself as protecting the tradition, the young monks little understood this position and thought the old monks ignorant and jealous. When the young monks appealed to the royal family, King Sisowath and his son, the future King Monivong, took the reformists' side. Through the support of Finot the careers of Chuon Nath and Huot Tath were then secured, and both went on to become the supreme patriarch in Cambodia, in 1948–1969 and 1969–1975 respectively.[58]

Traditional Buddhism and with it *borān kammaṭṭhāna* continued in rural areas that were beyond the everyday influence of

Phnom Penh, Thailand, and France, particularly in areas to which Western medicine had not spread. Its protective practices were taken up by soldiers of all ranks right up to the 1970s.[59] However, it had by this time been actively discouraged by the Sangha hierarchy of both the Thammayut and the Mahanikay. As supreme patriarch, Chuon Nath continued to issue prohibitions against *borān* practices and to purify traditional rites and rituals from what were now seen as non-Buddhist accretions. The reformist agenda in which Buddhism was understood as a universal religion in an essentialized form, and in tune with the European view of Buddhism, was privileged at the hierarchical center. Chuon Nath's position takes our story of *borān kammaṭṭhāna* in Cambodia, where it is suppressed at the center, but continues at the margins, up to the period of the Marxist revolution under Pol Pot. In Laos, meanwhile, it remained the centrally authorized practice as late as 1974. We shall return to this subject in the next chapter, when looking at meditation in twentieth-century revivals.

Shifting Power and Partial Survival in Thailand

Neither traditional medicine nor traditional meditation would ever recover from the political and religio-political measures that undermined and suppressed them between the first half of the nineteenth and first half of the twentieth century. However, in Thailand the pro-democracy coup of 1932 would at least interrupt those measures enough to allow for some evidence of the Buddhist meditation dominant before this period to be published. After the coup, the power of the palace and the concomitant dominance of the Thammayut hierarchy rapidly diminished. For a while King Prajadhipok (Rāma VII) (r. 1925–1935) had to live in exile, with the result that his two sons, Ananda (Rāma VIII) (r. 1935–1946) and the future King Bhumibol (Rāma IX) (r. 1946–2016), grew up in Switzerland. In 1938, for the first time in a century, a Mahanikay monk was promoted to the position of supreme patriarch, and four years later in 1942 the pro-democratic Sangha Act sought to redress the balance of power between the two *nikāya*.[60] With this change of affairs came three developments: traditional medicine was re-allowed and taught by traditional doctors in local areas (although, unlike Western medicine, it was still not taught at universities);[61] the imperiled *borān kammaṭṭhāna* teaching survived at least among some Mahanikay monks, such as Candasaro Sot; and Thammayut meditation monks were granted more support by monks in the Thammayut administration.

It may be the easing of controls and suppression in relation to meditation as well as monastic and textual variety that provided the context for the work on *borān kammaṭṭhāna* manuscripts facilitated by Jan (above), to come to fruition. When Yasothararat published Jan's collection of old meditation manuals in 1936, he took advantage of the assistance of a former Mahanikay monk working on related materials, Luangvisan Darunnakon, who had also published a collection of *borān kammaṭṭhāna* manuscripts the year before. Some of the manuscripts he used are available today in the meditation section at Wat Ratchasittharam. Darunnakon was a student of Chum (Phra Sangwaranuwonthera), the abbot and meditation master at Wat Ratchasittharam who continued the teaching lineage of Somdet Suk Kaitheun, the supreme patriarch who had brought the *borān kammaṭṭhāna* tradition from Ayutthaya. Darunnakon helped Yasothararat by providing, among other things, the distinctive meditation diagrams that help the practitioner understand the relative positioning of *nimitta* in the body, diagrams also found within the meditation manuscripts of the mid-eighteenth century used by Siyam Nikāya monks in Sri Lanka.[62]

Legacy

Although the 1932 coup interrupted the Thammayut dominance of Sangha affairs in Siam, it was not the end of the story of marginalization for *borān kammaṭṭhāna* and meditation monks. First, the rhetoric and understanding of orthodoxy, reform, and *pariyatti* over *paṭipatti* had established a firmly embedded culture whereby control and intervention in the practices of monks by the Sangha hierarchy and/or the state were accepted. This was readily used to stifle anything perceived as dissent or an independent power base. Second, the understandings of orthodoxy more commonly associated with the Thammayut had also infiltrated and now permeated the Mahanikay hierarchy.[63] Third, meditation became part of a claim to orthodoxy for monks seeking to exert their influence, and so we see the promotion of particular forms of meditation as a mark of political identity, when we look to the choices made in revivals of meditation in the twentieth century in the next chapter.

Conclusion

In this chapter we saw how *borān kammaṭṭhāna* was at the center of the first Theravada Buddhist revival of the modern period: the eighteenth-century revival of the ordination lineage in Sri Lanka from Ayutthaya, the then capital of Siam. Ayutthaya was also the source of a further dispersal of *borān kammaṭṭhāna* lineages to Thonburi and Bangkok through the court and Sangha elite. The subsequent disappearance of *borān kammaṭṭhāna* from the center was not only in response to change in hegemonic sciences, such as the rise of Western medicine, outlined in the previous chapter. It also reflected political changes, such as the Burmese sack of Ayutthaya, the modernization and centralization policies of the Chakri dynasty, the creation of the modern nation state of Thailand and its dominance in the region, the suppression of the culture of the northeast of Thailand—a process that would later be continued during the Cold War—and even the education of Thai royalty abroad.

Within this context, Buddhism was a tool in political rivalries as well as an object of protection and revival. This changed the nature of Buddhism. In Thailand, the focus on textual learning over practice, on canon over commentary, on the canonical texts of the Sutta Piṭaka and *Visuddhimagga* rather than Abhidhamma, and on exam-success and administration in authorizing practice and monastic status all conspired to sideline regional practice. This particularly affected practice that could not easily be recognized in the canonical Sutta and Vinaya texts. These reforms also impacted Cambodian Buddhism, with Thailand and France both seeking to influence the country by patronizing reform-oriented Buddhist lineages.

A change in the political context in the 1930s inspired a number of publications in Thailand that, against this backdrop of sidelining and disappearance, preserved crucial information about the long history of *borān kammaṭṭhāna* in the region, including at the highest levels of the monastic hierarchy. In the next chapter, we shall turn our attention to reforms from the late nineteenth century onward to find out how these changes influenced the selection of other meditations then, and why *borān kammaṭṭhāna* continued to be deselected. We shall observe the effect of Marxist revolutions on the remaining strongholds of *borān kammaṭṭhāna*, and what happened to those lineages that did survive into the late twentieth and early twenty-first century.

7
Meditation in Modern Revivals

> I kept these manuscripts tucked inside the rafters of the roof of my house because I realized that the soldiers could destroy them. I had learned that many manuscripts had been destroyed in different pagodas, and so I needed to keep them safe at the top of my roof. The destruction of manuscripts during the war, we believe that it had been predicted in Buddhist prophecies. So we cannot really say why soldiers would destroy them.
>
> —Achar Oun, *borān* practitioner, Cambodia 2012

In the previous chapter we saw how changes in Thailand (Siam) from the end of the eighteenth century to the early twentieth century ushered in periods of change, reform, and modernization, as well as the use of the Buddhist Sangha in the process of centralizing political control. These changes led to the marginalization, loss, and even active suppression of *borān kammaṭṭhāna*. In this chapter, we will look at what happened in subsequent periods of revival. While *borān kammaṭṭhāna* had been at the center of the mid-eighteenth-century Buddhist revival of Sri Lanka, how did it fare in the twentieth century?

Caste Restrictions and Monastic Lineages in Sri Lanka

Sri Lanka now has three monastic lineages, *nikāya*, with multiple subdivisions. The lineage that promoted *borān kammaṭṭhāna*, introduced from Ayutthaya in the mid-eighteenth century, is the earliest and became known as the "lineage from Siam," the Siyam Nikāya, to differentiate it from two later lineages introduced from Burma from the beginning of the nineteenth century. Initially the Siyam Nikāya embodied the spirit of radical reform, advocating a puritanical monasticism, in-depth canonical and commentarial study, scholarship, and preaching. It was also very much associated with royalty, aristocracy, and the center of court power in upcountry Kandy, serving as it did to bolster the power of the Kandyan kingdom even in the coastal areas officially within the territory of European colonial powers. It was this association that came to define it throughout its subsequent history.[1]

Although two of the pupils of Saraṇaṃkara, the leading light of the revival, were monks from other castes, ordination came to be restricted exclusively to the Goyigama caste, usually reckoned as the highest caste among the Sinhalese.[2] Hierarchical rank within the monastic order paralleled the feudal structure of temporal roles. Monastic lands were cultivated by Goyigama tenants who provided the monastery, which often also managed the large reservoirs and irrigation systems, with a share of the crop. Other castes had specific tasks in providing the monastery with its material, social, and festival requirements. The high status of abbots was indicated by their traveling in palanquins borne by the Paduvō caste, and by the annual presentation to them of gifts and betel leaves by those who rendered these services to them.[3] While the Siyam Nikāya began as a revivalist movement, its high-ranking monks ceased to be interested in reform.

The occupation of the coastal regions of Sri Lanka by successive European colonial powers had eroded the position of the Sangha there, and the consequent changes in economic and social structures created significant differences between the colonized regions and the still-independent interior. Lowland monks still received their titles and recognition from the Kandyan king in the Dutch and early British periods, and higher ordination was received in the royal ordination festival in Kandy, but the lowland monasteries did not have the advantage of receiving service and goods from feudal temple lands traditionally granted by the king. So while monks in the Kandyan kingdom acted as landlords, with a degree of autonomy, lowland monks depended on the strength of their relationship with their lay donors and needed to be responsive to their needs and concerns. Since ordination here brought relatively little material advantage or status, young men of the Goyigama caste were instead drawn toward government administration. This left a need for monks that could be fulfilled by other castes, if only higher ordination were permitted them.

A factor in the subsequent development of a new *nikāya* to fill this gap was the economic reliance of consecutive colonial powers on the lucrative cinnamon trade. The Salāgama caste, which included the cinnamon producers, grew relatively wealthy and powerful, and began to aspire to the same privileges for their monks as those allowed to monks of the Goyigama caste. While one could perform rituals and serve laypeople with only novice ordination, it was only as a fully ordained monk (*bhikkhu*) that one could pursue title, privileges, and a career through the monastic ranks: a novice of forty years' standing is hierarchically junior to a monk fully ordained only a single year. To become a novice one only needed a *bhikkhu*, a fully ordained monk, to give one the lower ordination, but becoming a *bhikkhu* required a formal ecclesiastical act conducted by at least five other *bhikkhu* in a formally consecrated area, called a *sīmā*. It often also required the permission of temporal authorities. The court and Sangha hierarchy at Kandy had the monopoly on higher ordination on the island and declined requests from members of the Salāgama caste to lift the caste restriction. The Salāgama and others turned elsewhere: to textual authority, and to the king and supreme patriarch of Burma.

They went to Amarapura, the then capital of Burma, now in greater Mandalay.

Burma as the Source of New Monastic Lineages

In Burma, too, this was a time of change and reform. The final dynasty of independent Burma before the British completed their annexation was the Konbaung (1752–1885). In the eighteenth century they oversaw a reform of the Sangha, appointing an ecclesiastical body known as the Thudhamma Council to govern the Buddhist Sangha of the entire kingdom, and granting it far-reaching powers.[4] The Thudhamma reform emphasized textual learning and correct monastic conduct in accordance with the Pali canon as interpreted through the commentaries; this required novices and monks to sit annual Vinaya examinations. From 1783 the Council could also prevent monks from making their living through traditional monastic occupations such as astrology and medicine, which were now deemed inappropriate.[5] The new Amarapura Nikāya of Sri Lanka received their ordinations and instruction under the head of the Thudhamma reform, the first Maung Taung Sayadaw Saṅgharāja Ñāṇa, and so it was these elements of reform—textual scholarship and Vinaya practice—that influenced the type of reform Buddhism established in Sri Lanka. The Amarapura Nikāya was founded in stages from 1803 onward as members of different caste groups regarded as unfit for ordination by the Siyam Nikāya sought ordination in Amarapura. Everyone knew that caste restriction had no authority in the Pali canon or commentaries, and it was this issue that allowed the Amarapura monks to challenge the Siyam Nikāya monks' authority. It made their focus on textual knowledge particularly apposite.

To conduct their own ordinations in Sri Lanka independently of the Siyam Nikāya, the Amarapura Nikāya needed their own sacred ordination enclosure, *sīmā*, independently of the one in Kandy to which they had previously been denied access. To deflect any possible accusation that their *sīmā* was invalid, an accusation that could undermine the validity of the ordination that took place within it, the monks who returned to Sri Lanka from Amarapura needed to establish their *sīmā* with uncontested legal accuracy. This required in-depth commentarial knowledge, the very area of Thudhamma expertise. The Amarapura succeeded in establishing their new *sīmā* at Balapiṭiya using a specific type known as an *udakukkhepa* "splashing of water" *sīmā*. Choosing this type cleverly allowed the monks concerned to establish a *sīmā* independently without the permission or cooperation either of other monks in the area or of the "king," or, in the absence of a king, the state authorities, cooperation they would have needed had they wanted to consecrate a *sīmā* on land.[6]

For the Amarapura monks, then, textual knowledge and correct Vinaya application were what made for authority, reform, and revival. The Amarapura Nikāya was described to Europeans in the middle of the century as seeking "to bring back the doctrines of Buddhism to their pristine purity, by disentangling them from caste, polytheism and other corruptions to which they had been subject for ages."[7]

Meditation in the New Lineages from Burma

At the time that the first Sri Lankan Amarapura monks trained in Burma, meditation was yet to be popularized there among monks, let alone the laity. Moreover, to have undertaken meditation would have required patronage, and at least temporary withdrawal from their everyday duties, potentially disrupting their close day-to-day relationship with the lay supporters on whom they were reliant. These Sri Lankan monks were consciously breaking from the Siamese lineage in Ceylon, where *borān kammaṭṭhāna* was still practiced by some, and perhaps it was also for this reason that they did not adopt the practice. So although *borān kammaṭṭhāna* was still practiced in Siam, Laos, and Cambodia and for a time even in Sri Lanka, and although *borān kammaṭṭhāna* had been a feature of reform and revival in Sri Lanka half a century earlier, it was not part of the reform Buddhism of the early Amarapura Nikāya. One hundred and fifty years later, however, the spread of a different form of meditation to Sri Lanka, the Burmese Vipassanā that would be developed later in the nineteenth century, and popularized internationally in the 1950s, was facilitated through the connections initiated between Burma and the Amarapura monks at this time.

While meditation was not a part of the early Amarapura Nikāya, it was a part of the foundation of the next *nikāya*, the Rāmañña Nikāya, in 1864. Initially this was not intended to be a separate *nikāya*, but a fresh branch of the Amarapura Nikāya when the older branches had become tangled in contention. The reformist stance of the Amarapura Nikāya had attracted Goyigama men in both the upcountry and the low country who were disaffected by the ritualism and infighting of the Siyam Nikāya. However, the Amarapura Nikāya in the low country soon began to fracture as much as the Siyam Nikāya that these Goyigama had discarded. The low-country Goyigama who had joined the Amarapura Nikāya found themselves disillusioned once again.

The contentions that arose reflected the high value placed by both Amarapura and Siyam Nikāya hierarchies on detailed textual scholarship particularly in the realm of Vinaya (monastic discipline). The crucial issue for the Amarapura was again the *sīmā*. A debate arose over technical points concerning whether a bridge-section temporarily placed over the gap between the water *sīmā* at Balapiṭiya and the walkway to the shore, even though lifted during ecclesiastical rituals, had invalidated the *sīmā* and therefore the entire Amarapura ordination lineage. At stake were issues of control, autonomy, and caste status, as well as the status and identity of the monks already ordained there.

The monk who started the debate was Laṅkāgoḍa Dhīrānanda, a student of the monk Kapugama Dhammakkhandha. Dhammakkhandha had introduced the second Amarapura lineage in 1809, but in 1816 became the darling of Christians for disrobing and converting to Christianity.[8] Dhīrānanda took over the leadership of this second lineage, which had its own *sīmā*. When a unification of the two Amarapura lineages briefly took place it was decided that there should be, as an indication of unity, only one *sīmā*. The Balapiṭiya *sīmā*, as the first *sīmā*, was the obvious choice, but Dhīrānanda balked at the control this would give the first Amarapura lineage over his, just as the Siyam Nikāya in Kandy had previously been able to exercise authority over all monks in the island. Dhīrānanda was from one of the higher sub-castes within the Salāgama caste. He later went on to create an autonomous splinter lineage, at which point he again expressed this concern with autonomy and status by imposing a caste restriction. Just as the Siyam Nikāya had excluded non-Goyigama, so Dhīrānanda restricted ordination in his lineage to his own Salāgama sub-caste.

Meanwhile, an expert on Vinaya matters, Dhīrānanda started the *sīmā* controversy by questioning the validity of the Balapiṭiya *sīmā* once it had been enlarged to accommodate the larger number of monks who would need to attend ecclesiastical rituals after the unification. This was also the occasion on which the offending bridge was built.

Initially Dhīrānanda's complaint stirred up sufficient doubt for monks who had been ordained in the one *sīmā* to go for re-ordination in the other, but there was resistance to his view. Soon there were large-scale debates, the exchange of scholarly tracts, and the sending of competing missions to the supreme patriarch Ñeyya, the second Maung Taung Sayadaw, in Burma for a ruling, since he was an authority recognized by both sides.[9] The dispute escalated to such an extent that for decades almost all the high-ranking monks in the Amarapura Nikāya of the low country were embroiled in the controversy, repeatedly debating the point with detailed reference to commentarial literature. Even a ruling from Ñeyya was to no avail, and the debate only died with its initial protagonists.

For all parties, to interpret the Vinaya correctly was to be true to the original teaching of the Buddha, but as we can see, the issue of *what* was correct only arose because of rivalry for power and control. The Goyigama monks who had joined the Amarapura Nikāya had, by doing so, already indicated their willingness to subordinate themselves to monks of lower castes. Caste hierarchy was not therefore of primary importance to them. Among the disaffected was Ambagahavattē Saraṇaṃkara, who as a young monk had been ordained in the Siyam Nikāya and observed the previous controversy, in 1844–1845, which had been over a different matter, the astrological calculations that influenced the timing of a particular ritual. When he then joined the Amarapura in 1857 he walked right into the *sīmā* debate. So in 1860 he set off with four other ex-Siyam Amarapura companions in search of direct contact with the Burmese supreme patriarch, Ñeyya. In Burma, some took higher ordination, while some had their previous ordination confirmed through a special strengthening ritual. By going to the source of the Amarapura lineage, they circumvented the strife over *sīmās* that had arisen within the Sri Lankan branch after its departure from Burma. More monks followed them.

The returnees were still in the same ordination lineage as other Amarapura monks but their identity as a separate *nikāya*, the Rāmañña Nikāya, emerged gradually toward the end of the 1860s. These monks were deeply interested in the purity of their monastic lineage. To assure them of the validity of their ordinations, the Burmese supreme patriarch's pupil, Paññasāmi, composed for them the famous Pali chronicle of the lineage, the *Sāsanavaṃsa*. Like the reformist monks of the Siyam Nikāya a hundred years earlier, Paññasāmi was convinced of the possibility of enlightenment in the present age. He was also aware that at the time meditation was growing in popularity in the Sagaing hills a short distance from Mandalay.[10] Meditation was therefore part of reform Buddhism in Burma at this time, and some of the Sri Lankan monks gained a reputation for serious and extensive forest practice and meditation after their return. Monks from other *nikāya* interested in this aspect of Buddhism switched their allegiance to the Rāmañña Nikāya.[11]

Meditation in the Rāmañña Nikāya

To what extent the meditation practice pursued by members of the Rāmañña Nikāya was a close reflection of the practices that were emerging within Burma is not entirely clear. This was a quarter of a century before Ledi Sayadaw, associated with the popularization of Vipassanā, would retreat from Mandalay to begin his own meditation practice. However, a description of the meditation practice of one of the later generations of monks, Harumalgoḍa Sīlālaṃkāra, who lived in the early to mid-twentieth century, indicates a meditation similar in emphasis to that of Burmese Vipassanā. He is described by his biographer as practicing meditation on the eighteen *dhātu*, one of the Abhidhamma categories that form the basis of meditations designed to bring about insight, *vipassanā*.[12] It is found in the *Paññā* "Insight" section of the *Visuddhimagga* as well as in Burmese Vipassanā, discussed in chapter 2.

Early Rāmañña Nikāya monks were clearly keen to experiment, honing their Vinaya practices to regain what they felt to be the lost spirit of early Buddhism. If they also sought out different meditation teachers then *borān kammaṭṭhāna* was still available from two immediate sources. One was the Sri Lankan *borān kammaṭṭhāna* tradition that had been imported with the establishment of the Siyam Nikāya in 1756, and which would still be practiced to some extent for a few more decades. Another potential source of knowledge on *borān* practice was directly from Siam. By this point in Sri Lanka the Siyam Nikāya hierarchy had been weakened by the loss of royal backing after the British had removed the last king of Kandy in 1815 and then reneged on their promise of support to the Buddhist establishment. It was therefore to authorities in Siam (Thailand) that the Siyam Nikāya monks in Sri Lanka turned as an authority at times of dispute.[13] However, it was the increasingly powerful future king Mongkut, then still a monk, who was the primary contact. He was sought out as a source of both royal and Vinaya authority.

The new reformists in the proto-Rāmañña Nikāya, then still

part of the Amarapura Nikāya, felt that they shared an agenda with the relatively new Thammayut Nikāya, the branch of Buddhism recently created by Prince Mongkut, and their Vinaya experts also exchanged letters with him. At one point it even seemed that the Thammayut might be established in Sri Lanka.[14] One of the monks from the 1844 delegation concerning astrological calculations stayed with Mongkut until the latter's disrobing to become king in 1851. He had reordained in the Thammayut and on his return to Sri Lanka was invited to participate in performing the ordination ceremony at a new *sīmā*. This event is generally accepted as marking the start of the Rāmañña Nikāya of Sri Lanka as a lineage separate from the Amarapura Nikāya.[15] The influence of Mongkut at this point in Sri Lanka's history makes it unlikely that *borān kammaṭṭhāna* was introduced as part of the uptake of meditation within the Rāmañña Nikāya. Mongkut had already dismissed its validity.

Mid-Twentieth-Century Meditation Revival in Sri Lanka

The early monks of the Rāmañña Nikāya in Sri Lanka shared Mongkut's interest in the original teachings of Buddhism and also had access to the Vipassanā tradition emerging in Sagaing in Burma. In Sri Lanka the Rāmañña lineage continues as a minority tradition, retaining to this day its reputation for strict Vinaya observance. Its current forest lineage, while heir to activities of the nineteenth century, is however the product of a crisis in the 1950s, at which point a new forest meditation center was established and an advertisement published for suitable recruits to become its resident monks. The forest lineage was the mission of the monk Kaḍavädduvē Jinavaṃsa (1907–2003), who from the late 1940s waged a war of words against what he saw as the inadequate state of the Sri Lankan Sangha at the time.[16] His new center was founded on the basis of the clearly advertised premise that enlightenment is possible in this life. In setting it up, Jinavaṃsa enlisted the help of Mātara Ñāṇārāma, a monk who had withdrawn to develop his own meditation practice after failing to reinvoke the forest tradition at a previous mission. Jinavaṃsa's fraught relationship with the Sangha authorities of the time and the lack of a strong, existing meditation lineage on which he and Ñāṇārāma felt they could rely is reflected in their turn to a new origin narrative for their center rather than to a living meditation tradition:

> On the advice of a hunter, they discovered a few miles from Tissamahārāma, the site of an ancient temple . . . This temple, to the immense satisfaction of all concerned, was associated with an ancient saint, Dhammadinna, a noted meditation teacher and miracle worker.[17]

Tissamahārāma is a sacred site associated with the conversion of the island to Buddhism by the monk Mahinda, the son of the Indian emperor Ashoka, in the third century B.C.E. It is believed to have been visited by the Buddha himself, who meditated there in the company of five hundred enlightened disciples. The new meditation center was thereby authorized with direct reference to a site of incomparable importance in Sri Lankan history and to an ancient, long-dead meditation master, as well as indirect reference to the Buddha himself practicing meditation on the island.

By the time this new forest meditation center was studied by anthropologist Michael Carrithers in the 1970s, Mātara Ñāṇārāma had had many years of developing his own meditation practice on the basis of his textual explorations and experimentation. He had also tried out the Burmese Vipassanā that was imported in the 1950s. Buddhaghosa's *Visuddhimagga* was important in his studies, but he was critical of gaps in it. In creating his system on a mainly textual basis, Ñāṇārāma was clear that there was no living tradition, even though theoretically he was in a teaching lineage from one of the earlier meditation monks. He believed that Buddhism had ossified and that forest meditation practitioners had, by virtue of their choosing to live remotely, become not only hard to access but scarce, too, with the result that their knowledge had been lost:

> He quotes from a letter written by the great scholar-monk Polvattē Buddhadatta: "We receive no help from history of written sources to show that a meditation tradition came [to us] unbroken." The chief reason for this break in the tradition was nearly four centuries of internal dissension and external colonisation that preceded the founding of the Siyam Nikāya in 1753. Meditation flourished briefly under monks from Thailand then, but their methods, like the older ones, were written down in books which were then forgotten by the village monks. His first task, therefore, was to marshal those written methods available to him.[18]

The assessment by Mātara Ñāṇārāma and, following him, Michael Carrithers of the works from the 1756 Siyam Nikāya's *borān kammaṭṭhāna* lineage is intriguing. We explored their response in chapter 1 but return to it here in order to understand why these works were not influential in the revival of the twentieth century. In response to a work entitled the *Amṛtākara Varṇanāva* (Sinhala; the equivalent of the Pali *Amatākaravaṇṇanā*), they claim it was

> descended from Thai monks of the eighteenth century, and . . . preserved in Kandy by the Bambaragala line of monks . . . It gave a fairly circumstantial account of meditation, and went into some detail about mindfulness of breathing. Ñāṇārāma found this very useful, if not conclusive. And indeed one may say generally of these texts that they can be quite effectively compared and corrected by referring to the canon and commentaries.[19]

Ñāṇārāma assesses *The Yogāvacara's Manual*, published by Rhys Davids in 1896 on the basis of the copy of the Bambaragala manuscript given to him by Anagarika Dharmapala and translated as *The Manual of a Mystic*, differently: "It is not a method of meditation." Carrithers expands on this:

> This method [also] arrived from Thailand in the eighteenth century, and its author(s) succumbed to the fascination of the meditative absorptions (*jhāna*), which are so extensively treated with the *kasiṇa* meditations. I suspect that here we have an example of an imaginative but not very insightful attempt to revive meditation from the texts, for the texts seem to have been treated as repositories of magical lore.

Carrithers here seems to have picked up on the extensive use of *nimitta* discussed earlier, but not on its links with Abhidhamma categories of reality. He adds a note about similarities he observes between this text and a work published in Thailand:

> There is a Thai book on meditation which does much the same for the analytic categories so important to the *Visuddhimagga*. This is what happens when the sense of such categories is lost. See *Sammā-Samādhi*, presented by T. Magness (Bangkok n.d.).[20]

These statements are significant for a number of reasons. The dismissive comments that *The Yogāvacara's Manual* is about "magical lore," the product of imagination without insight, and the suggestion that a similar Thai text has lost the sense of the true analytical meaning of the categories of the *Visuddhimagga* are surprisingly reminiscent of the kind of comments seen in mid-to-late nineteenth-century European writings on Buddhism. Another curiosity is that *The Yogāvacara's Manual* is, like the *Amatākaravaṇṇanā*, from the Bambaragala tradition. They are in fact closely related. It is hard to see how the one is accepted as "conclusive" but the other an "imaginative but not insightful attempt." Ratnajoti and Ratnapāla published both texts together in 1963. Although they published the *Amatākaravaṇṇanā* under a different name, *Vimuttimagga-uddāna*, I have established the identity through comparison with manuscript versions. They make the same comparative assessment of the two texts as Ñāṇārāma. The material, presumably the somatic aspects and use of *nimitta*, obviously confounded them, but it remains unclear what aspects Ñāṇārāma found conclusive and useful. Finally, the similarity observed by Carrithers between *The Yogāvacara's Manual* and the Thai text translated by T. Magness in 1961 is not coincidental: they, too, are related, as we shall see below.

For the forest monks of the Rāmañña Nikāya in the 1970s, we can see that although Ñāṇārāma claimed to have taken some inspiration from one of the *borān kammaṭṭhāna* texts brought to Sri Lanka two centuries earlier, his studies were based on texts rather than part of a living master-pupil lineage. He believed that no genuine living tradition of meditation had survived. Initially, when Vipassanā was introduced from Burma in the mid-twentieth century as a practice for both monks and for laypeople as part of their everyday lives, it was through the Burmese lineages. The first head of the highly successful Kanduboda retreat center was a Sri Lankan member of the Amarapura Nikāya.[21] Since the 1950s, meditation in Sri Lanka has been dominated by Burmese Vipassanā and other practices revived on the basis of canonical and commentarial textual sources.

The Cold War Period in Cambodia and Laos

While revivals of meditation inspired by texts such as the *Visuddhimagga* and by the introduction of Burmese Vipassanā began to thrive in Sri Lanka in the decades after independence, a different situation was unfolding in mainland Southeast Asia. As we have seen, in 1974 the Sangha authorities in Laos published a text that confirms that *borān kammaṭṭhāna* was still seen as a valid form of meditation there, while in Cambodia, those at the highest levels of the Sangha were the modernizers who had suppressed *borān* practice, leading to it become primarily a rural practice of the periphery.

This was how things stood at the brink of the civil war that would usher in the Pol Pot, Khmer Rouge, or Democratic Kampuchea period. Although many of the leaders of Cambodian communism had Buddhist backgrounds and had been former monks, and Buddhism had been used to recruit people in rural areas to the communist cause, after the communist victory Buddhism and traditional religion were dismantled. Villagers were threatened with execution if they fed monks. Monks were put on meager rations and had to be economically self-supporting. Leading monks, especially any that offered any criticism or resistance, were executed. Chuon Nath had died in 1969 at the age of eighty-six. Huot Tath, the last survivor of the three modernizers of the 1920s, now supreme patriarch, was executed in 1975 for issuing a call for a cease-fire during a radio broadcast. Estimated to number 65,000 before the Pol Pot period, by the time of the traditional three months' rains retreat that same year those monks who had not managed to flee the country had disrobed, died, or been killed, and most monasteries had been closed. The mass relocations of people had also disrupted other traditional religious practices such as the worship of guardian spirits and ancestors, dislocated as people were from the place of the spirits and ancestors connected to them.[22] It is estimated that over 90% of Cambodia's literary heritage was also destroyed. Practitioners, practice, and the material basis of the practice were gone.

For some Cambodians on the traditionalist side of the *borān* (traditional)–*samay* (modernist) factions that had emerged in the modern period under Thai and French influence, the catastrophic war, starvation, and killing of the period confirmed the importance of preserving the traditional Dhamma that they had witnessed being dismantled. One such person was Achar Moun Oun from Kampong Cham Province. Fearing the predicted demise of the *sāsana*, he risked his life and that of his family to preserve what evidence he could of the tradition. I met him in 2012, when he performed one of the embryology-based rebirthing rituals at night near a temple I was visiting not far from his village.[23] Though in his eighties and rapidly losing his hearing, he was still in demand for performing such *borān*-related rituals and cycled to different locations to perform them. He and his family explained how, amid all the warfare, he had managed to preserve an extensive collection of manuscripts.[24]

Achar Oun recollected,

> I received these manuscripts from my teachers. I had many more manuscripts but I shared and distributed to the pagodas [that had lost their manuscripts during the war]. During the war in Pol Pot's time, I decided to collect as many manuscripts as possible from everywhere and I wrapped and tied them together.

Achar Oun then related the events of the war to the prediction of the eventual, inevitable decline of the Buddhist teaching, quoted at the head of this chapter, the same prediction that had inspired the Burmese revival of meditation in the form of Vipassanā nearly a century earlier. His daughter, then forty-three years old, was sitting nearby as her father related this account. She interrupted to emphasize her father's concern to protect the manuscripts:

> My father did not care about anything during war, but he cared about his manuscripts, he wanted to keep them safe. When this area was caught up in the conflict [after 1979, the ongoing fighting between Khmer Rouge and Vietnamese forces in the area], and fighting was all around, he decided to collect the manuscripts from different places and he hid them in the oxcart in case the house was burnt down. Everyone else gathered together what food they could, because they were afraid of not having anything to eat, but not my father. He cared more about the manuscripts than even his own children, and decided to keep them safe. After the war was over, some people realized he had kept many manuscripts so that they came here and asked to borrow them but didn't return what they borrowed.

Achar Oun continued,

> I kept these manuscripts. I have had several teachers and I always dedicate my respect to them. I always dedicate my respect to my parents as well. As a result, it seems that I have power, and wherever I go people respect and love me. Many people always come to me and ask me to guide them in performing ceremonies; they want me to serve as Achar [lay officiant] for the ceremony. For example, people as far away as Phnom Penh and Pursat province invite me to lead the ceremony. I can say many people respect me in this life, but I believe that I will be even better in the next life.

Achar Oun also explained that in the past teachers kept *kammaṭṭhāna* secret and warned him that he should not teach those who ask him, but that he teaches whoever asks in the hope of passing on these endangered traditional practices to future generations.[25]

Initial *Borān* Revival Following the Restoration of Buddhism in Cambodia

In the immediate aftermath of the Pol Pot period, it looked as if *borān kammaṭṭhāna* might have died out in Cambodia, but soon there were signs of its resurrection. Following the Vietnamese taking control of Phnom Penh at the end of the 1970s, monastic ordination was once more permitted, but it was soon restricted to those over fifty-five years old: soldiers were needed by both the Vietnamese and the Khmer Rouge, who still controlled areas such as Kampong Cham. As the age restriction took effect, younger men who had received ordination disrobed, with the exception of a particularly determined few.[26]

In Kampong Cham and neighboring regions *borān kammaṭṭhāna* was revived almost immediately after the height of the

Pol Pot period. At Wat Pras Meas, "Temple of the Golden Deer," in Kampong Cham, the Khmer Rouge territory where Achar Oun had protected his manuscripts, a monk returned to the robes in 1979 and immediately resumed the practice. From conversations, it seem this was a pattern found elsewhere in rural areas, the practice being undertaken for a period of just over a week after the rice harvest and for three months during the annual rains retreat each year.[27] By the time I visited in 2012 the practice had discontinued at Wat Pras Meas, and also at other temples: people could recall an initial but abortive revival.

At a temple called Wat Damrei Sar, "Temple of the White Elephant," in neighboring Kandal Province, northeast from Phnom Penh on the road to Vietnam, the revival has lasted longer. A former monk called Phong Vorn also took the opportunity to become a monk once more in 1979. He was in his late fifties at that time, so the age restriction did not affect him, and he became the abbot until his death at the age of eighty-two in 2002. Ven. Phong Vorn had been a student of Ven. So Kheav, the previous head monk of Wat Damrei Sar, who had been killed by the Khmer Rouge. His teacher in turn was Achar Keo, a layman, as indicated by the title Achar, literally, "teacher," often used to refer to laymen who perform ritual and other services at temples in Cambodia. After reordaining, Ven. Phong Vorn began to teach the practice once more at the temple.

Also in 1979, just after his reordination, Phong Vorn took in forty-five-year-old mother Oun Sophy and her twenty-two-year-old son. They had traveled from neighboring Kampong Cham Province, one of the heartlands of *borān kammaṭṭhāna*. Her husband and her nine other children including her newborn baby had been killed by the Khmer Rouge. She had nothing left, nowhere to go. The abbot ordained the son, who would stay a monk for two or three rainy seasons.[28] Oun Sophy would stay for forty years, until her own death, outliving both Ven. Phong Vorn and her son. Initiated by Ven. Phong Vorn into the *borān* meditation system, she became a highly experienced meditator, saying it gave her inner peace and security after so much loss. Soon she was joined by lay practitioners, usually those in their fifties and above, who began to enter the temple temporarily each year to undertake the practice during the three months Buddhist rains retreat, as had been the tradition in Cambodia. Both she and the temporary practitioners occupied a set of traditional huts built in a corner of the monastic compound for this purpose.

Oun Sophy declined to teach the imperiled practice, because to have done so would have contravened Cambodian *bpap srei*, the code of conduct for women: women should not be teachers.[29] The teaching lineage passed to the new deputy abbot, Ven. Neang Sam Ol, then in his late thirties. Now in his early fifties, he began to learn the tradition shortly before the death of Phong Vorn, initially out of curiosity: "What are these things that people see when they meditate?" he had wondered. To commence teaching so soon was, Neang Sam Ol himself suggested, a departure from the more lengthy, staged initiation process of the past. Now he is hoping to preserve the tradition: "I want to prevent the knowledge handed down by past ancestors from being lost."[30]

Neang Sam Ol was supported in his role by Achar Te Tong Yi (Achar Yi) (d. 2018), who, like Ven. Kheav, had studied with Achar Keo. Achar Yi, in his early eighties when I first met him in 2012, worked hard to support the revived teaching of *borān kammaṭṭhāna* at a number of temples in Phnom Penh and surrounding Kandal Province. According to Achar Yi, it took longer for people to resume meditation in Phnom Penh. Most people were too preoccupied with the practicalities of survival and rebuilding. Also, the city did not celebrate the rites of the agricultural cycle that traditionally prompt communal *kammaṭṭhāna*. It was nearly a decade later, in the late 1980s, that people in the Phnom Penh area also began to return to the tradition.[31]

Achar Keo, the teacher of both Achar Yi and So Kheav, had also taught Ven. Ros So, the previous head monk of Wat Russei Chrouy in Kandal Province at which Achar Yi was still teaching when I first interviewed him in 2012. Another of Achar Yi's pupils is Ven. Noun Soth, the monk who undertook the teaching of *borān kammaṭṭhāna* at Wat Champukaek in Phnom Penh. Another well-endowed and wealthy temple that retains these practices is Wat Preak Brang, also in Kandal Province. The abbot there, Samdech Oudam Ponha Doung Phang, is a well-known meditation teacher, and renowned for his blessings. Both temples are attended by senior members of the government and military.[32]

The nature of the resumed practice seems to be at the physically more gentle end of the spectrum. While the rebirth rituals that I witnessed performed by Achar Oun were resumed, I have not heard accounts of anything like the physically demanding initiation rituals described by Ven. Vanarot Ken Vong (1924–1994) as taking place in the 1950s and recorded by Olivier de Bernon.[33] Thus there seems to have been a shift within *borān kammaṭṭhāna* toward focus on just the sitting form of meditation, in other words to become closer to the more globally accepted conception of what meditation should entail. Nonetheless, with increasing numbers finding time to take up the practice or seek out practitioners to perform the related rituals for them, it looked by the 1990s as if at least some elements of the practice lineages that the Khmer Rouge had done so much to annihilate were poised to flourish once more.[34]

Borān kammaṭṭhāna had a number of factors in its favor, which seem to promote this revival: in contrast to Vipassanā, which at the time was still regarded by some as a foreign intrusion, it was seen by Cambodians as being fundamentally Khmer in character.[35] It also had a reputation for providing healing, longevity, and protection.[36] Furthermore, it was embedded in the traditional ritual calendar: the rainy season, the rice harvest, and funerals; the crucial role played at Cambodian funerals by monks and the lay temple officiators (*achar*) who are trained in *kammaṭṭhāna* is still a motivation for undergoing training.[37] While they have different roles at funerals, both monks and laymen can act as teachers in the *borān* meditation tradition.

Further Decline in Cambodia

Despite these positive signs, by the 2010s the initial flames of enthusiasm had died down to a flicker, and few are those with the commitment required to master the method and ensure its continued transmission to future generations. When I first tried to track down living lineages, attendance at the training that a few temples put on annually for short periods, typically during the monastic rainy season in October/November and after the rice harvest in January/February, was fairly strong, and many people, particularly from the older generations, continue to request the rituals that practitioners are empowered to conduct. By 2015, I was unable to find any temple hosting the practice after the rice harvest.[38] The teaching lineages and the ability to deal with the texts are at risk. In other words, there are insufficient experienced practitioners and few able to understand the texts and manuscript manuals handed down from teachers of previous generations. Even some of the temples most associated with the practices, both historically and more recently, struggle to sustain the tradition. In other temples it has disappeared entirely as elderly *achar* have died with no one qualified to take their place.

In spite of the efforts and aspirations of elderly teachers such as Achar Oun and the late Achar Yi, and the work of the vice-abbot Neang Sam Ol at Wat Damrei Sar, hopes of reviving the *borān* tradition at present seem unrealistic. It is not clear that there is a sustainable teaching lineage even at the wealthy and powerful temples, Wat Champukaek and Wat Preak Brang. After two centuries of suppression and marginalization, *borān kammaṭṭhāna* had survived into the second half of the twentieth century mainly in those areas that were then those most affected by communist revolution. In Laos there has been no comeback, although recently attempts have been made to secure other aspects of traditional Lao Buddhism. It also seems to me that the method of practice used, while valuing *nimitta*, does not sustain the movements in the body described in the manuals that have come down to us from the eighteenth century.

When examining the reasons for the lack of a widespread revival several factors become apparent. *Borān* meditation was divorced from other branches of learning and occupations, such as medicine, in the 1920 ordinance. That affected how it was perceived but also meant that those who made their living by applying what they learned in meditation to medical treatments could no longer do so. This undermined its attractiveness for young men seeking a career in medicine. Its close relationship with medicine is confirmed by it surviving longest where modern (Western-derived) biomedicine remained absent the longest. Wat Preah Thomlanga, not far from Achar Oun's home, is among the cluster of temples in Kampong Cham that used to be well known for *borān* rituals and meditation, some of which initially hosted a revival. It no longer hosts *borān kammaṭṭhāna* or its related rituals, but it did so in living memory. The abbot and the group of *wat achar* who manage the temple confirmed that the disappearance of *borān kammaṭṭhāna* coincided with the advent of modern medicine. In spite of being only a few hours' drive from Phnom Penh, this area still feels relatively remote—although this is changing with the completion of the new, high-speed road between Phnom Penh and Vietnam—and was one of the last regions to receive Western medicine. Meditation teachers of non-*borān* methods in rural Battambang, an area more under Thai influence and a relatively early recipient of Western medicine, confirmed that there too *borān kammaṭṭhāna's* disappearance coincided with the acceptance of Western medicine during the pre-revolutionary period of reform.[39] The initial post–Pol Pot revival in some areas may have been because it was a resource for medicine and healing, and there was a dearth of medical expertise. Those with Western-style education, including medics, had been among those first targeted for elimination by the Khmer Rouge.

However, there are additional reasons for the demise of *borān kammaṭṭhāna* in Cambodia today. Even for those seeking out meditation, it is not to *borān kammaṭṭhāna* that they turn. Two particularly successful Buddhist teachers since the restoration of Buddhism in 1989 have been Ven. Sam Buntheoun (1957–2003) and Buth Savong (b. 1960);[40] both have been critical of *borān kammaṭṭhāna* and related practices.

The Rise of Vipassanā in Cambodia

Sam Buntheoun was a key figure in the popularization of Vipassanā after the restoration, presumably—since he remained in Cambodia during the Khmer Rouge period—drawing on forms that had reached Cambodia in the 1950s. Although other traditions, especially Goenka, have begun to open centers in Cambodia, Sam Buntheoun's meditation center at Udong has continued to grow in popularity and success even since his assassination in 2003. Numerous groups of monks, lay adults, and school children have gone on courses there or at the many regional branch centers set up by those who have trained there. When the topic of meditation arises in Cambodia more generally, it is invariably to Vipassanā within this tradition that people now allude. Vipassanā has now eclipsed *borān kammaṭṭhāna* to such an extent that the younger generation of monks in Kandal Province is largely unaware of the existence of *borān kammaṭṭhāna*.[41]

Sam Buntheoun was conscious of the difference. Indicative of his modernist stance was his criticism of water blessing. Water sprinkling using empowered water is the usual way for monks in Cambodia, Laos, and Thailand to give blessings and protection to laypeople, parallel to the more ubiquitous use of *paritta* string in Sri Lanka. To be critical of it is a standard modernist stance in that water blessing suggests that good fortune can be gained in this way, rather than through one's own karmic efforts. However, according to *borān* practitioners, Sam Buntheoun was also directly critical of *borān kammaṭṭhāna* itself and had asked Saṅgharāja Thep Vong to put a halt to it, a request that the latter declined.[42]

Another influential Buddhist teacher of recent decades is Buth

Savong. Buth Savong had taken ordination as a monk when Buddhism was restored at the end of the Democratic Kampuchea period but in 1984 succumbed, like Oun Sophy's son, to the pressure for young men to disrobe. He nevertheless continued be a religious teacher after his disrobing. He follows monastic precepts, dressing in white with his head shaved. His centers, radio preaching, and YouTube videos are very popular. Originally from Battambang, his criticism of the *borān* monks led to a split at the temple where he was based, with the *borān* monks leaving to establish a separate temple. Because of Buth Savong's popularity, people accepted his criticisms and made it hard for the *borān* monks to receive support. One informant reported,

> At the time when Achar Buth Savong gave Buddhist sermons between 1991 and 1993, *borān kammaṭṭhāna* gradually disappeared. Actually, the intention of his sermons was not to provoke people to give up *borān kammaṭṭhāna* or *thudong* [ascetic practice, associated with meditation while living in the forest]. Rather, he meant that to do *kammaṭṭhāna*, people do not need to stay only in the forest; they can do it anywhere. But laypeople misunderstood his teaching: his followers came to look down on people doing *kammaṭṭhāna* in the forest or *thudong*; and some people said that Achar Buth Savong was promoting Thai Dhamma in Cambodia.[43]

We can see in this speaker's account of Buth Savong's effect on *borān kammaṭṭhāna* a desire to minimize the suggestion that Buth Savong was actually hostile. When I was conducting interviews in 2012, there was a move to be more conciliatory when talking about the relationship between Vipassanā and *borān kammaṭṭhāna*, though now the further decline of *borān kammaṭṭhāna* seems to have made this redundant. This move reflected the lead taken by the current supreme patriarch Thep Vong, who declined to side with one or the other. *Borān* practices are still sought out as a source of blessing and power including by members of the government and military, but with the declining practice, particularly among young people, the difficulty will be finding the next generation of teachers.

Even if open animosity is a thing of the past, the religious teachings and practice of Sam Buntheoun and Buth Savong are part of the cause of the further decline of *borān kammaṭṭhāna*. Although both men are Cambodian and both were in Cambodia during the Pol Pot period and so cannot be dismissed as foreign impositions, they both offer an approach to Buddhist practice that seems to provide a welcome fresh start unconnected with Cambodia's recent past. Moreover, Sam Buntheoun taught a form of meditation that can be practiced in everyday life without the need to retreat from the world (although many do attend retreats). The practices are taught in large classes that are well-organized. One does not need to enter a formal relationship with an individual teacher. There is no need to enter into lengthy and, for the average Cambodian, relatively costly initiation stages that also take one away from income-generating work. Even *borān* practitioners themselves were appreciative of these qualities and the speed with which one can experience benefits in the newer meditation systems. Some former *borān* practitioners have switched to the new methods in recent decades, just as people did before the Pol Pot period.

Meditation and Monastic Rivalry in Thailand in the Cold War Period

In the preceding chapter we saw that the modernizing and reform of Thailand had been particularly significant for the marginalization of *borān kammaṭṭhāna* earlier in the twentieth century because of its impact through the Theravada world. This had already pushed *borān* practice from the center in Cambodia, though it remained the recognized practice of the Sangha hierarchy and government in Laos. Despite this pattern, interest in *borān kammaṭṭhāna* had revived to some extent in Thailand in the early decades of the twentieth century. The disruption to the Thammayut control of the Sangha following the coup of 1932 seems to have contributed to publications of *borān* texts and collaborations with *borān* practitioners that followed. As we saw in the previous chapter, the senior Thammayut meditation monk Jan Sirijantho (Ubāli) was instrumental in the most significant of these publications, through his collecting of manuscripts, his students, and the networks he had forged between the northeast of the country and Bangkok. In Bangkok, he had discussed *borān* practices with representatives of at least two living traditions, the lineage at Wat Ratchasittharam and that of Candasaro Sot (1884–1959), the abbot of Wat Paknam. Both lineages continue to this day. What then of developments in Thailand in the post-war period? Did a more relaxed or interested approach to non-reform meditation methods allow for a revival, and did those practices remain true to the complex Abhidhamma structure of their precursors in the Ayutthaya period?

Again, global and monastic politics shaped the unfolding situation in Thailand. How these factors played out can be seen in the case of Phimonlatham, the most prominent monk in Thailand in the 1950s. In this period, Burmese Vipassanā was beginning to spread throughout the region among both monks and laypeople, following its popularization, the new phenomenon of urban meditation centers, and the upbeat expectations of the Buddha Jayanti, the celebration of 2,500 years since the death of the Buddha, marking the halfway point in the lifespan of the *sāsana*, the Buddhist religion.

Phimonlatham (also known as At Asapho) was the third-most powerful monk in the national Thai Sangha, and the second-most powerful monk in the Mahanikay sect. Successful at home and abroad, he developed good relationships with influential Buddhist monks in several Southeast and South Asian countries.[44] In 1952 he sent his assistant, Chodok Yannasittho, to study meditation with Mahasi Sayadaw in Rangoon (now Yangon). After Chodok returned, Phimonlatham established the National Office of Vipassanākammaṭṭhāna (Insight Meditation) at Wat Mahathat in

Bangkok, the temple that had since the eighteenth century been the national administrative center of the Mahanikay. Phimonlatham appointed Chodok as the head of the new National Office, and over the following decade Chodok's teaching of Mahasi Sayadaw's "rising and falling" meditation technique attracted many followers.[45]

In many of his public talks in the 1950s, Chodok criticized two meditation techniques still popular in Thailand at the time. One was the *ānāpānasati*, mindfulness of breathing meditation, as taught in the Thammayut forest lineage of Man Bhūridatto largely on the authority of Pali canonical texts. The other was the *vijjā dhammakāya*. This is the term that Candasaro Sot, the abbot of Wat Paknam, gave to his practice of *borān kammaṭṭhāna*. The main criticism made by Chodok relied on the new dichotomy between *samatha* and *vipassanā* created in Burma, which usurped their formerly complementary status. Many of the modern Burmese Vipassanā lineages promoted *vipassanā* without *samatha* support. Chodok, on this basis, claimed that the *ānāpānasati* and *vijjā dhammakāya* techniques could only help practitioners attain *samatha* (the calming and *jhāna* outcomes) while Chodok's "rising and falling" technique could lead to liberating insight, *vipassanā*.[46] The comment appears to be a misreading of both traditions, and in the case of *vijjā dhammakāya* possibly reflects a modernist projection of meditation as mind-science, which therefore assumes that somatic, body-based practices relate to *samatha*. Chodok's position indicates how thoroughly a reformist, modernist agenda had permeated the highest ranks of the Mahanikay. The difference was that he was now taking authority from Vipassanā, with his criticism of both the post-reform forest tradition and the older, pre-reform *borān* style of meditation practice.

When Phimonlatham himself became an object of adverse political attention, it again affected practitioners within the lineages criticized by Chodok. This happened in the 1960s, when Phimonlatham was defrocked and put in jail on charges of being a communist sympathizer, which had been criminalized in the

1930s. As Phibul Choompolpaisal has shown, the accusations were primarily due to ecclesiastical rivalry and a power struggle among the higher echelons of the Sangha hierarchy. In Thailand at that time, just as it had been in the United States of America a decade earlier, the accusation of communist sympathy was an easy way to attack an enemy. One of the after-effects of Phimonlatham's downfall was the official promotion of monks who had not been close to Phimonlatham, such as the Mahanikay monk Kittivuddho (Kittiwuttho). Kittivuddho famously made his anti-communist sympathies extremely clear.[47] Phimonlatham's imprisonment meant that his followers and activities at Wat Mahathat, the Mahanikay headquarters, also fell from grace.[48] This turn of events appears to have meant that the Burmese Vipassanā method introduced by Chodok became less popular than before, while the Thammayut's *ānāpānasati* method and Sot's *vijjā dhammakāya* method became more widely accepted, although Sot himself had died in 1959.

We see similar rivalry affecting meditation in response to Sot's internationalization of his *vijjā dhammakāya* method in the context of increasing levels of Western convert Buddhism in the 1950s. Andrew Skilton has documented how events in Bangkok led to the alternating popularities of these same three traditions—Vipassanā, Thai forest *ānāpānasati*, and Sot's *vijjā dhammakāya* (a form of *borān kammaṭṭhāna*)—in the United Kingdom in the early years of the English Sangha Trust (EST). Inspired by the missionary monk Ṭhitavedo, sent to London by Sot, the first British monks of the EST had been ordained by Sot at Wat Paknam in the 1950s including Kapilavaḍḍho, ordained in 1954. He was taught *vijjā dhammakāya* directly by Sot, and also observed the high number of experienced meditation nuns (*mae chi*) at Wat Paknam.[49] He returned to Thailand with three further men who wanted to receive ordination in 1956. However, after their ordination, Kapilavaḍḍho fell out with Sot and left Wat Paknam for the Thammayut temple Wat Thathong. Soon after that, Kapilavaḍḍho returned to the United Kingdom, and although he initially continued teaching the *vijjā dhammakāya* method, he later switched to teaching

Burmese Vipassanā, promoted at the EST during the 1960s by the then-incumbent Ananda Bodhi, who had studied in Burma under Mahasi Sayadaw as well as in Thailand at Wat Mahathat under Phra Rajasiddhimuni. The EST then switched again, perhaps in part as a result of Vipassanā's decrease in popularity after the fall of Phimonlatham. This time it took up the transmission of the Thammayut northern Thai forest tradition, which by now also had followers in the Mahanikay, such as Ajan Chah (1918–1992). The EST follows Ajan Chah's method to this day, with the Thai forest tradition being widespread among Western converts, especially ordained monastics, globally.[50] As in the case of the fate of *borān kammaṭṭhāna* in Sri Lanka, the interplay of personal, monastic, national, and international politics shaped the choices of meditation method taken up in a region, even if the meditators themselves have had little interest in such matters.

Thailand's position on the Cold War frontline in the international politics of this time would have a more serious and lasting effect on the densely forested regions of the northeast. These were the last remaining territories available to forest monks in northeastern Thailand, the area from which Jan had collected *borān kammaṭṭhāna* manuscripts, and the heartland of the wandering forest monks. The area's poverty, isolation, and proximity to China, Laos, and Cambodia meant that it was targeted for communist insurgency by the military. To counter this it was also provided with American development aid. As a consequence, the indigenous forest habitat that supported the forest monks rapidly altered; the military targeting and economic development of the 1950s–1970s culminated in the closure of the forests in the 1980s with the forcible relocation of three to five million forest-dwellers.[51] Given that *borān kammaṭṭhāna* was still promoted by the senior monks in neighboring Laos in the mid-1970s, it seems likely that up until this time, although Thammayut forest monks had dominated interactions with Bangkok, a wider variety of practice had continued.

The Global Spread of Sot's Method

Sot's approach to meditation inspired other followers and gave an international flavor to meditation lineages that see him as their founder. Another foreigner who began to study meditation at Wat Paknam around the same time as Kapilavaḍḍho was Terence Barnett Magness (1929–2012), initially as a layman over the course of a dozen years in the 1950s and '60s. Magness was born into an English Catholic family in Penang in what was then British Malaya and managed to survive the Japanese invasion, although other members of his family did not. Despite the British withdrawal, he stayed in Southeast Asia, living and working in Thailand. In 1970 he became a monk at Wat Doi Suthep in Chiang Mai where he lived for most of the rest of his life. For a few years shortly after his ordination he left Wat Doi Suthep to resume his study of Sot's *vijjā dhammakāya* under the nun Ajan Kayawadee, one of the late Sot's most experienced students. In response to the perceived need to provide English-language materials for foreigners, Magness translated a number of Sot's teachings as well as a biography of him.[52] It was one of these works that anthropologist Michael Carrithers criticized in the early 1980s, little realizing that Magness and the Sri Lankan texts shared their descent from the meditation practices of Ayutthaya at the height of its power. Many followers of Sot have been unaware of the relationship between Sot's *vijjā dhammakāya* and earlier *borān kammaṭṭhāna* methods because of the importance of the account of Sot's own direct realization of the truth in the year 1916, which provides an origin narrative and confirms for practitioners the validity of his method.[53]

Some lineages of Candasaro Sot's spread directly from Wat Paknam into the wider world.[54] However, it was not until more than three decades after Sot's death, in the early 1990s, that one of these temples, Wat Phra Dhammakaya in Pathumthani outside of Bangkok, set up its international missionizing project.[55] This project has spread Sot's modified form of *borān kammaṭṭhāna* globally. Interestingly, one of the reasons for its success is that it has taken Sot's mission to make meditation accessible to another level, harnessing modern technology and pioneering the provision of online instructions, even creating cartoons to teach it to children. In simplifying the technique and making it available to a broader public, Sot and Dhammakaya have echoed the further expansion of modern Vipassanā in Burma four decades earlier.[56]

The method taught at Wat Paknam and temples derived from it is again criticized as unorthodox. This is partly for the reasons we have already identified: the changes in expectations in what meditation should be, which stem from the colonial period and the reformist responses to it; the lack of awareness of its relationship with the methods promoted by the Sangha hierarchy and royal court of Ayutthaya; the failure to recognize how the methods promoted by Ayutthaya reflect a detailed working out of the Abhidhamma path of liberation. However, politics and rivalry also contribute to this criticism. Since the end of the twentieth century, the wealth and success of the network of temples headed by Wat Phra Dhammakaya have made it an object of suspicion, a potentially powerful player in the red shirt–yellow shirt factions of Thai politics, and a possible source of revenue. Dhammakaya's meditation—its long history and Abhidhamma underpinnings unfamiliar to most—is seen as emblematic of the movement, part of its identity. We must therefore see criticism of it as unorthodox within this broader context.

Conclusion

This chapter has traced the fortunes of *borān kammaṭṭhāna* from the late nineteenth century to the present day. We observed how caste politics, changing relations with lay supporters, and rupture both in and with Thailand, meant that *borān* meditation was not a feature of the new ordination lineages in Sri Lanka, which, when they were interested in meditation at all, drew on Burmese Vipassanā and texts such as the *Visuddhimagga*.

We had learned in previous chapters of the effect on Cambodia of reforms and modernization inspired by Thailand and France in the late nineteenth and early twentieth centuries, pushing *borān kammaṭṭhāna* to the margins away from direct government and Sangha hierarchy control. The only place where it remained at the center was in Laos. The last bastions of *borān kammaṭṭhāna* were then precisely those places where Buddhism and local traditions were devasted during the Cold War period, by the Marxist revolutions of Laos and Cambodia, and the anti-communist forest closures and forced migrations in northeast Thailand.

Global and monastic politics in Thailand for a while conspired to promote Vipassanā in Burma, which has also dominated the revival of meditation in post–Pol Pot Cambodia. This changed, and some *borān kammaṭṭhāna* lineages have survived there to this day, though the most popular form is widely criticized as unorthodox, partly because of monastic rivalry and politics within Thailand, partly because the history of these practices has been forgotten.

Those *borān kammaṭṭhāna* lineages that have survived seem to have adapted to the modern period, so that they are less somatic, less detailed, and not recognizable as the detailed working out of the Abhidhamma path to becoming an arhat. The closest living tradition to the pre-modern lineages appears to be that taught at Wat Ratchasittharam, which continues to use the movements of the *nimitta* around the body. However, even here we find a change. The practices using these movements are regarded as *samatha* practices only, a preparation for *vipassanā*. Skilton and Choompolpaisal comment, "Future comparative study may be able to shed light on whether or not this is a concession to the reformist prioritizing of the meditation structure outlined in Buddhaghosa's *Visuddhimagga*."[57] We know from the Sri Lankan manuals that the incorporation of meditation attainments into the fabric of the practitioner's body was practiced at all stages of the path. How else could it enact the complete the transformation of the individual through the step-by-step progression of *citta*, *cetasika*, and *rūpa* provided by Abhidhamma?

Conclusion

This book has revealed the extensive existence of a form of meditation system that dominated the Theravada Buddhist world at the dawn of the modern period. We have examined its characteristics and followed its trajectory as, over the course of the past century and a half, it has disappeared to the verge of extinction.

In the late nineteenth century, when evidence for this tradition first came to the attention of Western scholars, meditation was misunderstood through the lens of Theosophy or even despised. We find it described as "a cloudland" or an invented system of "multiplied ridiculous distinctions, . . . which, in lieu of expanding the mind, tends to contract it almost to idiocy."[1] While the esoteric nature of these practices hindered a proper understanding, these dismissive attitudes reflected a colonial worldview: the expectations of Buddhism as a this-life philosophy and negative attitudes to Buddhists as backward, colonial subjects awaiting the Progress of imperial governance and civilization.

Within fifty years, this form of esoteric Theravada meditation had been displaced by text-based revivals of meditation from within the Thai reform wing of the monastic community and the spread of Burmese Vipassanā, so much so that writers in Thailand then labeled it as the "old method," *borān kammaṭṭhāna*. Tied as it was to funerary rites and the religious and harvest calendar, it continued to thrive in Laos and—despite attempts at its suppression—in rural Cambodia, until the 1970s. At that point the massive upheavals of the Cold War period destroyed the final remnants there and in Thailand's far northeast. Initial attempts at revival in Cambodia after the restoration of Buddhism have proved abortive—only a few temples retain the practice.

Back in the eighteenth century, *borān kammaṭṭhāna* was introduced to Sri Lanka from Thailand as part of the revival of Buddhism there, accepted as the valid means to enlightenment. The manuscripts left behind by the monks who learned the practice reveal that it entails an in-depth working out of the Abhidhamma path to liberation. Abhidhamma provides the most thorough presentation of Theravada Buddhist doctrine, explaining causality, and how to harness causality to bring about personal transformation. By the fifth century C.E., Abhidhamma analysis of the early Buddhist doctrine of impermanence had led to a theory of relative momentariness, whereby all the constituents of reality, *dhammas*, are constantly replaced, giving the appearance of continuity and the actuality of incessant change. These constituents of reality are categorized into four kinds: materiality, *rūpa*; states of consciousness, *citta*; aspects of consciousness, *cetasika*; and nibbana. As individuals, we are constituted of materiality, states of consciousness, and aspects of consciousness that mutually condition each other, constantly disappearing at different speeds, only to be replaced by other *dhammas*. *Borān kammaṭṭhāna* seeks to harness this process of constant substitution by directing it, generating higher states of consciousness to replace lower states in a detailed progression from ordinary mortal to enlightened being, to the attainment of nibbana.

All Theravada meditation systems, beyond the elementary practices of the initial stages, relate to Abhidhamma. So what is different about this system? The key points of contrast are that *borān kammaṭṭhāna* as a meditation system describes the process of transformation in detail and relates that transformation to changes in consciousness, mentality and materiality, or, in Western terms, mind and body. The body is the locus of change. Other Theravada meditation systems familiar today emphasize the transformation of mind, leaving the transformation of the body implicit or ignored. In the latter, the body is object, not subject.

The treatment of meditation as purely a mind-science arose during the European colonial period, a reaction to the Western dominance in areas of physicality. It corresponded to the Cartesian divide between *psyche* and *physis*, and the related rift between religion and science, then prevalent in the West. This adaptation of meditation in the modern period allowed for its revival and eventual widespread adoption, even by the West, once feared as the cause of Buddhism's demise.

Amid the changing worldviews, power structures, and politics of the modern period, the fear that colonialism was ushering in the long-prophesied apocalyptic demise of Buddhism led to attempts to protect it. The shape of these revivalist movements varied from place to place. One reaction was the idea that genuine meditation is mind-science and that in psychology lies the superiority of Buddhism and Buddhists. This approach circumvented the colonial dominance of the physical realm. The resulting types of meditation practice, labeled Vipassanā because of their focus on cognitive insight, gained widespread popularity, ousting other forms. Theravada monastic and doctrinal expertise relating to material culture was sidelined.

While the Burmese revival emphasized the importance of Abhidhamma, text-based revival elsewhere, in emphasizing a return to the early canonical texts, regarded Abhidhamma as a developed form of scholasticism. Such textual fundamentalism shaped the reform of Buddhism in those regions where the evidence for *borān kammaṭṭhāna* is substantial: Cambodia, Laos, Sri Lanka, and Thailand. While the colonial powers of France and Britain set the rapidly changing scene, Thailand was the fastest to modernize and the only country to retain an autonomous royal family and successfully resist colonization. The Thai royal family was at the forefront in shaping this fundamentalist reaction and highly influential in changes throughout the region.

In this context, *borān kammaṭṭhāna's* highly complex somatic practices were misunderstood. It was rejected by both internal reformers and external observers as a corruption or fundamental misunderstanding of Buddhism. Vipassanā and text-based meditation filled the voids created by these changes and by the subsequent ramifications of the Cold War. The longest living tradition of Theravada meditation, which can be traced back at least as far as the late fifteenth century, and may even reach back to the early commentarial period, was displaced by practices that, though newly developed, were authorized with reference to the Pali canon of early Buddhism.

But is it a corruption? Or is *borān kammaṭṭhāna* the only Theravada system of meditation that seeks to complete the process of transformation laid out in Abhidhamma, based on serious consideration of the transformation attained by the Buddha? *Borān kammaṭṭhāna* not only accepts the genuine nature of the Buddha's enlightenment, but provides an extremely detailed, technical method for practitioners to reach it in their current embodiment in this lifetime. We have shown how it employs the progressive substitution of our corrupt states by consecutive skillful, resultant, and functional mental states found in the Abhidhamma, which provides an analysis of consciousness as composite and explains the complex relationship between consciousness and form. We have also shown that *borān kammaṭṭhāna* displays features not recorded in Abhidhamma treatises to bring about transformation.

Since Buddhist practice is centrally concerned with transformation, it was inevitable that close attention would be paid to other methods used to bring about change within its broader cultural milieu. Where appropriate and possible, it is natural that such methods be integrated with soteriological purposes. It is likely that some or most of this was as much a matter of shared development and cultural assimilation as conscious adaptation. On close inspection, we can see that *borān kammaṭṭhāna* applies a range of theories and technologies of transformation to provide a delivery method for its transformative practices, a delivery method that allows the supramundane (*lokuttara*) to be realized in the present life by an individual within the mundane (*lokiya*) world.

The technologies of transformation on which it drew—or with which it shares techniques—include generative grammar, letter alchemy, ayurvedic pharmacy and obstetrics, and the chemistry of mercury purification. In this book we have examined these technologies to see how their methods correlate with those in found in pre-modern Theravada meditation. These technologies also share with Abhidhamma and *borān kammaṭṭhāna* a sophisticated principle of substitution and the use of group theory mathematics to predict change and maximize the effectiveness of substitution in their different domains. Examining these sciences explains many of the features of *borān kammaṭṭhāna* unrecognized in the modern world.

The lack of recognition of these features in meditation reflects the changing position of the sciences from which they are drawn. These sciences with their common principles of transformation were ousted, indeed outgunned, during the colonial period by a competing set of technologies introduced from Europe. European science was a competing knowledge system: a new and powerful means of understanding the world, exploiting causality, and predicting outcomes. Although in many ways European "science" was demonstrably inferior in a number of areas and still learning from Asian sciences, the political rhetoric was otherwise. This rhetoric had the backing of the more advanced military technology of the West, as well as ways in which Western players took advantage of local rivalries. The technologies developed in the period on the basis of European empirical science began to seem, and in some cases to be, more reliable or effective than those based on traditional knowledge systems. Even where they were not more effective, they were sometimes implemented at the expense of traditional technologies for political, economic, or other reasons.

The marginalization and disappearance of these technologies of transformation, with which *borān kammaṭṭhāna* resonated, inevitably left this older system of meditation isolated and vulnerable in the new world order. While the Buddhist truth of "the way things really are," *yathā-bhūta-ñāṇa-dassana*, is unchanging, we have seen in this book how competing worldviews and technologies altered the systems that Theravada Buddhists employed for realizing it.

While some meditation lineages derived from pre-modern

esoteric Theravada have survived into the modern period, their adaptation and simplification make the historical process and experience of esoteric Theravada difficult to comprehend. The use of *nimitta* and other outcomes of meditative experience to incorporate attainments into the body more naturally aligns with contemporary understanding of *samatha* practices used to improve the receptiveness of the mind. Situated as we are in a post-Cartesian world, it may be unimaginable to inhabit the pre-Cartesian consciousness of the practitioners who used these methods for the full sequence of the path, including the deep insight and profound purification that culminate in enlightenment and freedom from samsara. Cognitive science has allowed us to reevaluate the transformative effectiveness within a single lifetime even of simplified meditation practice, identifying mechanisms and evidence unimagined back when such practices were first devised.[2] It will take advanced practitioners able to inhabit both worlds, or new understandings of consciousness to pervade modern culture, for us to fully appreciate what this sophisticated system of transformation had and has to offer.

Notes

Introduction

1. Crosby 2013.
2. Crosby, Skilton, and Kyaw 2019.

Chapter 1. The Colonial Gaze

1. Copleston (1892) 1908: 60. For his discussion of aspects of meditation such as the *jhāna* and *kasiṇa*, see Copleston (1892) 1908: 130–131.
2. Copleston (1892) 1908: 88–89.
3. Copleston (1892) 1908: 130.
4. Complicating the picture are two things. First, meditation manuscripts indicate the presence of Burmese meditation before the revival. Second, *samatha* meditation that has implications for the physical body is also understood to be practiced by another form of esoteric Theravada, not addressed in this work, namely *weikza*. *Weikza* lineages of practice emerged within Theravada Buddhism in Burma in the late nineteenth and twentieth centuries, away from the urban centers of power and colonial political and medical influence (Rozenberg, Brac de la Perrière, and Turner 2014). *Weikza* is associated with longevity practices. Little represented in scholarship until recently, yet pervading Burmese Buddhist culture once one's eyes have been opened to its presence, its meditation practices may in any case be hard to recover or examine because of the restrictive normalizing lens of Vipassanā methods imposed by Burmese Sangha authorities (Kyaw 2019; Ashin and Crosby 2017).
5. At least one living lineage continued in Copleston's time, sadly unrecognized by outsiders interested in the subject until after it had died. See Kemper 2019 and Harris 2019 for the struggles of internal and external observers respectively to comprehend meditation, or to make contact with living traditions.

6. Alabaster 1871.
7. Alabaster 1871: xxiii.
8. Alabaster 1871: xxviii–xxix, cited with this ellipsis in Skilton 2019: 62. See Skilton for an extensive analysis of Alabaster's portrayal of Buddhist meditation and how it was informed by both colonial orientalism and Thai reformist attitudes of the period.
9. Draper 1874: vi.
10. Barker 1886: 375.
11. Draper 1874: 11. For a modern example, see Dixon 2008: 1 and 16. On nineteenth-century attitudes to Buddhism see Almond 1988, and on the teaching of Galileo to school children, ibid., 91.
12. For a more nuanced discussion of the development of the representation of Theravada Buddhism by missionaries and other colonial-period outside observers see Elizabeth Harris (2006). She documents how even individual authors' attitudes changed toward Buddhism and locals during this period, becoming more antagonistic. On the acultural understanding of "Progress," i.e., that modernity is a natural outcome toward which all cultures progress, rather than variable, reversible (in the form of regression), and culturally specific, see Taylor 1995. For a discussion focusing on the impact of the acultural notion of "Progress" on colonial attitudes to war, technology, and religion in the Theravada region, see Crosby 2017.
13. Perreira 2012. On the problematic nature of this identification, see also Crosby 2014: Introduction and *passim*.
14. Almond 1988: 90. The cofounders of Theosophy, Madame Blavatsky and General Olcott, would reinterpret the rebirth theory in the light of evolutionary theory to dismiss the notion of humans being reborn as animals, further down the evolutionary chain. This revisionary attitude was symptomatic of how confidently Westerners laid claim to ownership of "true Buddhism." For an example of the uptake of this attitude to rebirth in Theravada see Ashin and Crosby 2016.
15. Draper 1874: 138.
16. See Crosby 2017 on the growth and application of Social Darwinism in this period.
17. Countess of Jersey 1884–1885 and J.M.M. 1865. Both cited in Almond 1988: 39.
18. Bornaetxea, Fernando, and Morón 2014.
19. On the largely forgotten earlier influence, see Hickey 2019.
20. Kyaw 2014: 113–121.

21. Min 2018. The book was his translation of the *Abhidhammatthasaṅgaha*, which was published as *Compendium of Philosophy* by the Pali Text Society in 1910 and is still in print.
22. Aung 1918: 102.
23. Aung 1918: 103. Shwe Zan Aung is referring on the Buddhist side to meditation, as can be seen from his observation, "The Western method begins with a subject, while the Buddhist method begins with the operator himself."
24. Aung 1918: 103.
25. For an extensive explanation of these responses, see Turner 2014.
26. Braun 2013: 31–33.
27. Yasothararat 1936: 2.
28. Skilton 2019. In a survey article, I also referred to these marginalized practices as "tantric Theravāda" and "*yogāvacara*" (Crosby 2000a). The term *yoga*, literally "union," means practice or discipline and can refer to a range of technologies including medicine and meditation. The term *yogāvacara*, "practitioner of *yoga*," means a meditator in Pali. I used it because of the title of the first published manual of the tradition by Rhys Davids (1896) and because of the frequent reference to the *yogāvacara* in it and related Sri Lankan texts. Additionally, François Bizot has also used the terms non-Mahāvihāra, Mahanikay (Pali *Mahānikāya*), non-reform, and traditional/indigenous Southeast Asian Buddhism (e.g., Bizot 1989: 16), to refer to the range of practices related to *borān kammaṭṭhāna* that he observed in Cambodia and in Southeast Asian texts. He has used them in contrast to terms such as Mahāvihārin, Dhammayutika Nikāya, Sinhalese orthodoxy, and reformed Buddhism to denote normative contemporary Theravada. These terms make sense from a Cambodian context, but not in relation to Sri Lanka: much of our evidence for *borān kammaṭṭhāna* there comes from within the eighteenth-century Siam Nikāya reform tradition that was heir to the Mahāvihāra monastic and literary lineage that had dominated Theravāda since the twelfth century. During fieldwork in Cambodia in the early 2000s, some informants made a distinction between *borān* methods as *kammaṭṭhāna* and the newly popular Burmese-derived Vipassanā, although only the relatively few familiar with *borān kammaṭṭhāna* were able to make this distinction. Since the restoration of Buddhism in Cambodia from the 1990s onward the terms *borān* and *samay* have been extended to have rather general meanings of more traditional/Cambodian (*borān*) and modern/imported (*samay*), although the definition of "modern" should not be taken too literally—

borān practitioners do not eschew modernity or modern technology (Marston 2008).

29. Skilton and Choompolpaisal 2014.
30. Kemper 2019.
31. Hickey 2019: 24–27, 68.
32. Cited in Somadasa 1987–1995, 1:241. Nevill made the comment in reference to the manuscript now catalogued in the British Library as Or.6601(6), which is related in content to a number of other manuscripts collected by him (see chapter 3). Nevill made no claims to understand the subject of meditation: the opinion expressed here is preceded by, "the subject is so little understood by me, I make these remarks with diffidence as to their utility." It is not clear to me what Nevill intended when using the Pali term *paramattha* "ultimate reality/truth" in this context. It could be a reference to the Abhidhamma, regarded as expressing a *paramattha* perspective, and thus indicate that he recognized the Abhidhamma vocabulary that pervades these texts.
33. C. A. F. Rhys Davids 1916: vi–vii, citing the authority of Don Martino de Zilva Wickremasinghe of the British Museum.
34. C. A. F. Rhys Davids 1920.
35. T. W. Rhys Davids 1896: V.
36. Hickey 2019: 85–87.
37. Carrithers 1983: 232.
38. Carrithers 1983: 232.
39. Bowers 1996: 33–45. Mackenzie 2007: 16, 105–109.
40. See works by Bizot, Lagirarde, and Bernon in the bibliography. See Crosby 2000a for a bibliographic essay on Bizot's writings.

Chapter 2. Abhidhamma and Practice

1. Randall 1990: 28. The phrase *sammā arahaṃ* in Pali means "perfectly worthy one," a description of the Buddha contained in the *itipiso* formula that lists the Buddha's qualities and is the basis of meditation on them. The five-syllable formulae may also be given an esoteric meaning representing important groups of five. Some *borān* lineages, such as the one at Wat Damrei Sar in Cambodia, think it wrong to use the phrase *sammā arahaṃ*, preferring instead the phrase *arahaṃ*, while the initial phrase used at Wat Ratchasittharam is *bu-ddho* "Buddha."
2. This analysis of the subdivision providing a gradual path is taken from Andrew Skilton 2016.

3. Kong 2015: 47. Kong provides an extensive discussion of beliefs concerning the differences between subtle and gross food, cosmology, and fetal nutrition.
4. Some of these elements will be discussed in greater detail in this book, but here I am primarily concerned with meditation, so for a survey of the broader ritual aspects, see Crosby 2000a and works by Bizot and Bernon.
5. *Buddhanorakan* 1.3, quoted in Urkasame 2013: 29–30.
6. Urkasame 2013: 345–368.
7. This is the title provided by Ñāṇamoli Bhikkhu 1956 (reprint 1991), whose translation I shall be using. Page references are to the 1991 reprint.
8. The *khandha* are *rūpa*, form; *vedanā*, feeling; *saññā*, apperception; *saṅkhārā*, volitional responses; and *viññāṇa*, consciousness.
9. Anālayo 2012: 32–35; 42–43.
10. *Satipaṭṭhāna Sutta* is *Majjhima Nikāya* No. 10 and *Mahāsatipaṭṭhāna Sutta* is *Dīgha Nikāya* No. 22. For a translation of the former and partial translation of the commentary, see Soma Thera 1949, revised online edition 2013.
11. Anālayo 2012: 29.
12. Bodhi et al. 1993: 9.25.
13. For a more nuanced discussion of *samatha* and *vipassanā* in modern Myanmar, see Kyaw's study of the Theinngu and Sunlun traditions which challenge this simple classification (Kyaw 2019). On the origins and popularity of Vipassanā see Braun 2013 and Jordt 2007.
14. Karunadasa 2010: 79–81.
15. Vism IV 27–31, Ñāṇamoli (1956) 1991: 119–121.
16. See Crosby 2019 for a more in-depth discussion of the importance of the different types of *samādhi*, including how absorption *samādhi* relates to interrupting continuity in samsara.
17. *Amatākaravaṇṇanā* (unpublished manuscript) chapter 1, verses 65–66. Translations are my own and unpublished unless otherwise stated.
18. Ñāṇamoli (1956) 1991: 145; 277–279.
19. For an understanding of *nimitta* in terms of cognitive processes such as responses to sensory deprivation, see Lindahl et al. 2014.
20. I do not know what kind of stone or gem *kālaguṇa* is.
21. *Amatākaravaṇṇanā* chapter 10, verse 6.
22. Bodhi et al. 1993: 56.
23. Greene forthcoming: chapter 2, citing the translation of the *Visuddhimagga* by Ñāṇamoli 1991: 276–277.
24. See Crosby 2019 for more details of the place and role of *nimitta* in this tradition.

25. Patrick Ong reports that it was explained to him that this initial stage generates energy "possible because of the location of the body's elements (the four elements of earth, wind, fire, water) around the navel, which comprise the basic constitutions of the human body." Ong 2011: 171.
26. Choompolpaisal 2019: 176–177.
27. Skilton and Choompolpaisal 2014: 93.
28. Choompolpaisal 2019.
29. The right-male, left-female instruction is not given in the *Amatākaravaṇṇanā*, which was transmitted in an entirely male monastic context, but is known from other texts and from living practice.
30. For a survey of these other manuals, see Crosby 2019.
31. The presentation of causality there is on the basis of the twenty-four conditions, *paccaya*, that the Buddha understood through his omniscience; Kyaw 2014: 89–90.
32. The mention of the places of articulation is an interesting feature that I have yet to fully understand, in part because I have come across no discursive explanation of it and no use of it in a living practice. While it may in general relate to the overall understanding of the potency of the Pali language, I suspect its interest is because of speech as a medium between consciousness and physicality according to Abhidhamma: the intention to speak leads to articulation using the six places associated with sound formation in the mouth, nose, and throat; the sound then produced, which is physical, an aspect of *rūpa*, then causes understanding in the recipient.
33. Choompolpaisal 2019.
34. Bernon 2002: 150–151.
35. Choompolpaisal 2019: 156.
36. Urkasame 2013: 246–256.
37. Choompolpaisal 2019: 158–160.
38. Crosby 2014: 35–39.
39. Urkasame 2013: 318–320. Urkasame provides a more detailed exploration of the significance, variation, and understanding of these rays. One use is that the rays are the basis for prognostication, as the color of the rays of light seen by those who are about to die is indicative of their future state of rebirth, a theme important in *borān* culture and the application of meditation. Since the Buddha here is examining the complex workings and ramifications of causality, it makes sense that he would experience all these lights, while ordinary mortals will only experience what is directly relevant to their own destiny.

40. Extracted from the translation of the *Atthasālinī* by Pe Maung Tin 1920: 17–18.

Chapter 3. Documenting the Esoteric

1. British Library manuscript Or6600(90).
2. Crosby, Skilton, and Gunasena 2012.
3. See also Bizot 1976: 117.
4. For the text, see Hallisey 1993. For the illustrations, see Terwiel 2019.
5. Bizot 1989. See Crosby 2000a: 153–156 for a summary.
6. Bizot 1973 and 1989.
7. Hansen 2007: 81.
8. On the *Amatākaravaṇṇanā's* length and abbreviation techniques, see Crosby 2007.
9. Coedès 1956; Urkasame 2013: 245–246 and Urkasame's Figure 24.
10. See Urkasame 2013 for further inscriptions that postdate the Phitsanulok inscription.
11. Skilling 2018: 181–182. See also Urkasame 2013.
12. On its extensive medical uses in Ayurveda and modern evidence-based assessment see Rastogi, Kulshrestha, and Rawat 2006. I would like to thank David Wharton for explaining the difference between these two plants and their use in papermaking.
13. Becchetti 1994. See Crosby 2000a: 166–167 for a summary.
14. Bizot 1976: 43–44.
15. For more on this mission, see Crosby, Skilton, and Gunasena 2012. For more on the manuscripts resulting from the mission, see Crosby 2019. On the revival more broadly and on Saraṇaṃkara, see Blackburn 2001.
16. Bechert 1989.
17. FEMC, http://khmermanuscripts.efeo.fr, accessed April 21, 2020.
18. Interviews, December 2012.
19. Digital Library of Lao Manuscripts, www.laomanuscripts.net/en/index.
20. An example in the Staatsbibliothek in Berlin is Ms.or.fol. 3276, part 6, Wenk 1975: 74–75.
21. Bernon 2000. For the extensive writings by Bizot, see the bibliography.
22. On the development of the term and title *Mūlakammaṭṭhāna*, see Skilton 2019.
23. The travels during which the Russian scholar Minayeff collected manuscripts are recorded in his memoir translated into English in the 1950s (Minayeff n.d.).

24. For a brief survey see Crosby 2019, or individual entries in Somadasa 1987–1995. The story of the development of Nevill's collection, with the inclusion of a high number of relatively rare texts, and its acquisition by the British Library exemplifies the forces that shaped such acquisitions at the time. Hugh Nevill (1847–1897) worked in the Ceylon Civil Service. He rose to the position of district judge and police magistrate by the time of his premature retirement. These were not considered high achievements, and he seems to have been far more interested in research and the advancement of knowledge than in his career in the civil service. In spite of his interest and detailed knowledge of Sri Lanka, he retained an assumption that superior knowledge was to be found in Europe, and it was there that he sent his identifications and collections, which were primarily zoological. He also worked on comparative linguistics and the anthropology of ethnic and caste groups in Sri Lanka. In collecting and providing detailed descriptions of all his manuscripts, Nevill was helped by a Sri Lankan called Wijeratne. With his help he developed considerable expertise and was in a position to seek out rare manuscripts. His collection in the British Library consists of 2,227 manuscripts, including at least 11 manuscripts containing 17 *borān kammaṭṭhāna* texts. For a survey, see Crosby 2019. One of these texts is the subject of Crosby, Skilton, and Gunasena 2012; two are discussed in Crosby 1999a, chapter 6 of which provides an edition and translation of one of the works, a litany for the devotional practices that precede meditation. The manuscripts ended up in Europe after Nevill was forced to retire with injuries incurred fulfilling his official duties during a cholera epidemic. Whenever smallpox and cholera broke out in Sri Lanka, the general population preferred treatment with local herbs and indigenous medicine. They distrusted government medicine and sanatoriums, and so resisted the government's attempts to enforce the reporting of cases. Reporting became a legal requirement in 1897, the British administration in Sri Lanka acting to protect exports to Europe from the harm it feared the plague epidemic in India might inflict on the reputation of the island's produce. Cholera and smallpox had been brought into Sri Lanka repeatedly by plantation workers migrating from India. Migration escalated in the 1890s as the more labor-intensive tea began to replace the failed coffee crops. The enforcement of a quarantine period on new arrivals had previously been considered too costly (5 days for cholera and 18 days for smallpox). It was also easy to circumvent. The number of migrant workers who became ill and were discarded en route to the main plantation areas in the south was so high that it led to depop-

ulation in the north as locals then contracted the diseases also (Meegama 1986: 13–14). The importance of quarantine and water sanitation was well understood by the British by this time, but through a combination of racism—whereby plantation workers were seen as having a quite different physical make-up and as being uninterested in hygiene—and short-term economic gain, British plantation owners failed to provide sanitation for their workers (Meegama 1986: 19). In 1891, in response to a cholera outbreak in his district, Nevill and his fellow officers sought to impose a range of measures. It is unclear exactly what they were, but presumably they included quarantine. The general resistance from the locals (which Nevill attributed to ignorance) escalated into a riot in which Nevill was stoned. He never fully recovered, and six years later he retired to Europe with his collection. As the climate in France was regarded as more beneficial to his health, he retired there rather than England, but he died later the same year. At the time Don Martino de Zilva Wickremasinghe was working at the British Library, cataloguing its Sri Lankan printed books (de Zilva Wickremasinghe 1901). He arranged for the purchase of Nevill's collection by the library and its transportation to London.

25. Strong 2010.
26. This account is based on personal communication from Phibul Choompolpaisal of conversations he had since October 2011 with Dr. Prachark Wattananusit, former senior librarian of National Library of Thailand and current vice president of the Thai Library Association, and other library staff, as well as on conferences and discussions held by the Manuscript Conservation Association of Thailand established in 2015. See also Matt Reeder's summary of the collection (2016).
27. For a discussion of these manuscripts and illustration, see Terwiel 2019, to whom I am indebted for this explanation.
28. Printing in East Asia developed through a combination of available materials and technologies with Daoist and Buddhist religious beliefs. For Buddhists, maintaining the presence of Buddha relics and the Buddha's teaching was important to stem the decline of Buddhism and the attendant apocalyptic consequences of such decline (Barrett 2008a). Its precursors, beyond the use of stamps for reproducing designs on coins and religious sealings, were the use by Daoists of talismanic forms of Chinese characters to cast "spells" that controlled the spirit world, and the stamping of skin, known also to Indian Buddhists (Barrett 2008b: 50). The wood technology to develop printing on paper was in place in China from the end of the fifth century (Barrett 2008b: 51). However,

it was the belief that the words of the Buddha represented the Buddha himself, i.e., were his "essence" (*dhātu*)—usually translated into English as "relic"—that was reported to Empress Wu of China by the monk Yiching (635–713) and led to mass printing on paper (Barrett 2008b: 86–89). The mid-third-century-B.C.E. Emperor Ashoka is regarded in Buddhist literature as the archetypal Buddhist ruler, a "universal emperor" with unsurpassed dominion and a cosmological right to rule. He is also famed for redistributing the Buddha's funerary relics (*dhātu*) and re-enshrining them in 84,000 *stūpas* (funerary mounds). Empress Wu had adopted Ashoka's title of "universal emperor." Concerned to undertake religious works to ensure her well-being after death as she approached old age, and keen to reassure her subjects of her right to rule and her ability to maintain the presence of Buddha relics like Ashoka, she had 100,000 copies of a text called the *Great Spell of Unsullied Pure Light* printed and distributed. Between 764 and 770 a Japanese empress followed this model by distributing one million small *stūpas* containing printed copies of potent passages excerpted from the same text (Barrett 2008b: 94). While the print culture established by Empress Wu in China was disrupted by the restoration of the Tang dynasty, commercial printing for the meritorious reproduction of Buddhist texts in order to maintain the Buddha's Dhamma and relics in the world had developed by the end of the ninth century, leading to the invention of movable type by the twelfth century (Barrett 2008b: 130–131).

29. Merit-making is the performance of positive actions that store up "merit," an intangible form of benefit or good fortune, which then leads to a better experience and fortune in this life or the next. One may make merit for oneself or on behalf of others, especially the recently deceased. Having a book copied, or—in the modern period—printed, is traditionally done as part of the funeral or death commemoration rites, although this is not the only occasion for the copying of texts.
30. Barrett suggests that the technology could have arrived through several routes, including via Tangut slaves brought into Italy from northeastern Tibet (Barrett 2008a: 36–39).
31. MacCulloch 2003: 71–76.
32. Charney 2006: 182; Olson 1992: 280.
33. Olson 1992: 280–281.
34. Gombrich and Obeyesekere 1988: 203.
35. Becchetti 1994: 47.
36. Despite attempts by U Nu, the first prime minister of independent

Burma, to set up state-backed monastic courts in the 1950s, this only proved successful in the early 1980s under military dictator General Ne Win (Ashin and Crosby 2017).

37. During fieldwork in Cambodia in 2012, Long Sarou and I began many of our interviews with a short slideshow showing evidence of practice elsewhere, from Sri Lankan manuscripts through to the early twentieth century and living practice in Cambodia and Thailand. Most of the information was new to most of our informants. While the response of Thais within *borān* and *borān*-derived traditions was to see authority for their practices as lying with the origins of Buddhism, in India, Cambodians tended to see Cambodia as the original source of their practices and were on the whole inclined to dismiss the validity of the other branches outside of Cambodia. Preserving aspects of Buddhism identified as *borān* has a history of being defended with reference to preserving Khmer culture. Curiously, Wat Damrei Sar in Kandal Province, now one of the few places in Cambodia where these practices are still taught, sees its particular branch as in part deriving from a monk who returned from Thailand, and relates this to some Thai features of their litanies.
38. Hansen 2007: 105–107. Mongkut had also chosen Vinaya as his first publication (Olson 1992: 281). This emphasis on correct and accessible Vinaya developed in Cambodia after Khmer monks, pursuing their studies in Thailand, were influenced by Mongkut and new ways of teaching Buddhist texts (Hansen 2007: 101–102).
39. Hansen 2007: 79.
40. T. W. Rhys Davids 1896; Woodward 1916.
41. Leclère 1899. More has been written on this by François Bizot (1976: 224–225).
42. I understand from Phibul Choompolpaisal that there were journal publications on the subject in Thailand in the two decades preceding this, which may modify this picture. This is the subject of Choompolpaisal's ongoing research, and I have not yet seen such materials. Choompolpaisal (2019) provides summaries of the different methods of meditation recorded in the Thai publications from the 1930s.
43. On some ways in which association with spiritually advanced meditation monks has been seen as a means to enhance secular status more recently, see Gabaude 2003a and 2003b.
44. Choompolpaisal 2019.
45. Mettanando 1999.
46. Olivier de Bernon did not have access to this manuscript. The temple

librarian says that the manuscript had been borrowed by a French scholar and never returned (Skilton, personal communication, May 2019).

47. Bernon 2002: 150.
48. Ratnajoti and Ratnapāla 1963. The first of the three texts in the volume is unrelated. It is a translation into Pali of a modern summary of the *Vimuttimagga* by Bapat based on its translation from Chinese (Bapat 1972), although in their introduction Ratnapāla and Ratnajoti seem unaware of its origins. Their story of the interruption in their work at least explains how the two separate types of material they had in their papers came to be seen as a part of the same manuscript.
49. For a biography and bibliography of Terence Magness, see www.triplegem.net/phra-terry, accessed May 20, 2019.
50. Choompolpaisal 2019.
51. Bizot 1976.
52. Choompolpaisal 2019.
53. Sermchai 1991.
54. http://meditation.dmc.tv/.
55. Choompolpaisal forthcoming.
56. Thanaveero 1994.
57. A handlist of manuscripts in his collection may be downloaded from the Bodleian website: www.bodleian.ox.ac.uk/bodley/finding-resources/special/projects/hidden-collections, accessed April 17, 2019. Academic works assisted by Veera Thanaveero include Bernon 2000, which also covers a much broader range of material, then Newell 2011, Ong 2011, and Skilton and Choompolpaisal 2014 and 2015. These last are a direct engagement with the textual materials under Veera's guidance.
58. Urkasame's thesis (2013) provides detailed analyses of several *borān kammaṭṭhāna* texts, identifying substantial concordance with Theravada canonical and commentarial texts as well as further evidence of the distinctive features of *borān* meditation discussed in this book.
59. For a recent attempt to consider variety in Theravada meditation, see Crosby, Skilton, and Kyaw 2019.
60. Choompolpaisal 2019.

Chapter 4. Technologies of Transformation

1. *attho akkharasaññāto. sabbavacanānaṃ attho akkhareh' eva saññāyate. akkharavipattiyaṃ hi atthassa dunnayatā hoti; tasmā akkharakosallaṃ bahūpakāraṃ suttantesu.* These are the opening lines of Kaccāyana's

grammar. On these lines of Kaccāyana and the later divergence between forty-one and forty-three phonemes through the addition of a short *e* and *o*, see Gornall 2012: 139–140 and 2020: 70.

2. These are specialized technical terms from the Abhidhamma commentarial tradition. *Rūpa*, "form," and *nāma*, literally "name/naming," refer to physical and mental processes other than consciousness. The *saṅkhāra* are volitional, so contain skillful and unskillful mental states, which contrasts with the neutral or functional *kiriya* mental states.
3. I have adapted and translated this passage from the translation of Bizot and Lagirarde 1996: 224–227.
4. Becchetti 1991: 71.
5. European awareness of the relationship between Sanskrit and other languages and on Sanskrit grammar goes back to Italian observations in the sixteenth century (Shendge 1996: 311). Indian surgery also influenced Italian surgery in the sixteenth century.
6. Bizot 1988: 60–86; von Hinüber (1987) 1994; Crosby 2000b; Gornall 2012: 168–169.
7. Gornall 2012: 176; Nagasena 2012: 273–276.
8. Bode 1909, cited in Ruiz-Falqués 2012, who discusses this convergence of Abhidhamma and grammatical interest.
9. Terwiel notes this rift in relation to tattoos. The apotropaic usage of diagrams is still popular throughout Southeast Asia, particularly among ordinary people, and contrasts with a rejection of the practice by the urban elite (Terwiel 1979).
10. Chomsky repeatedly acknowledged his debt to and the primacy of Sanskrit generative grammar, reflecting its continued place in linguistic history to this day.
11. It is tempting to think that Waskaḍuwē Subhūti, in characterizing Sanskrit, Pali, and Sinhala as "cultivated" because they have grammars—in contrast to uncivilized languages with no grammar—was making an adverse comparison with the European languages of those scholars for whom he provided manuscript and Pali-language assistance, such as Robert Childers (1838–1876), Wilhelm Geiger (1856–1943), and Viggo Fausbøll (1821–1908) (Subhūti 1876: i).
12. The related mathematics of trigonometry also developed early in South Asia. See Shaw 2007: 237–253 on the sophisticated hydrology of Indian Buddhist sites such as Sanchi in the first millennium C.E., enabling the single-phase construction of dams to enable rice production.
13. As a highly inflected language, word position is considerably less

important for meaning in Sanskrit and Pali, thus allowing this flexibility without loss of semantic content.

14. Filliozat 2004: 139.
15. Becchetti 1991.
16. Filliozat 2004.
17. See Kyaw 2014: chapter 5.
18. Von Rospatt 1998: 471.
19. Von Rospatt 1995: 11, 81.
20. Nārada 1969 and 1981.
21. Cousins 1981.
22. Kyaw 2014: 88 and 274. The commentaries analyze the ways the *dhammas* can relate to each other in terms of twenty-four *paccaya*, conditional relations or causal factors, that together determine the trajectory of causality.
23. Ratnajoti and Ratnapāla did not recognize this triggering process when editing a version of this text, and so assumed the text was ungrammatical and needed correcting, meaning that the system no longer works in their redactions (Ratnajoti and Ratnapāla 1963, discussed in Crosby 2005).
24. For discussion of Pali grammarians and variations between them see Gornall 2012 and 2020, and work by Ruiz-Falqués.
25. Internally each of these groups is organized according to the manner or effort (*prayatna* in Sanskrit) required to say them, i.e., voiceless, voiced, non-aspirate, aspirate, nasalized.
26. The final phoneme in each set of plosives is produced in two places, one of the first five places plus the nose. Because of this the nasal consonants are distributed across the first five *sthāna* groupings as the final sound. The nasalization thus corresponds with one of the "efforts" (see previous note).
27. Pāṇini invents the codeword *it* to refer to the *anubandha* in his *Aṣṭadhyāyī*, whereas the term *anubandha*, literally "tagged on," is used by later grammarians.
28. Not all of them can act as final consonants in the real Sanskrit language, but only here when used as codes by Pāṇini. Note that the simple long vowels *ā*, *ī*, and *ū* are not included in Śiva sutras, but their use is taught in the grammar.
29. The final rule of the *Aṣṭadhyāyī* is "*a a*." This is in itself releasing a substitution that had been effective throughout the entire grammar. The short vowel *a*, pronounced as the *u* in the English word "cup," is regarded as the short version of the long vowel *ā*, pronounced like *a* in "car." However, the shape of the mouth for producing these two vowels is in fact different.

They differ by more than just duration. Nonetheless, for the grammar to work, we must accept not only the fiction of *a* simply being a short version of *ā* throughout the grammar, but also their difference in order to be able to use it in the real language.

30. Joshi and Roodbergen 1985: 469–472. Joshi and Roodbergen helpfully summarize their interpretation of *alvidhi* (which becomes *alvidhau* when inflected in the seventh case), a procedure applying to phonemes, as follows: "To sum up, the new interpretation proposed for *alvidhi* in P. 1.1.56 assumes that class properties which are not conditioned by a sound or sequence of sounds of the *sthāṇin*, that is, by specifically phonemic properties of the *sthānin*, are transferable. But individual properties of the *sthānin*, that is, sound properties, like *vyañjanatva* 'being a consonant,' *udāttatva* 'having *udātta* accent,' *hantva* 'being (the sequence) *h-a-n*' are never transferable" (Joshi and Roodbergen 1987: 476). In other words, when substituting phonemes, some aspects of the substituted items may transfer, just not aspects of sound—the sound is replaced and does not continue.
31. Kahrs 1998: 188–189.
32. Piera Candotti and Pontillo 2013.
33. Cousins 1981: 23.
34. Kitchai Urkasame discusses how some of the syllabic identifications work by means of a phonetic similarity with the name for the substituted item, such as the syllable *na* in *na mo bu ddhā ya* representing the element water, the word for which is *nam* in Thai (Urkasame 2013: 306), though it is hard to know whether this phonetic similarity is primary to the association between water and *na* or coincidental and retrospective, given that we do not know the local language at the time and place of *boran kammaṭṭhāna's* origins.

    It is possible that the principle of substitution is relevant to understanding the esoteric interpretation within *borān kammaṭṭhāna* of the term *kammaṭṭhāna* itself. It literally means "place or locus of work" (*karmasthāna* in Sanskrit), or occupation, coming to have the meaning of meditation after the Buddha described meditation as the *kammaṭṭhāna*, occupation, of the monk just as other occupations are the work of different laypeople. (See *Dīghajāṇusutta, Aṅguttara Nikāya* 8.54, cited by Skilton 2019 where this development is explained.) The esoteric interpretation provided by the *borān* tradition is that this "locus of work" is the body (Bernon 2000: 23). The body then becomes the locus, *thāna/sthāna*, onto which different aspects of the meditation practices and stages on the path to arhatship (enlightenment) may be transferred (becoming the *sthānin* in the language of the grammatical rule) and substituted in sequence until the desired outcome is achieved.

35. Ruiz-Falqués examines the development of this aspect of Buddhist philosophy of language further in relation to the *Saddatthabhedacintā*, a grammatical philosophical work composed by the monk Saddhammasiri in thirteenth–fourteenth-century Pagan, making the link between Abhidhamma and generative grammar clear. The *Saddatthabhedacintā* identifies speech sounds as a type of materiality (*rūpa*) born of consciousness, *citta-ja*, an understanding of the relationship between mental processes and materiality found in Abhidhamma. The commentary explains, "What the masters mean is that word/sound is manifested in articulatory organs such as the throat, etc. but it is actually originated when a verbal intimation in consciousness (*vacīviññatti*) enters into contact with the earth element [of action]" (Ruiz-Falqués 2012: 9). Ruiz-Falqués also observes that in this text, "We also find the remarkable statement that phonemes are the highest reality (*paramattha*) whereas words are only conventional concepts (*paññatti*)" (Ruiz-Falqués 2012: 10).
36. Crosby 2006. This treatment of Buddhaghosa as the primary authority for Theravada dates back at least to the twelfth-century reform led by the Mahāvihāra monastery in Sri Lanka, and possibly earlier.
37. Norman (1976) 1991: 87.
38. Crosby 1999a: chapter 5. On attitudes to Pali in Theravada from Buddhaghosa onward, see Crosby 2003.
39. Bizot and von Hinüber 1994: 39.
40. White 1984: 49.
41. The final three words are a phrase taken from a popular tale, *Jātaka* 400, in the context of one fisherman telling another to catch hold of large fish firmly (Fausbøll [1883] 1990: 334). The meaning of the term *cetaso* here is unclear to me, unless it is simply to add a further example. The description of the *grū's* activity is from Bizot and von Hinüber 1994: 44–46.
42. The English is my translation from the Pali and French.
43. Bizot and von Hinüber 1994: 49–84.
44. Ruiz-Falqués 2017: 251. For an edition, see Pind 2013.
45. My telling based on the Sanskrit text in Lanman 1884: 50. For a new edition and full translation of the text, see Mallinson 2007: 150–151.
46. The error is thus a hypercorrection, one mistake made while trying to avoid making another (Hitchings 2011: 187). This is explained as the underlying issue by Norman in relation to another version of the story

found in the Chinese version of the *Mūlasarvāstivādavinaya*. There Ānanda hears "a monk reciting a *Dharmapada* verse which ended with the words, 'It were better that a man live only for one day, and see a water-heron.' Ānanda's efforts to persuade the monk that the verse should have ended with the words 'and see the principle of coming into existence and passing away' were unsuccessful. This Chinese version was following a tradition based up on a Sanskrit form **udaka-baka*, which could only come from a Gāndhārī-type dialect (cf. *udaka-vaya*, GDhp 317) which inserted a non-historic *-k-*, in the place of a glide *-y-*, in the compound *udaya-vyaya* 'arising and passing away'" (Norman [1997] 2006: 90–91). Bizot considers possible north Indian sources for aspects of traditional Cambodian Theravada in the light of these connections (Bizot and Lagirarde 1996: 49).

47. Ruiz-Falqués 2014.
48. D'Alwis 1863: xxi–xxii.
49. Adapted and translated from Bizot and Lagirarde 1996: 223–224.
50. Crosby 1999a: chapter 6.

Chapter 5. Transformation of the Body

1. Bizot 1980: 238–239. My translation into English.
2. I am using the term *Ayurveda* to refer to traditional Indian medicine, rather than in the more technical sense in which it refers to one particular branch of traditional Indian medicine in contrast to others, such as Siddha medicine.
3. Unschuld 1979.
4. Wujastyk (1998) 2001: 4.
5. Wujastyk 2000: 485.
6. Wujastyk 2000: 479.
7. Weiss 1980: 94.
8. Wujastyk 2000: 486.
9. Mulholland 1989.
10. Chhem 2007: 107.
11. Naono 2009: 121–122.
12. These are three robes, an alms bowl, a waistband, a razor, a sewing kit, and a water strainer, and were not just permitted but required. The list of permitted items increases as the Vinaya progresses.
13. Rhys Davids and Oldenberg (1882) 1982: 51–55.
14. Gunawardana 1984.

15. On resistance to modernization in colonial Burma see Turner 2014, and, for a counter-example, see Ashin and Crosby 2016.
16. Mettanando 1999: 52–54.
17. See Andrew Skilton and Phibul Choompolpaisal's translation of the section of his medical work that deals with illnesses stemming from an imbalance in the air or wind element (2017).
18. See Bizot 1981a; Bizot 1980; Urkasame 2013: 322–333; and Becchetti 1994. Crosby 2000a provides a short summary.
19. Mulholland 1989: 20–38. In obstetrics the term *embryo* is used in the first eight weeks from conception, and the term *fetus* thereafter. However, I have used the terms interchangeably to refer to the unborn child.
20. This is not the case for the Buddha-to-be when in the womb.
21. Weiss 1980: 99–100.
22. Mulholland 1989: 37.
23. Weiss 1980: 101.
24. Weiss 1980: 104.
25. Weiss 1980: 108.
26. Weiss 1980: 105.
27. Weiss 1980: 108.
28. Crosby 2014: 153–154.
29. Zysk (1991) 1998: 42–49.
30. Gunawardana 1984: 13–14. For the *Milindapañha* references, see Horner (1963) 1996: 172–181.
31. Gunawardana 1984: 14–15. Since the pathway of repeated combinations between heart and navel suggests that the earlier heart-to-heart model of fetal nutrition, before the recognition of the role of the umbilical cord in Pali commentaries, may underlie *borān kammaṭṭhāna* practice, this may provide us with a date before which *borān kammaṭṭhāna* must have developed, with the inclusion of the *hadayavatthu* found in Abhidhamma commentaries indicating that the practice did not emerge before the commentarial period.
32. Gunawardana does not consider—and it is not known—whether or not nuns were involved in the development of these texts. The nuns order continued in Theravada Buddhism until as late as the thirteenth century.
33. For the parallels between ayurvedic and Theravada commentarial understandings of the stages of development of the womb, see Gunawardana 1984: 19, which also reveals that the Buddhist accounts are relatively close to modern embryology. Terms shared between medical and Buddhist texts on embryology and the meditation texts of *borān kammaṭṭhāna*

include the stages in the development of the embryo and the terms for the father depositing or "placing" (*ṭhapeti*) his semen (*bīja*, *dhātu*) in the womb/embryo (*gabbha*—the term *gabbha* can mean both) found as early as the first century B.C.E. *Milindapañha* (Trenckner 1928: 125). These terms are the same as those used for the *borān* practitioner placing (*ṭhapeti*) the elements (*dhātu*) of the path in his womb/the embryo (*gabbha*) that becomes the future enlightened being. There is a possible parallel between the *ghana* "compact" stage of fetal development in Ayurveda and *borān kammaṭṭhāna*, at which the embryo is fully formed prior to the emergence of gender distinctions, and the most advanced *ghana* level of recitation using permutations, but this is only a speculation at present.

34. Bizot and von Hinüber 1994: 40.
35. Crosby 2014: 203. We see it still in Tai-Khmer Buddhism in the association of lower ordination at age twelve with one's mother (twelve being the number of female constituents in the body) and higher ordination at age twenty with one's father (twenty being the number of male constituents in the body).
36. White 1984: 50.
37. White 1984: 51–52.
38. White 1984: 66.
39. White 1984: 66.
40. White 1984: 51–52.
41. Crosby 1999a: 188, cf. Bizot 1992: 214. The transformative effect of suffusion of one substance with another would also have been familiar to Buddhist monks from water irrigataion, another expertise that may have been important for monks in propagating the religion and ensuring healthy supplies for the monastery. See Shaw 2007.
42. On the longstanding relationship between Buddhist medicine and alchemy in Cambodia, see Chhem 2007: 112.
43. This antagonism has often been construed in religious terms. However, in its impact on Buddhism in Indochina, France was more representative of secularism than Catholicism. While Catholicism was strongly represented in the army and by missionaries, the administrators of French colonialism tended to be secularists and freemasons, particularly after the formal separation of church and state in 1905 (Ovesen and Trankell 2010: 25–26).
44. The History of Vaccines, www.historyofvaccines.org, accessed May 27, 2013.
45. Naono 2009: 137.

46. Putheti, Patil, and Obire 2009: 11.
47. Meulenbeld 1999–2002, vol. 1A: 13. The advantages only began to receive recognition in modern biomedicine in the 1980s. These include direct access to the blood stream through the rich vascular plexus of the nasal cavity and bypassing the possibility of gastro-intestinal destruction. It also avoids the risks and pain of intravenous catheters. It is currently of interest for a range of applications including the potential to bypass the blood-brain barrier and treat the central nervous system, and thus neurodegenerative diseases such as Alzheimers (Alsarra et al. 2010: 175; intranasal.net, accessed February 8, 2020).
48. Naono 2009: 117, 121. Recent developments in modern transdermal delivery using ultrasound to remove the top layer of the skin's surface to make it more permeable are refined versions of the method for delivering ink in tattooing, also long associated with delivering medicine and other forms of protection in Southeast Asia as elsewhere (Kearney 2012). The earliest known tattoos are the fifty-seven tattoos of "Oetzi the Ice Man," whose mummified remains date back at least 5,000 years. The tattoos, coinciding with acupuncture points, are believed by many to be a medical map of the body for curative purposes (Pabst et al. 2009). The permanence of tattooing that makes it useful for this purpose also underlies its use in other contexts: protective *yantras* branding criminals, and marking affiliation. There may be an overlap between the concept of tattoo as an indication of belonging and that of it as protection, i.e., one is protected by, rather than a possible victim of, the more powerful group/individual with whom one is thereby affiliated. Attitudes in China (where tattooing is associated more with the branding of criminals) may explain changes in Thailand in the nineteenth and twentieth centuries, where the use of tattoos at court was no longer required and it became associated with the non-elite classes (Terwiel 1979).
49. Naono 2009: 121. An interesting example comes from Sri Lanka, where smallpox was thought to be inflicted by gods and particularly associated with the goddess Pattini to whom one made offerings for protection from it.
50. Glynn 2004: 20–21. In late eighteenth-century America, variolation continued to be prescribed alongside purging and alchemy using mercury and antimony, as in the case of U.S. President John Adams, who recorded his experience of being inoculated against the Boston epidemic in 1764 (Blinderman 1977).
51. Brimnes 2004.

52. Brimnes 2004.
53. Entrican, *Triennial Report on Vaccination in Burma for 1917–18 to 1919–20*, cited by Naono 2009: 128–129.
54. Glynn 2004: 118.
55. Naono 2009: 129.
56. Naono 2009: 100–101.
57. Naono 2009: 16–39, 85.
58. Ovesen and Trankell 2010: 27, 55–59.
59. Mulholland 1989: 11.
60. Highet 1914.
61. Meulenbeld 1999–2002, vol. 1A: 352.

Chapter 6. From Center to Periphery

1. Translated in Woodward 1916: 150.
2. Although *borān kammaṭṭhāna* manuals provide more than the forty *kammaṭṭhāna* of the *Visuddhimagga* and both *samatha* and *vipassanā* outcomes, as outlined in chapter 1, the terms used in the passage cited here, namely *vidarśanā* and "forty *karmasṭhāna*," are among the most common descriptive names found on Sinhalese manuscripts of this tradition (see Crosby 2019). This may relate to the *Visuddhimagga's* position as an exoteric text, while the more detailed breakdown of *borān* methods are esoteric aspects of the practice.
3. Na Bangchang 1988: 1.
4. *Rājādhirājasiṃha Katikāvatā*, cited by Jayatilaka 1916: 149–150, manuscript catalogued Somadasa 1987–1995, vol. 4: 270–271. For translations of the edicts of Sri Lankan kings, see Ratnapala 1971.
5. Anne Blackburn, in her study of the nature of the Siyam Nikāya revival under Saraṇaṃkara, notes that the leading lights of the revival such as Saraṇaṃkara himself are described as meditators and that Saraṇaṃkara wrote on aspects of meditation in his commentaries (Blackburn 2001: 95). She does not discuss the nature of the meditation that he practiced. No *borān kammaṭṭhāna* manuals have been identified in the temple libraries she documents, and the identification of the tradition within the Siyam Nikāya, though suggested by Jayatilaka (1916) and reported by the Rāmañña Nikāya meditation monk Ñāṇarāma (studied by Carrithers 1983: 232–233), was only confirmed more recently from evidence within the manuals themselves (Crosby, Skilton, Gunasena 2012). Some of the *paritta* verses found in the *Vākkapprakaraṇa* text of litanies (chapter

3) to accompany *borān kammaṭṭhāna* practice have been identified by Amal Gunasena (personal communication, 2009) as compositions by Saraṇaṃkara.

6. It is possible that the tradition continued longer, but I have no firm evidence. Some monks from Sri Lanka visited Wat Ratchasittharam in Thonburi, Bangkok, in 2012 and reported the continued existence of such practice to Veera Thanaveero, the head of the *borān kammaṭṭhāna* meditation tradition there, even though such practice was not their own. Unfortunately, they did not leave their details, so I have been unable to contact them to verify these claims (personal conversation, Veera Thanaveero, January 2013).
7. Ratnajoti and Ratnapāla 1963; Crosby 2005.
8. "The bhikkhu Doratiyāveye, Thera, was incumbent of the Hangurangketa Wihāra in the Western [*sic*] Province of Ceylon, and was living so recently as 1900" (Woodward 1916: xviii). Although Woodward identifies this as being in Western Province, this monastery is in Central Province (correction from Amal Gunasena, personal communication, September 5, 2013).

   For the extent to which Madame Blavatsky continued to influence Anagarika Dharmapala's meditation and personal spiritual quest throughout his life, see Kemper 2015 and 2019.
9. Fernando 1960; Suraweera 1968; Blackburn 2001: 54–55. It seems to have been specifically in the modern era, as colonial powers and court and Sangha hierarchies each sought to enhance their own power, that monks who might prove non-compliant were disempowered through both rhetoric and regulation that confined them to "non-worldly" activities. In Thailand and Cambodia, during the Bangkok and Phnom Penh periods, a major motivation for reform was the fear of militant monks who lay beyond royal control. Even among those who accept a stark lay-monastic divide, the anxiety to protect the Dhamma and the rhetoric that anxiety inspires perennially motivate enterprising and ambitious monks to engage directly in politics. This anxiety may justify an interpretation that connects the conspiracy against Kīrti Śrī with his status as an "alien" king, a Śaiva from South India, although political intermarriage with Nayakkars of South India since the seventeenth century meant that he was not the first king in this dynasty.
10. Choompolpaisal forthcoming.
11. Terwiel 2019: 8–13. Phibul Choompolpaisal and Andrew Skilton have also found a manuscript of a text called the *Lakkhaṇadhamma* ascribed to King Taksin and previously thought lost (Skilton 2019: 54).

12. Taylor 1993: 24.
13. Taylor 1993: 30.
14. For different types of monastic dress in Thailand, see Bizot 1993.
15. Choompolpaisal 2011: 189.
16. Choompolpaisal 2011: 259–263, 268–269, 280–281.
17. It seems possible that Mongkut had no immediate facility in meditation. One may speculate that his status and his personal identity, divided between patriotic traditionalism and modernist reform, compromised the usual incentives for a monk to make progress in the absence of the rewards that some practitioners gain more easily. On the one hand, as crown prince, Mongkut hardly needed incentives of status; on the other hand, his reformist convictions were at odds with the "spiritual" attainments on offer. Most of all, potential long-term subordination to a meditation teacher may have been unappealing to an ambitious young man already endowed with political influence and intellectual ability.
18. Taylor 1993: 42.
19. Ñāṇamoli 1956: III, 64.
20. For an example of this process in relation to Burma, see Kyaw's discussion of the Theinngu Sayadaw's meditation practice and the necessity and manner of its authorization (Kyaw 2019).
21. Taylor 1993: 43; Crosby 2014: 91.
22. Choompolpaisal 2019: 155.
23. Taylor 1993: 42.
24. For example, manuscripts call number *pho* 20 and *ko* 8; personal communication, Phibul Choompolpaisal, July 2013.
25. Kittivuttho 2003: 64–65. I have not yet seen this text of the *Paṭhamasambodhi*, nor do I know if the manuscript by him corresponds with the book version published in 1923, and republished 1925–1926. I therefore do not know the nature of the *borān kammaṭṭhāna* elements thought to be contained in it.
26. Laulertvorakul 2003: 27–30.
27. Malasart 2019: 45 and in preparation.
28. Hansen 2007: 94.
29. During this and later periods when no *sangharat* was appointed the highest-ranking monks in the kingdom were members of the royal family ordained in the Thammayut Nikāya.
30. Choompolpaisal 2011: 268–269.
31. Choompolpaisal 2011: 267–269.
32. Taylor 1993: 33.

33. Taylor 1993: 42–43.
34. Nagasena 2012: 23.
35. Wyatt 1969: 234–242.
36. Taylor 1993: 34.
37. Choompolpaisal 2011: 279–286.
38. Taylor 1993: 32.
39. Skilton 2019. Skilton's article includes a detailed discussion of Mongkut's criticism of the Buddhism of his compatriots.
40. There seem to be some common elements between *borān kammaṭṭhāna* and Thammayut forest tradition practice, including in the litanies used for worship, the use of the preparatory recitation of "*buddho*," and the simplified visualization of a sphere of light, all of which warrant further consideration.
41. Tiyavanich 1997: 172–198, 252–273.
42. Taylor 1993: 53; material in square brackets is my addition.
43. www.dhammathai.org.
44. Taylor 1993: 57.
45. Yasothararat 1936: 10.
46. Yasothararat 1936: 2.
47. Taylor 1993: 57.
48. Yasothararat 1936: 4–8.
49. Article by Assistant Prof. Huan Phinthuphan of the Faculty of Education, Srinakarinwirot University: http://facstaff.swu.ac.th/huan, accessed August 11, 2013. www.vajira.org/index.php/temple-public-news, accessed April 20, 2019. The latter is the website of the Thai temple Vajiradhammapadip, which follows the meditation lineage from Wat Paknam.
50. Unfortunately, the websites that mention this do not specify the source either of the accusation or of the information about the accusation. Further details of attacks on Sot, including an apparent attempted shooting, are given on the website of the Dhammakaya Foundation, which also draws authority for its meditation practices from Sot: www.dmc.tv/pages/phramongkolthepmuni/2007-04-21-1.html, accessed August 11, 2013, confirmed April 20, 2019. The shooting incident is recounted in print in Anonymous 2010: 54–55.
51. Harris 2005: 106.
52. Bernon 2012: 379.
53. On the development of modernist Buddhism among Cambodian monks in the nineteenth and twentieth centuries, and the role played by new approaches to textual studies, see Hansen 2007: chapter 3.

54. Harris 2005: 105–109.
55. Harris 2005: 110.
56. Translated with my additional comments in square brackets from the French of Bizot 1976: 11–12.
57. Hansen 2007: 102–103.
58. Bernon 2000: 32; Harris 2005: 117–119.
59. Harris 2005: 168.
60. Choompolpaisal 2011: 288–289.
61. Matpimon 2009: 3.
62. Darunnakon 1935; Choompolpaisal 2019.
63. We can see this most obviously with monastic robes. In Cambodia modernizing Mahanikay monks began adopting the simpler robes of the Thammayut Nikāya around 1918 (Harris 2005: 107). Those who wanted to retain the old *borān* practices also retained the old method of dress and the older generation of conservative monks sought to prevent the adoption of the simplified robes with an ordinance in 1918 under which several modernizing monks were prosecuted (Hansen 2007: 106). In Thailand the adoption of Thammayut dress style was more widespread. Monks who practice *borān kammaṭṭhāna* in Cambodia today, on seeing photographs of *borān kammaṭṭhāna* practitioners in Thailand, confirm that they are doing the correct devotional rituals (judged from a photograph of the standard five-candle offering), but say with conviction that their practice must be wrong since they are wearing incorrect monastic dress (Crosby and Long fieldwork December 2012).

Chapter 7. Meditation in Modern Revivals

1. Blackburn 2001.
2. Malalgoda 1976: 91. As the Salāgama caste rose in power it developed a self-narrative claiming descent from a very high brahmin caste, a claim presumably made to indicate that they were higher status than the Goyigama (Malalgoda 1976: 102).
3. Malalgoda 1976: 89–90.
4. Sudhamma in standard Pali transcription. On the Thudhamma reform, see Charney 2006: 96–105. The council's powers included the authority to defrock monks for infringements other than the four *pārājika* offenses, in monastic *vinaya* law the exclusive grounds for expulsion (Pranke 2004: v–vi). The four *pārājika* offenses are sexual intercourse, murder, theft of a substantial amount, and falsely claiming superhuman powers. State and state-sponsored hierarchies have frequently sought to defrock monks for

reasons other than these four. However, a state-sanctioned defrocking is only recognized within the state that organizes it, leading such hierarchies to prefer to pin the universally recognized *pārājika* offenses on those whom they wish to disempower, particularly those with an international following outside local state control (see Crosby 2014: 208 and 278). (Here I use the term "defrock" to mean "expel someone from the Sangha," and "disrobe" to mean "leave the Sangha voluntarily," although the ritual process of returning to lay life is the same.)

5. Pranke 2004: 5.
6. Nagasena 2012: 166, 224–233.
7. De Silva 1847, cited in Malalgoda 1976: 103. Although the Amarapura Nikāya was described as being anti-polytheist by de Silva, it is not clear to me how true this is and how much it was part of the Amarapura Nikāya when first formed. Although the worship of local gods instead of the Buddha is an accusation that appears against the mythical "Ari heretical monks" in the chronicles that the Thudhamma hierarchy wrote, even Ledi Sayadaw, the epitome of Burmese reform Buddhism and author of an important anti-monotheist work, accepted the belief in non-human beings (Pyi Phyo Kyaw and Patrick Pranke, personal communication, August 2013). In the twentieth century dismissing the importance or ultimate validity of worship was a fairly consistent feature of scholarly Buddhism in Burma and Sri Lanka. The third Sri Lankan *nikāya*, the Rāmañña Nikāya, would later criticize both the Amarapura and the Siyam Nikāya for their tolerance of polytheism. While polytheism does not, then, appear to have been an issue for the Thudhamma monks or the initial founders of the Amarapura Nikāya, it was an aspect deemed un-Buddhist by Christian observers. The adoption of this stance could have been a response to the Christian missionary context within which Amarapura monks were working, based as they were in colonial territory. Later it facilitated their alliance with the theosophists, important in supporting aspects of the Buddhist revival, including financial support for Anagarika Dharmapala's project to restore Buddhist sites in India to Buddhist control through the Mahābodhi Society.
8. Malalgoda 1976: 152.
9. Malalgoda 1976: 151–161. As an aside, it was this extensive practice at writing tracts and debating that stood the Sangha in good stead for the debates with the Christians later, particularly the Pānadura debate of 1873.
10. Pranke 2004: 28–29.

11. Malalgoda 1976: 166–169.
12. Carrithers 1983: 236. Carrithers offers the following comment, indicating that his negative views of the meditation practices of Sri Lanka were not confined to the *borān kammaṭṭhāna*: "If I am correct in assuming that the line of meditation advice began to take on a purely dogmatic—rather than experiential—character, this is a manifestation of that tendency. . . . And indeed, if one really 'begins with attention to the eighteen elements,' one may never get past learning them by heart. The point may very easily be obscured behind a mass of scholastic detail, never to emerge" (Carrithers 1983: 236–237).
13. Malalgoda 1976: 133–134, 155; Kariyawasam 1973: 4–5.
14. Blackburn 2010: 147.
15. Malalgoda 1976: 165–166.
16. Carrithers 1983: 113.
17. Carrithers 1983: 210–213.
18. Carrithers 1983: 232.
19. Carrithers 1983: 233.
20. Carrithers 1983: 233 with note 16.
21. Bond 1988: 133.
22. Harris 2005: 174–178.
23. These rituals are described in Bizot 1981a.
24. Achar Oun was concerned about the future of his collection of *borān kammaṭṭhāna* texts, which Long Sarou and I arranged to be copied by the staff of EFEO in Phnom Penh. While we also arranged for a cupboard suitable to protect the manuscripts, it does not seem to have been used for this purpose for long, and we are not sure what happened to the originals as his eyesight then clarity deteriorated over the following years.
25. Crosby and Long, interviews throughout December 2012.
26. The restriction in the Khmer Rouge–controlled area was only in place there for four or five years, but nearer to ten—i.e., until 1988—in the Vietnamese-controlled areas. This picture of a more flexible approach in the Khmer Rouge territories of Kampong Cham was confirmed by several sources. Possibly the nun's son disrobed once restrictions in the Vietnamese-controlled area began to be enforced.
27. Ven. Sopheap, interview, Wat Pras Meas, December 12, 2012.
28. The nun, Oun Sophy, or Yey Phy ("Grandma Phy"), when first recounting her relationship with the abbot told me that the abbot had shown his recognition of her achievement by ordaining her—not in the simple clothing of a nun, but the robes of a monk dyed white, distinguishing her from the

other women who become nuns, usually just for the annual three-month rainy season retreat. A few years later, when I had joined the rains retreat meditation myself, Yey Phy clarified that the abbot did not bestow these robes during her lifetime but after his death, when they met in her meditation. For Cambodians, the access the practice gives one to beings in other realms, particularly the deceased, is very important and one of the reasons for its survival. Regarding the robes, although the full ordination of nuns, *bhikkhunī*, has been revived in Sri Lanka, nuns in Southeast Asia, called *don chi* in Cambodia, are "precept nuns" rather than "fully ordained." This means that on the whole they follow the ten precepts of a novice monk, *sāmaṇera*, rather than the full set of *vinaya* rules followed by monks, *bhikkhu*, who have undergone the higher ordination, *upasampadā*. Precept nuns wear simple white robes rather than the set of three yellow, brown, or orange robes of the monks. The process of ordination for precept nuns is flexible and can be performed by a single monk, whereas a *bhikkhunī* must be ordained both by other *bhikkhunī* and *bhikkhu*. For a discussion of the history of *bhikkhunī* and precept nuns see Crosby 2014: chapter 9.

29. Interview, December 31, 2012, and ongoing discussions in subsequent years.
30. Interview, December 31, 2012. Since 2015 I have undertaken the practice under Neang Sam Ol's guidance.
31. Interview, Wat Champukaek, December 18, 2012.
32. Interview, December 25, 2012. On Wat Preak Brang, see Marston 2008: 110–112. Samdech Preah Krou Om Bunheng, the head monk at Wat Champukaek, does not teach *borān kammaṭṭhāna*, but has made great efforts to ensure there is always such a teacher there. At the time of the interviews that my colleague Long Sarou and I conducted at these temples in December 2012, both temples were providing services for individual members of the then-ruling Shinowatra family of Thailand.
33. Bernon 2000: 19–21.
34. The nature of the resumed practice seems to be at the physically more gentle end of the spectrum. While I have witnessed the "rebirth rituals" described by Bizot (1981a), I have not heard accounts of anything like the physically demanding initiation rituals described by Ven. Vanarot Ken Vong (1924–1994) as taking place in the 1950s and recorded by de Bernon (2000: 19–21). Thus there seems to have been a shift within *borān kammaṭṭhāna* toward a focus on sitting meditation, in other words to become closer to the more globally accepted conception of what meditation should entail.
35. Marston 2008: 108.

36. Group interview at Wat Champukaek, 2003.
37. The *wat achar*, the lay men who manage and perform important services at temples, often provide continuity and consistency across the generations of monks. One that we met at a temple in Kandal Province had traveled a long way to stay at the temple and learn the practice in response to the collective decision of all the *achar* at his temple (there are often around 7–8) that one of them should acquire sufficient expertise in *borān kammaṭṭhāna* to help with funerals (interview, December 31, 2012).
38. In 2017 I heard of the revival of the practice by a former and reordained monk in the Kulen mountains but have yet to verify the nature of this revival. I have not come across the practice among the younger generations, though this was still widespread in the first half of the twentieth century.
39. Crosby and Long interviews, December 2012.
40. Marston 2009: 238–247.
41. Crosby and Long interviews, Kandal Province, December 2012.
42. Interviews, December 2012. In asking the supreme patriarch to suppress *borān kammaṭṭhāna*, Sam Buntheoun was in a sense invoking the pre–Khmer Rouge antagonism between *borān* and *samay*, i.e., modern Buddhism (Marston 2008: 99), just as his teaching of Vipassanā seems to have drawn on its developing popularity prior to the Khmer Rouge period.
43. Email interview, Battambang, December 2012. In the light of the ongoing border disputes with Thailand and the earlier history of conflict between the two nations, to claim that someone promotes Thai Dhamma is a criticism in the modern period. It is accurate to associate Vipassanā with Thailand in that pre-war Vipassanā teachers had trained there (interview with Achar Long Bok, a senior Vipassanā meditation teacher, Kos Krolor District, Battambang Province, December 26, 2012), but it is not clear to me that Buth Savong promoted Vipassanā. I would like to thank John Marston for replying to my questions about Buth Savong. In terms of the view of *borān kammaṭṭhāna* as originating in Cambodia, the picture is quite complex. In the case of Wat Damrei Sar, the pronunciation of the litanies and the oral history of the temple suggest that while the practice is clearly related to other *borān kammaṭṭhāna* in Cambodia, their particular branch at some point came from Thailand.
44. Choompolpaisal 2011: 293–296.
45. Akaramahabhandit 2003: 9–21.
46. Soundclips of Chodok can be found at www.youtube.com/watch?v=B-VGBLGwjC9Y, accessed May 21, 2019.
47. Much has been written on Kittivuddho's infamous anti-communist state-

ments, including in books discussing Buddhism and violence. See, for example, Suksamran 1982: 132–157.
48. Choompolpaisal 2011: 296–309, 315–319.
49. Randall 1990: 23. *Mae chi* is the Thai prase for "precept nuns" who usually take the same ten precepts of novice monks. The full ordination of nuns as *bhikkhunī* is not permitted in Thailand.
50. Skilton 2013b. Kapilavaḍḍho wrote about his experiences in the posthumously published *Life as a Siamese Monk* under the name Richard Randall (1990). For film footage of the ordination of the three monks, see www.youtube.com/watch?v=SZwxJyfJ3Oo, accessed May 20, 2019.
51. Crosby 2014: 162. The death toll is still unclear, with widely different estimates.
52. www.triple-gem.net/phra-terry, accessed May 20, 2019.
53. Mettanando 1999: 2.
54. Cadge 2004.
55. In 1992 Wat Phra Dhammakaya established its first international branch in California.
56. It is possible that the simplification attributed to Sot is only at the early stages, in which case he popularized meditation rather than changed it, for the early stages are also relatively simple in other traditions of *borān kammaṭṭhāna*. Other factors usually emphasized in the success of Dhammakaya are its business model, encouragement of large donations, and high level of organization. See Scott 2009.
57. Skilton and Choompolpaisal 2014: 112.

Conclusion

1. See the discussion of Copleston and Alabaster in chapter 1.
2. I am thinking here of such developments as the identification of telomeres, the effect of meditation on them, and their role in the retention of cognitive reserve.

Bibliography

Akaramahabhandit, Phrasophonmahathera. 2003 [2546 B.E.]. *Lakkarn Patibat Vipatsana Kammatthan* [The Principles of the Practice of Vipassana-Kammatthan]. Bangkok: Mahachula University Publication.

Alabaster, Henry. 1871. *The Wheel of the Law: Buddhism Illustrated from Siamese Sources*. London: Trübner & Co.

Almond, Philip C. 1988. *The British Discovery of Buddhism*. Cambridge: Cambridge University Press.

Alsarra, Ibrahim A., Amel Y. Hamed, Fars K. Alanazi, and Gamal M. El Maghraby. 2010. "Vesicular Systems for Intranasal Drug Delivery." In *Drug Delivery to the Central Nervous System*, edited by K. K. Jain, 175–203. Neuromethods 45. New York: Humana Press.

"Amatākaravaṇṇanā." Unpublished manuscript, number Or6601(85)I, around late 1750s. London: Nevill Collection, Asia and Africa Collections, British Library.

Anālayo, Bhikkhu. 2012. "The Dynamics of Theravāda Insight Meditation." In 佛教禪坐傳統國際學術研討 會論文集 [Buddhist Meditation Traditions: An International Symposium], edited by Kuo-pin Chuang, 23–56. Taiwan: Dharma Drum Publishing Corporation. www.semanticscholar.org/paper/The-Dynamics-of-Theravada-Insight-Meditation-An%C4%81layo/30bccc6816d0b17712b1815c2555 6d9e73be5820, accessed September 13, 2013.

Anonymous. 2010. *The Life and Times of Luang Phaw Wat Paknam*. 4th ed. Pathumthani: Dhammakaya Foundation.

Ashin, Janaka, and Kate Crosby. 2016. "All Too Human: The Impact of International Buddhist Networks on the Life and Posthumous Conviction of the Burmese Nationalist Monk, Shin Ukkaṭṭha (1897–1978)." *Journal for the Irish Society for the Academic Study of Religions* 3: 219–235.

———. 2017. "Heresy and Monastic Malpractice in the Buddhist Court Cases (*Vinicchaya*) of Modern Burma (Myanmar)." *Contemporary Buddhism* 18 (1): 199–261.

Aung, Shwe Zan. 1910. *Compendium of Philosophy Being a Translation Now Made for the First Time from the Original Pali of the Abhidhammattha-saṅgaha*. London: The Pali Text Society.

———. 1918. "Buddhism and Science." *Journal of Burma Research Society* 8 (1): 99–106.

Bapat, P. V. 1972. Review of Galkätiyagama Ratnajoti and Karalliyaddē Ratnapāla (1963). *Journal of the Vidyalankara University of Ceylon* 1 (1): 172–190.

Barker, George F. 1886. "Memoir of John William Draper 1811–1882." (Read before the National Academy, April 21, 1886.) Offprint, *National Academy of Sciences Biographical Memoirs* 2: 349–388. Washington, DC: National Academy of Sciences.

Barrett, T. H. 2008a. *The Rise and Spread of Printing: A New Account of Religious Factors*. 2nd ed. Watford, UK: Minnow Press.

———. 2008b. *The Woman who Discovered Printing*. New Haven and London: Yale University Press.

Becchetti, C. 1991. *Le Mystère dans les Lettres*. Bangkok: Éditions de Cahiers de France.

———. 1994. "Une ancienne tradition de manuscrits au Cambodge." In *Recherches nouvelles sur le Cambodge*, edited by François Bizot, 47–62. Paris: École française d'Extrême-Orient.

Bechert, H. 1989. "Vimuttimagga and Amatakaravannana." In *Amalā Prajñā: Aspects of Buddhist Studies: Professor P. V. Bapat Felicitation Volume*, edited by N. H. Samtani and H. S. Prasad, 11–14. Bibliotheca Indo-Buddhica 63. Delhi: Sri Satguru Publications.

Bernon, Olivier de. 2000. "Le Manuel des Maîtres de *kammaṭṭhān*, Études et présentation de rituels de méditation dans la tradition du bouddhisme khmer." PhD thesis, Institut National des Langues et Civilisations Orientales.

———. 2002. "Le *mūl kammaṭṭhān* du Wat Ratchathiwat daté de 1661 A.D.: Présentation et traduction." *Journal of the Siam Society* 90–91: 149–160.

———. 2012. "Circulation of Texts in Mid-Nineteenth Century Cambodia: A New Reading of Inscription K. 892 (Vatt Tā Tok, CE 1857)." In Skilling et al. 2012: 371–399.

Bizot, François. 1971. "La figuration des pieds du Bouddha au Cambodge." *Asiatische Studien: Zeitschrift der Schweizerischen Asiengesellschaft = Études asiatiques: revue de la Société Suisse-Asie* 25: 407–439.

———. 1973. *Histoire du Reamker. Rion ramakerti nai tā cak'*. Phnom

Penh: École française d'Extrême-Orient. Reprint, Bangkok: École française d'Extrême-Orient, 1980, 1983; and Phnom Penh: Éditions sauvages, 1991, 1993.

———. 1976. *Le figuier à cinq branches*. Recherches sur le bouddhisme khmer I, Publications de l'École française d'Extrême-Orient 107. Paris: École française d'Extrême-Orient.

———. 1980. "La grotte de la naissance." Recherches sur le bouddhisme khmer II, *Bulletin de l'École française d'Extrême Orient* 67: 222–273.

———. 1981a. *Le don de soi-même*. Recherches sur le bouddhisme khmer III, Publications de l'École française d'Extrême-Orient 130. Paris: École française d'Extrême-Orient.

———. 1981b. "Notes sur les *yantra* bouddhiques d'Indochine." In *Tantric and Taoist Studies in Honour of R. A. Stein*, edited by M. Strickmann, 155–191. Mélanges Chinois et Bouddhiques 20. Brussels: Institut Belge des Hautes Etudes Chinoises.

———. 1988. *Les traditions de la pabbajjā en Asie du Sud-Est*. Recherches sur le bouddhisme khmer IV. Göttingen: Vandenhoeck & Ruprecht.

———. 1989. *Reamaker ou l'Amour Symbolique de Rām et Setā*. Recherches sur le bouddhisme khmer V. Paris: École française d'Extrême-Orient.

———. 1992. *Le chemin de Lankā*. Textes bouddhiques du Cambodge I. Paris: École française d'Extrême-Orient.

———. 1993. *Le Bouddhisme des Thaïs*. Bangkok: Éditions des Cahiers de France.

———. 1994a. "La Consécration des Statues et le culte des Morts." In *Recherches nouvelles sur le Cambodge*, edited by François Bizot, 101–127. Paris: École française d'Extrême-Orient.

———, ed. 1994b. *Recherches nouvelles sur le Cambodge*. Paris: École française d'Extrême-Orient.

———. 2000. "La place des communautés du Nord-Laos dans l'histoire du bouddhisme d'Asie du Sud-Est." *Bulletin de l'École française d'Extrême-Orient* 87 (2): 511–528.

Bizot, François, and François Lagirarde. 1996. *Saddavimala: La pureté par les mots*. Paris and Chiang Mai, Thailand: École française d'Extrême-Orient.

Bizot, François, and Oskar von Hinüber. 1994. *La guirlande de Joyaux*. Textes bouddhiques du Cambodge II. Paris: École française d'Extrême-Orient.

Blackburn, Anne M. 2001. *Buddhist Learning and Textual Practice in Eighteenth-Century Lankan Monastic Culture*. Princeton, NJ: Princeton University Press.

———. 2010. *Locations of Buddhism: Colonialism and Modernity in Sri Lanka*. Chicago: University of Chicago Press.

Blinderman, A. 1977. "John Adams: Fears, Depressions, and Ailments." *New York State Journal of Medicine* 77: 268–276.

Bode, Mabel Haynes. 1909. *The Pali Literature of Burma*. London: Royal Asiatic Society.

Bodhi, Bhikkhu et al. 1993. *A Comprehensive Manual of Abhidhamma: The Abhidhammattha Sangaha of Ācariya Anuruddha*. Kandy: Buddhist Publication Society.

Bond, George. 1988. *The Buddhist Revival in Sri Lanka: Religious Tradition, Reinterpretation, and Response*. Columbia: University of South Carolina Press.

Bornaetxea, Rodriguez Fernando, and David Alvear Morón. 2014. "Construction of Reality or Dependent Origination? From Scientific Psychotherapy to Responsible Attention." *Contemporary Buddhism* 15: 216–243.

Bowers, Jeffrey. 1996. *Dhammakaya Meditation in Thai Society*. Bangkok: Chulalongkorn University Printing House.

Braun, Erik C. 2013. *The Birth of Insight: Meditation, Modern Buddhism, and the Burmese Monk Ledi Sayadaw*. Chicago: University of Chicago Press.

Brimnes, Niels. 2004. "Variolation, Vaccination and Popular Resistance in Early Colonial South India." *Medical History* 48 (2), April 1: 199–228.

Cadge, Wendy. 2004. *Heartwood: The First Generation of Theravada Buddhism in America*. Chicago: University of Chicago Press.

Carrithers, M. 1983. *The Forest Monks of Sri Lanka: An Anthropological and Historical Study*. Delhi: Oxford University Press.

Charney, Michael W. 2006. *Powerful Learning: Buddhist Literati and the Throne in Burma's Last Dynasty, 1752–1885*. Ann Arbor: Centers for South and Southeast Asian Studies, The University of Michigan.

Chhem, Rethy K. 2007. "La médecine au service du pourvoir angkorien: Universités monastiques, transmission du savoir et formation médicale sous le règne de Jayavarman VII (1181–1220 A.D.)." *Canadian Journal of Buddhist Studies* 3: 95–124.

Choompolpaisal, Phibul. 2011. "Reassessing Modern Thai Political Buddhism: A Critical Study of Sociological Literature from Weber to Keyes." PhD thesis, School of Oriental and African Studies, University of London.

———. 2019. "*Nimitta* and Visual Methods in Siamese and Lao Medita-

tion Traditions from the 17th Century to the Present Day." *Contemporary Buddhism* 20 (1): 152–183.
———. Forthcoming. "*Boran Kammaṭṭhan* (Ancient Theravāda) Meditation Transmissions from Late Ayutthaya to Rattanakosin Periods" (provisional title). *Buddhist Studies Review.*
Chulachomklao Tipiṭaka. 1893. Compiled in 28 volumes under the patronage of the Thai king Chulalongkorn, or Rama V.
Coedès, G. 1915. "Dhammakāya." *Adyar Library Bulletin* 20: 248–285.
Copleston, R. S. (1892) 1908. *Buddhism Primitive and Present in Magadha and in Ceylon.* London: Longmans, Green.
Cousins, Lance. 1981. "The Paṭṭhāna and the Development of the Theravādin Abhidhamma." *Journal of the Pāli Text Society* 9: 22–46.
Crosby, Henrietta Kate. 1999a. "Studies in the Medieval Pali Literature of Sri Lanka with Special Reference to the Esoteric Yogavacara Tradition." DPhil thesis, University of Oxford.
Crosby, Kate. 2000a. "Tantric Theravada: A Bibliographic Essay on the Writings of François Bizot and Other Literature on the *Yogāvacara* Tradition." *Contemporary Buddhism* 1 (2): 141–198.
———. 2000b. "*Uddis* and *Ācikh:* The Inclusion of the *Sikkhāpada* in the *Pabbajjā* Liturgy According to the *Samantapāsādikā*. *Journal of Indian Philosophy* 28 (5–6): 461–477.
———. 2003. "The Origin of the Language Name Pāli in Medieval Theravāda Literature." *Journal of Buddhist Studies,* Centre for Buddhist Studies, Sri Lanka, 2: 70–116.
———. 2005. "Differences between the Vimuttimagga-uddāna and the Amatākaravaṇṇanā." *Journal of Buddhist Studies,* Centre for Buddhist Studies, Sri Lanka, 3: 139–151.
———. 2006. "Sāriputta's Three Works on the *Samantapāsādikā*." *Journal of the Pali Text Society* 28: 49–59.
———. 2007. "*Saṅkhepasārasaṅgaha*." *Journal of the Pali Text Society* 29: 169–174.
———. 2013. *Traditional Theravada Meditation and Its Modern-Era Suppression.* Hong Kong: Buddha-Dharma Centre of Hong Kong.
———. 2014. *Theravada Buddhism: Continuity, Diversity, Identity.* Oxford: Wiley-Blackwell.
———. 2017. "The Impact of the Science-Religion Bifurcation on the Landscape of Modern Theravada Meditation." In *Theravada Encounters with Modernity,* edited by Steven Collins and Juliane Schober, 29–46. London: Routledge.

———. 2019. "Abhidhamma and *Nimitta* in 18th-Century Meditation Manuscripts from Sri Lanka: A Consideration of Orthodoxy and Heteropraxy in *Boran Kammaṭṭhāna*." *Contemporary Buddhism* 20 (1): 111–151.

Crosby, Kate, Andrew Skilton, and Amal Gunasena. 2012. "The Sutta on Understanding Death in the Transmission of *Borān* Meditation from Siam to the Kandyan Court." *Journal of Indian Philosophy* 40 (2): 177–198.

Crosby, Kate, Andrew Skilton, and Pyi Phyo Kyaw, eds. 2019. *Variety in Theravada Meditation*. Special issue, *Contemporary Buddhism* 20 (1).

D'Alwis, James. 1863. *An Introduction to Kachchāyana's Grammar of the Pāli Language*. London: Williams & Northgate.

Darunnakon, Luangvisan. 1935. [2478 B.E.]. *Samatha-Vipassana Kammathan*. A funeral publication in commemoration of Phraphuttha Vithi Nayok (Bun) at the Meru of Wat Klang Bangkaew (Bangkok). No publisher details.

De Silva, A. 1847. "On the Corruptions of Buddhism and the Different Tenets, Opinions and Principles of the Amarapoora and Siamese Sects." Appendix XII to Ribeyro's *History of Ceylon* (1685), retranslated from the French edition (with an appendix) by George Lee. Colombo.

de Zilva Wickremasinghe, Don Martino. 1901. *Catalogue of the Sinhalese Printed Books in the Library of the British Museum*. London: British Museum.

Dixon, Thomas. 2008. *Science and Religion: A Very Short Introduction*. Oxford: Oxford University Press.

Draper, John William. 1874. *History of the Conflict between Religion and Science*. London and New York: D. Appleton.

Fausbøll, Viggo. (1883) 1990. *The Jātaka together with Its Commentary Being Tales of the Anterior Births of Gotama Buddha*. III. Oxford: Pali Text Society.

Fernando, P. E. E. 1960. "Indian Office Land Grant of King Kīrti Śrī Rājasiṃha." *Ceylon Journal of Humanities and Social Sciences* 3 (1): 72–81.

Filliozat, Pierre-Sylvain. 2004. "Ancient Sanskrit Mathematics: An Oral Tradition and a Written Literature." In *History of Science, History of Text*, edited by Karine Chemla, 137–157, 360–375. Boston Studies in the Philosophy of Science 238. Dordrecht: Springer Netherlands.

Finot, L. 1917. "Recherches sur la littérature laotienne." *Bulletin de l'École française d'Extrême-Orient* 17 (5): 1–219.

Gabaude, Louis. 2003a. "Where Ascetics Get Comfort and Recluses Go Public: Museums for Buddhist Saints in Thailand." In *Pilgrims, Patrons, and Place: Localizing Sanctity in Asian Religions*, edited by Phyllis Granoff and Koichi Shinohara, 103–123. Vancouver and Toronto: University of British Columbia Press.

———. 2003b. "A New Phenomenon in Thai Monasteries: The Stūpa-Museum." In *The Buddhist Monastery. A Cross-Cultural Survey*, edited by Pierre Pichard and François Lagirarde, 169–186. Paris: École française d'Extrême-Orient.

Glynn, Ian, and Jennifer. 2004. *The Life and Death of Smallpox*. London: Profile Books.

Gombrich, R. F., and G. Obeyesekere. 1988. *Buddhism Transformed: Religious Change in Sri Lanka*. Princeton, NJ: Princeton University Press.

Gornall, Alastair. 2012. "Buddhism and Grammar: The Scholarly Cultivation of Pāli in Medieval Laṅkā." PhD thesis, University of Cambridge.

Gornall, Alastair. 2020. *Rewriting Buddhism. Pali Literature and Monastic Reform in Sri Lanka, 1157–1270*. London: UCL Press.

Greene, Eric M. Forthcoming. *Chan Before Chan: Meditation, Repentance, and Visionary Experience in Early Medieval Chinese Buddhism*. Honolulu: University of Hawai'i Press.

Gunawardana, R. A. L. H. 1984. "Obstetrics and Theories of Reproduction in Ancient and Early Medieval Sri Lanka." *Journal of Humanities and Social Sciences of the University of Kelaniya (Kalyani)* 3–4: 1–22.

Hallisey, Charles. 1993. "*Nibbānasutta:* An Allegedly Non-Canonical Sutta on Nibbāna as a Great City." *Journal of the Pali Text Society* 18: 97–130.

Hansen, Anne Ruth. 2007. *How to Behave: Buddhism and Modernity in Colonial Cambodia, 1860–1930*. Honolulu: University of Hawai'i Press.

Harris, Elizabeth J. 2006. *Theravāda Buddhism and the British Encounter: Religious, Missionary and Colonial Experience in Nineteenth-Century Sri Lanka*. London: Routledge.

———. 2019. "Buddhist Meditation and the British Colonial Gaze in Nineteenth-Century Sri Lanka." *Contemporary Buddhism* 20 (1): 200–222.

Harris, Ian. 2005. *Cambodian Buddhism: History and Practice*. Honolulu: University of Hawai'i Press. Reprint, Chiang Mai, Thailand: Silkworm, 2006.

Hickey, Wakoh Shannon. 2019. *Mind Cure: How Meditation Became Medicine*. New York: Oxford University Press.

Highet, Campbell H. 1914. "Small Pox Vaccination and the New Vaccination Law in Siam." *Journal of the Siam Society* 11: 13–32.

von Hinüber, Oskar. (1987) 1994. "Das buddhistische Recht und die Phonetik des Pāli." *Studien zur Indologie und Iranistik* 13/14 (Festschrift Wilhelm Rau): 101–127; English translation, "Buddhist Law and the Phonetics of Pāli," in *Selected Papers on Pāli Studies*, by Oskar von Hinüber, 198–232. Oxford: Pali Text Society, 1994.

Hitchings, Henry. 2011. *The Language Wars: A History of Proper English*. London: John Murray.

Horner, I. B. (1963) 1996. *Milinda's Questions*. Volume 1. Oxford: Pali Text Society.

Jayatilaka, D. B. 1916. "A Dhyāna Book." Appendix to Woodward 1916: 143–150.

Jersey, Countess of [Child-Villers, Margaret]. 1884–1885. "Buddhism and Christianity." *The National Review* 4: 577–591.

J. M. M. 1865. "Buddhism." *Journal of Sacred Literature* 35: 281–300.

Jordt, Ingrid. 2007. *Burma's Lay Meditation Movement: Buddhism and the Cultural Construction of Power*. Athens, OH: Ohio University Press.

Joshi, Shivaram Dattatray, and J. A. F. Roodbergen, trans. 1985. "On P. 1.1.56." *Journal of the American Oriental Society* 105 (3): 469–477.

Kahrs, Eivind. 1998. *Indian Semantic Analysis: The Nirvacana Tradition*. Cambridge: Cambridge University Press.

Kariyawasam, Tissa. 1973. "Religious Activities and the Development of a New Poetical Tradition in Sinhalese, 1852–1906." PhD thesis, University of London.

Karunadasa, Y. 2010. *The Theravāda Abhidhamma: Its Inquiry into the Nature of Conditioned Reality*. Hong Kong: Centre of Buddhist Studies, The University of Hong Kong.

Kearney, Christine. 2012. "Breakthrough Method of Delivering Drugs Under the Skin." *Medical News Today*, September 15, 2012. www.medicalnewstoday.com/articles/250296.php, accessed June 29, 2013.

Kemper, Steven. 2015. *Rescued from the Nation: Anagarika Dharmapala and the Buddhist World*. Chicago and London: University of Chicago Press.

———. 2019. "Anagarika Dharmapala's Meditation." *Contemporary Buddhism* 20 (1): 223–246.

Kittivuddho, Phrathepkittipanyakhun. 2003 [2546 B.E.]. *Thammakay*

Kaen Triphob [Dhammakaya as the Core of Three Worlds]. 4th ed. Bangkok: Abhidhamma Mahathat Foundation and Dhammakaya Foundation. First edition published same year by Abhidhamma Mahathat Foundation.

Kong, Man-Shik. 2015. "Food and Craving in Early Buddhist Monasticism Focusing on Pali Literature." PhD thesis, King's College London.

Kyaw, Pyi Phyo. 2014. "*Paṭṭhāna* in Burmese Buddhism." PhD thesis, King's College London.

———. 2019. "The Sound of the Breath: Sunlun and Theinngu Meditation Traditions of Myanmar." *Contemporary Buddhism* 20 (1): 247–291.

Lagirarde, F. 1994. "Textes bouddhiques du pay khmer et du Lanna: Un exemple de parenté." In *Recherches Nouvelles sur le Cambodge*, edited by F. Bizot, 63–77. Paris: École française d'Extrême-Orient.

———. 1996. "Les manuscrits en thaï du Nord de la Siam Society." *Journal of the Siam Society* 84 (1): 91–115.

———. 1998. "Une interprétation bouddhique des rites funéraires du Lanna et du Laos: Le sutta apocryphe de Mahā Kāla." *Aséanie, Sciences humaines en Asie du Sud-Est* 2:47–77.

Lanman, Charles Rockwell. 1884. *A Sanskrit Reader.* Cambridge, MA: Harvard University Press.

Laulertvorakul, Anant. 2003. "Paṭhamasambodhi in Nine Languages: Their Relation and Evolution." *Manusya: Journal of Humanities* 6 (2): 11–34.

Leclère, Adhémard. 1899. *Le Bouddhisme au Cambodge.* Paris: Ernest Leroux.

Lindahl, Jared R., Christopher T. Kaplan, Even M. Winget, and Willoughby B. Britton. 2014. "A Phenomenology of Meditation-Induced Light Experiences: Traditional Buddhist and Neurobiological Perspectives." *Frontiers in Psychology* 4, Article 973: 1–16. www.frontiersin.org.

MacCulloch, Diarmaid. 2003. *Reformation: Europe's House Divided, 1490–1700.* London: Penguin Books.

Mackenzie, Rory. 2007. *New Buddhist Movements in Thailand: Towards an Understanding of Wat Phra Dhammakāya and Santi Asoke.* London: Routledge.

Magness, Terence B. 1961. *Sammā Samādhi: Being an Exposition of the Method of Samatha-Vipassanā as Discovered and Attained by All Buddhas.* Bangkok: Ladda Valaya Vorapitaksanon.

Malalgoda, Kitsiri. 1976. *Buddhism and Sinhalese Society, 1750–1900*. Berkeley: University of California Press.

Malasart, Woramat. 2019. "The *Dhammakāyānussatti-kathā:* A Trace of 'Siam's Borān Buddhism' from the Reign of Rāmā I (1782–1809)." MA thesis, University of Otago, Dunedin.

———. In preparation. "The *Dhammakāya* Text Genre and Its Significance on 'Siam's Borān Buddhism' and Modern Suppression" (title provisional).

Mallinson, Sir James. 2007. *The Ocean of the Rivers of Story*. Volume 1. New York: New York University Press, JJC Foundation.

Marston, John. 2008. "Reconstructing 'Ancient' Cambodian Buddhism." *Contemporary Buddhism* 9 (1): 99–121.

———. 2009. "Cambodian Religion since 1989." In *Beyond Democracy in Cambodia: Political Reconstruction in a Post-Conflict Society*, edited by Joakim Öjendal and Mona Lilja, 224–249. Copenhagen: NIAS Press.

Matpimon, Krai. 2009. "Kwamru Buangton Keaw Kub Phesatchakam (Basic Knowledge Relating to Medical Treatment)." www.kmitl.ac.th [Official website of King Mongkut's Institute of Technology, Ladkrabang University]. Accessed July 31, 2013.

Min, Nitra Soe. 2018. "A Study on U Shwe Zan Aung, A Prominent Writer Who Made the First Translation of Buddha Abhidhamma into English." *Journal of the Myanmar Academy of Arts and Sciences* 16 (7): 245–264.

Meegama, S. A. 1986. "The Mortality Transition in Sri Lanka." Chapter 2 in *Determinants of Mortality Change and Differentials in Developing Countries: The Five-Country Case Study Project*, 1–32. New York: United Nations.

Mettanando Bhikkhu. 1999. "Meditation and Healing in the Theravada Buddhist Order of Thailand and Laos." PhD thesis, Hamburg University.

Meulenbeld, Gerrit Jan. 1999–2002. *A History of Indian Medical Literature*. 3 volumes. Groningen: E. Forsten.

Minayeff, Ivan Pavlovich. n.d. [1950s]. *Travels in and Diaries of India and Burma*, trans. Hirendranath Sanyal. Calcutta: Eastern Trading Co.

Mulholland, Jean. 1989. *Herbal Medicine in Paediatrics: Translation of a Thai Book of Genesis*. Canberra: Faculty of Asian Studies, ANU.

Na Bangchang, Supaphan. 1988. "A Pali Letter Sent by the Aggamahāsenāpati of Siam to the Court at Kandy in 1756." *Journal of the Pali Text Society* 12:185–212.

Nagasena Bhikkhu. 2012. "The Monastic Boundary (*Sīmā*) in Burmese Buddhism: Authority, Purity and Validity in Historical and Modern Contexts." PhD thesis, School of Oriental and African Studies, University of London.

Ñāṇamoli Bhikkhu, trans. (1956) 1991. *The Path of Purification*. 5th ed. Kandy: Buddhist Publication Society. First edition, Colombo: A. Semage.

Naono, Atsuko. 2009. *State of Vaccination: The Fight Against Smallpox in Colonial Burma*. Hyderabad: Orient Blackswan.

Nārada, U. 1969 & 1981. *Conditional Relations*. Volume 1, London: Luzac; volume 2, London: Pali Text Society.

Newell, Catherine. 2011. "Two Meditation Traditions from Contemporary Thailand: A Summary Overview." *Rian Thai: International Journal of Thai Studies* 4: 81–110.

Norman, K. R. (1976) 1991. "The Language in which the Buddha Taught." In *Collected Papers*, vol. 2, by K. R. Norman, 84–98. Oxford: Pali Text Society.

———. (1997) 2006. *A Philological Approach to Buddhism*. 2nd ed. Lancaster: Pali Text Society.

Olson, Grant A. 1992. "Thai Cremation Volumes: A Brief History of a Unique Genre of Literature." *Asian Folklore Studies* 51 (2): 279–294.

Ong, Pei Wen Patrick. 2011. "Examining and Analysing the Meditation System Passed Down by the Supreme Patriarch Suk Kaithuean, Now Taught at Wat Ratchasittharam." *Rian Thai: International Journal of Thai Studies* 4: 115–189.

Ovesen, Jan, and Ing-Britt Trankell. 2010. *Cambodians and Their Doctors: A Medical Anthropology of Colonial and Post-Colonial Cambodia*. Copenhagen: NIAS Press.

Pabst, M.A., I. Letofsky-Pabst, E. Bock, M. Moser, et al. 2009. "The Tattoos of the Tyrolean Iceman: A Light Microscopical, Ultrastructural and Element Analytical Study." *Journal of Archaeological Science* 36 (10): 2335–2341.

Pe Maung Tin. 1920. *The Expositor (Aṭṭhasālinī): Buddhaghosa's Commentary on the Dhammasaṅgani, the First Book of the Abhidhammapiṭaka*. Edited and revised by C. A. F. Rhys Davids. London: Pali Text Society.

Perreira, Todd LeRoy. 2012. "Whence Theravāda? The Modern Genealogy of an Ancient Term." In Skilling et al. 443–571.

Piera Candotti, Maria, and Tiziana Pontillo. 2013. "The Earlier Pāṇinian Tradition on the Imperceptible Sign." In *Signless Signification in*

Ancient India and Beyond, edited by Tiziana Pontillo and Maria Piera Candotti, 99–154. London and New York: Anthem Press.

Pind, Ole Holten. 2013. *Kaccāyana and Kaccāyanavutti*. Bristol: Pali Text Society.

Pranke, Patrick Arthur. 2004. "The 'Treatise on the Lineage of Elders' (*Vaṃsadīpanī*): Monastic Reform and the Writing of Buddhist History in Eighteenth-Century Burma." PhD thesis, University of Michigan.

Putheti, Ramesh R., Mahesh C. Patil, and O. Obire. 2009. "Nasal Drug Delivery in Pharmaceutical and Biotechnology: Present and Future." *e-Journal of Science & Technology* 12 (3): 1–21.

Randall, Richard. 1990. *Life as a Siamese Monk*. Bradford on Avon, UK: Aukana Publishing.

Rastogi, Subha, Dinesh K. Kulshrestha, and Ajay Kumar Singh Rawat. 2006. "'*Streblus asper*' Lour. (Shakhotaka): A Review of Its Chemical, Pharmacological and Ethnomedicinal Properties." *Evidence-Based Complementary and Alternative Medicine* 3 (2): 217–222.

Ratnajoti, Galkätiyagama, and Karalliyaddē Ratnapāla. 1963. *Vimuttimaggo: Bhadantārahanta-Mahāriṭṭha-Upatissa-tthera-vara-ppanīto*. Colombo: Government Press of Ceylon.

Ratnapala, Nandasena. 1971. *The Katikavatas*. Munich: R. Kitzinger.

Reeder, Matt. 2016. "The National Library of Thailand, Manuscript Collection." http://dissertationreviews.org/archives/13975, accessed May 14, 2019.

Rhys Davids, C. A. F. 1916. "Editor's Preface." In Woodward 1916.

———. 1920. *The Visuddhi-magga of Buddhaghosa*. London: Pali Text Society.

Rhys Davids, T. W. (1896) 1981. *The Yogāvacara's Manual*. London: Pali Text Society.

Rhys Davids, T. W., and H. Oldenberg. (1882) 1982. *Vinaya Texts*. Pt. 2. Oxford: Clarendon Press. Reprint, Delhi: Motilal Banarsidass.

Von Rospatt, Alexander. 1995. *The Buddhist Doctrine of Momentariness: A Survey of Origins and Early Phase of This Doctrine up to Vasubandhu*. Stuttgart: Franz Stainer Verlag.

———. 1998. "Momentariness, Buddhist Doctrine of." In *Routledge Encyclopedia of Philosophy*, edited by Edward Craig, 469–473. London and New York: Routledge.

Rozenberg, Guillaume, Bénédicte Brac de la Perrière, and Alicia Turner, eds. 2014. *Champions of Buddhism: Weikza Cults in Contemporary Burma*. Singapore: National University of Singapore Press.

Ruangsan, Phramaha Niras. 2015. "*Vijjādhammakāya:* Presentation of the Essential Elements and Core Doctrines through the Translation of Its Five Primary Texts." PhD thesis, University of Sydney.

Ruiz-Falqués, Aleix. 2012. "Saddhammasiri and His Philosophy of Language." Unpublished paper delivered at the International Burma Studies Conference, 2012.

———. 2014. "The Creative Erudition of Chapaṭa Saddhammajotipāla, a 15th-Century Grammarian and Philosopher from Burma." *Journal of Indian Philosophy* 43 (4–5): 389–426.

———. 2017. "On the Authorship of *Kaccāyana*, the Oldest Pāli Grammar." In *Pariyatti: Studies in Pāli Language and Literature*, edited by Bimalendra Kumar and Ujjwal Kumar, 251–268. New Delhi: Aditya Prakashan.

Scott, Rachelle M. 2009. *Nirvana for Sale? Buddhism, Wealth, and the Dhammakāya Temple in Contemporary Thailand*. Albany: State University of New York Press.

Sermchai, Jayamangalo. 1991. *The Heart of Dhammakaya Meditation*. Bangkok: Dhammakaya Buddhist Meditation Foundation Sala Karnparien (Wat Saket).

Shaw, Julia. 2007. *Buddhist Landscapes in Central India: Sanchi Hill and Archaeologies of Religious and Social Change in c. Third Century BC to Fifth Century AD*. London: The British Academy.

Shendge, Malati J. 1996. "Beginning of Scientific Observations: Founding of Linguistic Science in India." *Indian Journal of History of Science* 31 (4): 303–326.

Skilling, Peter. 2018. "Calligraphic Magic: Abhidhamma Inscriptions from Sukhodaya." *Buddhist Studies Review* 35 (1–2): 161–187

Skilling, Peter, Jason A. Carbine, Claudio Cicuzza, and Santi Pakdeekham, eds. 2012. *How Theravāda Is Theravāda? Exploring Buddhist Identities*. Chiang Mai, Thailand: Silkworm Books.

Skilton, Andrew. 2013a. "Theravada." In *A Companion to Buddhist Philosophy*, edited by Steven M. Emmanuel, 71–85. 1st ed. John Wiley & Sons, Inc.

———. 2013b. "Elective Affinities: The Reconstruction of a Forgotten Episode in the Shared History of Thai and British Buddhism—Kapilavaḍḍho and Wat Paknam." In *A Buddhist Crossroads: Pioneer European Buddhists and Globalizing Asian Networks, 1860–1960*. Con-

temporary Buddhism 14 (1): special issue edited by Alicia Turner, Laurence Cox, and Brian Bocking, 149-168.

———. 2016. "*Pīti* in the 'Old Meditation' (*Boran Kammatthan*), or Why Is *Pīti* Always the First Stage of the *Boran Kammatthan* Meditation Process?" Unpublished paper delivered at Traditional Theravada Meditation (*boran kammatthan*), Siem Reap, July 5–6, 2016.

———. 2019. "Meditation and Its Subjects: Tracing *Kammaṭṭhāna* from the Early Canon to the *Boran Kammathan* Traditions of Southeast Asia." *Contemporary Buddhism* 20 (1): 36–72.

Skilton, Andrew, and Phibul Choompolpaisal. 2014. "The Old Meditation (*Boran* Kammatthan), a Pre-reform Theravāda Meditation System from Wat Ratchasittharam: The *Pīti* Section of the *Kammatthan Matchima Baeb Lamdub*." *Aséanie* 33:83–116.

———. 2015. "The Ancient Theravāda Meditation System, *Borān Kammaṭṭhāna: Ānāpānasati* or 'Mindfulness of the Breath' in Kammatthan Majjima Baeb Lamdub." *Buddhist Studies Review* 32 (2): 207–229.

———. 2017. "How to Deal with Wind Illnesses: Two Short Meditation Texts from Buddhist Southeast Asia." In *Buddhism and Medicine: An Anthology of Premodern Sources*, edited by C. Pierce Salguero, 425–430. New York: Columbia University Press.

Soma Thera. 1949. *The Way of Mindfulness: Being the Translation of the Satipaṭṭhāna Sutta of the Majjhima Nikaya; Its Commentary, the Satipaṭṭhāna Sutta Vaṇṇanā of the Papañcasūdannī of Buddhaghosa Thera; and Excerpts from the Līnatthapakāsanā Tīkā, Marginal Notes, of Dhammapāla Thera on the Commentary*. Colombo: Vaijrama. Rev. online ed., "The Way of Mindfulness: The Satipatthana Sutta and Its Commentary," *Access to Insight (BCBS Edition)*, November 30, 2013, www.accesstoinsight.org/lib/authors/soma/wayof.html, accessed December 1, 2019.

Somadasa, K. D. 1987–1995. *Catalogue of the Hugh Nevill Collection of Sinhalese Manuscripts in the British Library*. 7 vols. London and Henley on Thames: British Library and Pali Text Society.

Strong, John S. 2010. "'The Devil Was in That Little Bone': The Portuguese Capture and Destruction of the Buddha's Tooth Relic." In *Relics and Remains*, edited by Alexandra Walsham, 184–198. Past and Present Supplement 5. Oxford: Oxford University Press.

Subhūti, Waskaḍuwē. (1876) 2001. *Nāmamālā or A Work on Pali Grammar*. Colombo: Government Printing Office. Reprint, New Delhi: Asian Educational Services.

Suksamran, Somboon. 1982. *Buddhism and Politics in Thailand: A Study of Socio-political Change and Political Activism of the Thai Sangha*. Singapore: Institute of Southeast Asian Studies.

Suraweera, A. V. 1968. "The Imprisonment of Sangharāja Saranaṃkara." *Vidyodaya Journal of Arts, Sciences and Letters* 1: 53–57.

Taylor, James L. 1993. *Forest Monks and the Nation-State: An Anthropological and Historical Study in Northeastern Thailand*. Singapore: Institute of Southeast Asian Studies.

Taylor, Charles. 1995. "Two Theories of Modernity." *Hastings Center Report* 25 (2): 24–33.

Terwiel, B. J. 1979. "Tattooing in Thailand's History." *Journal of the Royal Asiatic Society of Great Britain & Ireland* 111: 156–166.

———. 2019. "The City of Nibbāna in the Thai Picture Books of the Three Worlds." *Contemporary Buddhism* 20 (1): 184–199.

Thanaveero, Veera (Phrakhrusangkharak). 1994 [2537 B.E.]. *Kammatthan Kae Kam Raksa Rok* [Meditation: The Solving of Kamma, the Curing of Illnesss]. Nonthaburi, Thailand: Sampachanya Press.

Tiyavanich, Kamala. 1997. *Forest Recollections: Wandering Monks in Twentieth-Century Thailand*. Honolulu: University of Hawai'i Press.

Trenckner, V. 1928. *The Milindapanho: Being Dialogues between King Milinda and the Buddhist Sage Nāgasena*. London: Royal Asiatic Society.

Turner, Alicia. 2014. *Saving Buddhism: Moral Community and the Impermanence of Colonial Religion*. Honolulu: University of Hawai'i Press.

Unschuld, Paul U. 1979. "The Chinese Reception of Indian Medicine in the First Millennium A.D." *Bulletin of the History of Medicine* 53 (3): 329–345.

Urkasame, Kitchai. 2013. "A Study of Elements in Yogāvacara Tradition from Tham Scripts Palm-Leaf Manuscripts." PhD thesis, University of Sydney.

Weiss, Mitchell G. 1980. "*Caraka Saṃhitā* on the Doctrine of Karma." In *Karma and Rebirth in the Classical Indian Traditions*, edited by Wendy Doniger O'Flaherty, 90–115. London: University of California Press.

Wenk, Klaus. 1975. *Laotische Handschriften*. Wiesbaden: Franz Steiner Verlag.

White, David Gordon. 1984. "Why Gurus Are Heavy." *Numen* 31 (1): 40–73.

Woodward, F. L. 1916. *Manual of a Mystic: Being a Translation from the*

Pali and Sinhalese Work Entitled the Yogāvachara's Manual. London: Pali Text Society.

Wujastyk, Dominik. (1998) 2001. *The Roots of Ayurveda: Selections from the Ayurvedic Classics*. Rev. ed. Penguin Classics. New Delhi: Penguin Books.

———. 2000. "The Combinatorics of Tastes and Humours in Indian Medicine and Mathematics." *Journal of Indian Philosophy* 28 (5–6): 479–495.

Wyatt, David K. 1969. *The Politics of Reform in Thailand: Education in the Reign of King Chulalongkorn*. New Haven and London: Yale University Press.

Yasothararat, Phramaha Jai. 1936 [2478 B.E.]. *Nangsue Phuttha-rangsi-thrisadi-yan wa duai Samatha lae Vipassana-kammathan Si Yuk* [Book on Buddha-rangsī-trisadī-yan Relating to Samatha and Vipassanā Meditation During the Four Periods]. Bangkok: n.p.

Zysk, Kenneth G. (1991) 1998. *Asceticism and Healing in Ancient India: Medicine in the Buddhist Monastery*. Rev. ed. Indian Medical Tradition 2. Delhi: Motilal Banarsidass.

Index

About the Author

Kate Crosby's interest in Buddhism began as an infant, when she was enraptured by a large Kuan-yin she met in the courtyard garden of the Victoria and Albert Museum, London. The Kuan-yin has since moved to Fa-Yue Buddhist temple in Brierley Hill. Meanwhile Kate was introduced to Buddhist meditation and Indo-European languages at high school and went on to study Buddhism and related languages in Oxford, Hamburg, Kelaniya, Pune, and Varanasi. Her translations of Sanskrit works include the eighth-century Buddhist treatise, the *Bodhicaryāvatāra* (1995), and two books of the Indian epic, the *Mahābhārata*: *The Dead of Night and the Women* (2009). Her main research interest is the literature, history, and practice of Theravada Buddhism throughout Asia, reflected in publications such as *Theravada Buddhism: Continuity, Diversity, Identity* (2013), *Traditional Theravada Meditation and Its Modern-Era Suppression* (2014), and *Variety in Theravada Meditation* (ed., 2019). She is Professor of Buddhist Studies in the Department of Theology and Religious Studies at King's College London.